Where Did I Put My Glasses?

Best wishes to
Margaret Kaetsel

Ralph Mendelson

WHERE DID I PUT MY GLASSES?

**How You Can
Improve Your Memory
As You Grow Older**

Ralph Mendelson

Segno Books

P.O. Box 10818
Cleveland, Ohio 44110

Acknowledgements

Grateful acknowledgement is made for permission to reprint the following:

"I Remember It Well" p. 27
(Alan Jay Lerner, Frederick Loewe)
©1957 CHAPPELL & CO. (Renewed)
All Rights Reserved. Used By Permission

G. B. Shaw satire from *The Smithsonian Torch* p. 264
Reprinted by permission of Smithsonian Institution

Murray Suid: from *Demonic Mnemonics* p. 267
Reprinted by permission of the author.

ISBN 0-9635556-0-X

Printed in the United States of America

Where Did I Put My Glasses?

Table of Contents

To my parents, Ruth and Louis, and my children, Walton and Philip, who have given me memories that are the treasures of my later years.

Prologue

Who Are You?

Try this experiment: Close your eyes, remove all memories from your mind, then ask yourself who you are. Be sure you have removed every memory, even your memory of the past two seconds, your memory of the past instant. Everything —your childhood, youth, middle and older age. Your family, friends, home — every place you've ever lived, everything you've ever seen or done, everything you've ever read or heard about. Live only in the present instant without a single memory. Who are you now?

You are no one. You —without a single memory —do not exist. You *are* your memories. And that is why this book rambles far beyond strategies for finding your glasses or remembering names. Those things are important parts of memory, so they are included in the book, but they are not the whole.

You are the whole. Remember that.

Preface

How to Use This Book

When I first began teaching memory improvement for older persons at Cuyahoga Community College, the lady in the office that administers their Elders' Programs asked a question that took me aback: "Will your course *really* improve people's memory?"

Will it? I wondered. I knew that my advice was sound. I follow it myself, so I know it works. Now seventy-four, I am a graduate student in psychology at Cleveland State University, where my grades as are good as any of the twenty-and thirty-year-olds in my classes. But will people actually leave my memory improvement course with more efficient memories than they had before?

Suddenly inspired, I replied: "It's like taking piano lessons. The teacher can tell you how to play the piano, but unless you practice, you won't learn to play."

I can tell you exactly what to do to improve your memory. And it will work. The advice I offer has been tested for many, many years, in some instances for centuries, and has proved valuable. But you must practice the strategies that I explain if you want to improve your memory.

I have written this book with that in mind: all the information you need for intelligent, productive practice is here; the rest is up to you. Read the book through. Pick out the ideas that interest you most and try them. Practice them.

When you first read the book, you will not be able to remember all of it, so refer back to it to be sure you are practicing the right things in the right way. Some memory problems are complicated. Take names, for instance. I make several suggestions for improving your memory for names. You might want to try some of the easy ones first. They will improve your performance, but will leave plenty of room for further improvement. If you want to do even better, go back and tackle the more sophisticated strategies.

After you have mastered the memory strategies that were most important to you, browse through the book for ideas you overlooked at first reading, or ideas that seem more important now that you have mastered those you tried first.

I have written the book for older persons who are relatively healthy — that is, who read, who watch or listen to the news, who discuss the problems of the day with their friends, or who pursue a job or a hobby, or take part in civic affairs. Thanks to modern sanitation and modern medicine, that includes most of us. Clinical psychologists have worked out techniques for helping the less fortunate people who suffer from mentally crippling diseases such as Alzheimer's. Those techniques are wonderful, and they work, but they are beyond the scope of a self-help book.

Since it is never too soon to form good habits of thought and action, younger persons can profit from the book, too. The memory strategies that are explained apply to all — young and old — and the younger reader can simply skip those portions directed to readers of my age.

I have written the book informally for a few reasons. First, I wanted to make it easy to read and absorb. That means that information about any specific problem — say the problem of finding things — is scattered in different places. But the index and the section headings make it easy to pull together information on any topic.

Another reason for the style is that it involves some repetition, and repetition is important to memory. If you want to learn something, you had better accept the idea that you will have to repeat it one way or another. And that brings us back to the idea of reviewing the book from time to time. Repeated readings of the material in the book — selecting what interests you —will enable you learn it more thoroughly.

Finally, I have tried to make the book enjoyable to read. Please take the book seriously, but not somberly. I am convinced that we can improve our memory at any age and that doing it is fun. So — enjoy.

Chapter 1

Find Those Glasses

Dear Mr. Mendelson:

Perhaps you can answer a question that has been bothering me a great deal lately. I keep losing my glasses, and I have a lot of trouble finding them.

I never used to have this problem. Am I losing my memory?

Sincerely,
Mrs. A. W. Watson

Dear Mrs. Watson:

The evidence you have presented tells me nothing about any possible change in your memory. The reason you did not lose your glasses when you were younger is that you did not use reading glasses then.

Best regards,
Ralph Mendelson

Dear Mr. Mendelson:

How did you know that I did not use glasses when I was younger? I had almost forgotten that myself. And how did you know I use glasses only for reading? I didn't mention that in my letter.

Sincerely,
Mrs. A. W. Watson

Dear Mrs. Watson:

Elementary, my dear Mrs. Watson. People who cannot see at all without glasses always know where they are: on their noses. People who need glasses only to read, often misplace them. People usually don't need reading glasses till they are over forty. I suggest that you read my book, *Where Did I Put My Glasses?* to improve your chances of finding them when you need them.

Good luck,
Ralph Mendelson

In addition to giving me a chance to plug my book (and get off a feeble joke on her name), Mrs. Watson's letter illustrates a curious way of thinking — curious, but a way that many older people think. This way of thinking requires belief in two contradictory assertions:

1. I can *not* rely on my memory, because it is becoming undependable.

2. I *can* rely on my memory, and it tells me that I had a better memory when I was young than I have now.

How can we resolve this paradox? If both assertions are true, we have an impossible situation: memory is reliable and unreliable at the same time. The fact is, however, that we don't have a difficult situation at all because the second part of both assertions is not quite true. Let's take a closer look at them.

Aging and memory

In some respects our memory grows weaker as we grow older. Most psychologists agree on that. But psychologists do not agree so well on just what those respects are. The one thing we can say for sure is that memory — like everything else — changes over the years. And as with everything else, some of the changes are good and some are bad. We certainly remember *more*. We add to our store of memories every day.

We all know what memory is, but we do not always agree on where the boundaries fall, so I will explain some of the notions of memory that underlie this book. The reason we have a memory is that we could not survive without one. We must be able to remember how to get food or we could not continue to exist. In our civilized world, we must be able to remember such things as turning the stove off before leaving the house. What has *that* to do with survival? Well, money helps us survive — and it helps make survival worth while. Running the stove to no purpose wastes money. Under extreme conditions, there is always the danger that it could even burn the house down or use up all the oxygen so that we suffocate.

How does memory affect this situation? Usually the very act of leaving the house calls to mind the fact that we should be sure that the stove is off. If we have trouble remembering to turn it off, we may train ourselves to associate the act of opening the door with the thought of turning off the stove. That is the usual way of thinking of memory. We call it an internal memory strategy, because we have made a mental (internal) association between opening the door and turning off the stove.

But there is another way to avoid leaving the house with the stove burning. We could form the habit of leaving our car keys on the stove. That habit would be internal. Once that habit is formed (after all, we have to put the keys *somewhere*), then every time we leave the house, we will see whether the stove is on or off. Using the cars keys this way is not a matter of memory in the narrow sense of the word. You can think of it as an external aid to memory — as opposed to an internal aid like forming an association or a habit. In my opinion, the important thing is not whether we call this strategy "memory" or "an external aid to memory," but that the stove gets turned off.

I like to think of two kinds of memory: biological memory, which is limited to our minds, and functional memory, which includes all kinds of internal and external strategies for getting the job done. Alarm clocks that get us up and strings around the finger that remind us to buy milk on the way home are not part of our biological memory, but they help us get the job done, so I think of them as part of our functional memory.

If our biological memory deteriorates from age (and there is evidence pro and con) we can compensate by developing external strategies — part of our functional memory. If we do it right, we will have fewer memory lapses than we did when we relied on our biological memory alone.

The thrust of this book is to point out some of the ways we can compensate for any slippage that occurs in our biological memory, and to point out how we can build on the knowledge and skills we have acquired over the years. Parts of the book will cover ideas that you thought of long ago and have incorporated into your way of life. But you will find familiar ideas clarified and organized, and you will find new ideas that will help improve your memory.

What happens to brains when we get old

Did you ever hear that our brains shrink as we grow older? The first time I heard that, it scared the daylights out of me. Scientists know that the brain gets smaller with age, and they know that we never grow new brain cells. For many years they believed that we lose brain cells all the time, so that the brain of an older person has hundreds of thousands fewer brain cells than a young person.

Fortunately, there is a bright side to all this. The loss of brain cells does not seem to make any difference in the efficiency of the brain.

On top of that, recent investigations suggest that the brain does *not* lose cells over the years. Recent findings indicate that the cells shrink, but they do not die or disappear.

From my point of view as an older person who is not a physiologist, as long as my brain works I don't care what size it is. And I don't care whether I am losing brain cells or my cells are shrinking as long as they do what I want them to do.

I'm not scared any more. I hope that the scientists discover what really happens to the brain as we grow older, because knowledge is always better than ignorance, but I don't expect it to affect my life or my lifestyle.

Learning from Mrs. Watson's glasses

Mrs. Watson's problem with losing her glasses illustrates two interesting things about older persons' memory problems. The first is simply that the older we get, the more aware we are of the importance of remembering things. True, Mrs. Watson did not have a problem finding her glasses when she was young because she didn't have glasses to get lost. But it is more than simply the fact that now she *does* have glasses. We take things more seriously as we grow older, and that includes memory lapses. When I was young and misplaced my hat, I just went without a hat. At age 74, I am embarrassed and uncomfortable when I forget my hat, and I feel that I have somehow failed in a simple task — anybody should be able to remember his hat. And I can't just shrug off misplacing my reading glasses because I want very badly to read, and I can't read without them.

The older we get, the more we appreciate the importance of memory. We become more sensitive to memory problems, and we unwittingly place greater importance on memory. How many times, when I was young, did my mother complain that I would forget my head if it wasn't attached to my body? (Ever hear that when *you* were young?) She might have embarrassed me for a minute or two, but I continued to lose things and forget appointments with complete abandon. When we were young, things like punctuality meant little; we forgot appointments, and we forgot any embarrassment that resulted.

The second point is that all of us — young and old alike — have been brainwashed into believing that older people have memory problems that younger people don't have. We believe this unfortunate canard even though it has been discredited over and over through the ages. Two hundred years ago, Dr. Samuel Johnson, the great English literary personage said:

> There is a wicked inclination in most people to suppose an old man decayed in his intellects. If a young or middle-aged man, when leaving a company, does not recollect where he laid his hat, it is nothing; but if the same inattention is discovered in an old man, people will shrug up their shoulders and say, "His memory is going."

Two real-life illustrations

Dear seventy-eight-year-old Aunt Emily's family picnic would have been a huge success had she not put Chlorox in the salad dressing instead of vinegar. What to do with her? If she couldn't remember the difference between Chlorox and vinegar . . . If she couldn't remember that she was making a salad and not doing the laundry . . . Obviously she must be put in a home where she could not harm either herself or others.

Never mind that she had a houseful of guests. That the guests had "helped" her prepare dinner. That one of them (never identified) had put the Chlorox bottle where Emily always kept the vinegar and the vinegar bottle where she kept the Chlorox. And that the two bottles were practically the same size and shape.

Three weeks later, Emily's niece, Anne, who had suggested a nursing home for her aunt, spent a night at a friend's house. In the morning, she asked for some hair spray and was told that there was none. Several minutes later, she laughingly reported that she had found the hair spray she was looking for in the medicine cabinet — an aerosol can exactly the right size and shape. She had used it generously — and had drenched her hair with Lysol. Her friends got a good laugh out of that and kidded her about it for months.

This true story (except that names have been changed for the usual reasons) reported by psychologist Irene Hulicka, brings us back to our question: Why didn't Anne's friends suggest that *she* be put away where she could do no harm either to herself or others? She had far less excuse for her mistake than her aunt, but her friends did not take *her* mistake seriously.

Aunt Emily had not lost her memory. She had remembered only too well exactly where she always kept the vinegar — she remembered it so well that she had not bothered to read the label or to smell the contents.

I got my second real-life illustration of Johnson's complaint from my morning newspaper. "Vice President Dan Quayle mistakenly credited a moon landing to a congressman convicted of a sex charge, amusing a crowd of Young Republicans at the group's national convention yesterday.

"'This next Thursday, July 20, will be a historic date ... as America celebrates the 20th anniversary of Neil Armstrong and Buz Lukens walking on the moon,' Quayle said.

"He meant to say Edwin (Buzz) Aldrin ... "

We elected Mr. Quayle (in part) because we saw him as young and vigorous — someone who should have a memory far better than yours or mine — if the notion that memory deteriorates as we get older is true.

But the truth of that notion is not accepted by everyone. The article continues: "Joseph Canzeri, a Quayle 'handler' last year who once worked for Nelson A. Rockefeller, described Quayle's 'immaturity and lack of attention.'

"'He was like a kid,' Canzeri said. 'Ask him to turn off a light, and by the time he gets to the switch, he's forgotten what he went for.'"

The lesson in this story lies in Mr. Canzeri's remark: immature people have memory problems, and that some observers find the memory lapses of "kids" more glaring than those of old folks like you and me.

Some reasons for the belief that age affects memory

There *are* reasons for the belief that we lose our memories when we grow old. Some are good reasons; some are not so good.

Here's a reason that's not so good. Alzheimer's disease is big in the news these days. It destroys the memory of its victim progressively, till there is little left of the person we once knew. And Alzheimer's is not the only disease of its kind; there are other's that have the same horrible results. They are all called dementias, or, if they strike older people, senile dementias. But our chances of falling victim to any of them are slim. The best estimate is that fewer than six percent of us will ever get anything as serious as Alzheimer's. The trouble is that these diseases are so dramatic, and if you get one it is so devastating, that the mere possibility warps our view of old age.

Better than that, mental problems, both mild and severe, are no more frequent among old people than among the young. So it is not that we approach a disaster period of life as we grow older; it is just that we never know what the future may bring, and of course it may bring trouble.

Psychologist Alan Baddeley adds a bit of information that has both a pleasant and an unpleasant side:

> Senile dementia is almost invariably progressive and typically occurs shortly before death. Riegel and Riegel, who have carried out a series of studies of old people, testing their intellectual and physical competence over a period of several years, suggest that mental capacity declines at a relatively gradual rate through age up to a point about a year before death, when deterioration becomes rapid ...

If I have given the mistaken impression that I believe no changes occur with age, this quotation should correct it. Changes do occur, but we should not misjudge them. We should not expect them to make major changes in our lives because in almost every case they do not — or need not.

The best opinion at the present time is that the view of gradual aging must be displaced by the expectation of a vigorous adult life span followed by a brief and precipitous aging at the very end.

Don't find trouble where trouble does not exist

Psychologist Steven H. Zarit points out that "While memory deficits are prominent in persons with dementia, the extent of changes in healthy older persons has probably been exaggerated both by the elderly and by those who associate with them, including relatives and professionals." He also says that, "While many persons take forgetfulness as primary evidence of organic brain dysfunction, the issue is not whether someone is forgetful, but the extent and persistence of the problems. Since all persons are forgetful to some extent, one's assessment must be guided by some standards of how much forgetfulness is likely to indicate an organic problem."

Zarit illustrates the problem of mistaken diagnoses with a story about a daughter who arranged for her seventy-eight year old mother to visit a gerontology clinic. After an operation three years before, the mother had a period of acutely disturbed memory, and the daughter believed that her mother had never quite recovered. Examination of the mother did not reveal any noticeable intellectual impairment. When a second daughter was interviewed, it came out that the first daughter's relationship with her mother had always been difficult, so that there was a strong possibility that the problem lay in a conflict of personalities rather than in a psychological failing of the mother.

Aches and pains and slowing down

Age brings a slowing down and a growing susceptibility to all kinds of illness, aches, and pains. It is easy to generalize and say that if our physical health deteriorates, our mental health must deteriorate, too. There is some truth to that, but not enough. Individuals differ. We do not all deteriorate the same way or at the same rate. And physical illness may or may not affect our mental condition.

An actual acute illness will often interfere with memory, and that encourages the myth that age itself, regardless of health, brings a weakening of memory. But we should separate these two ideas. To the very small extent that age affects memory, we must learn how to compensate — and there are many ways to do that which we will explore. To the extent that poor health weakens memory, we must do what we can to stay fit. In writing this book, I have assumed that my readers are free from Alzheimer's and enjoy relatively good health.

Depression

Depression weakens memory. This may be another cause of the belief, because depression is said to be the single most common mental complaint of the elderly. Don't get me wrong, studies show that depression is probably no more common among old people than among young people. In fact, people who have not become depressed before the age of sixty are not likely to become depressed later. Most older people who are healthy, seem to be quite up-beat.

But it is not hard to understand why many older people do suffer from depression. They are more likely to have suffered bouts of ill health; they know what it's like, and they foresee more of it coming. Older people frequently have no job and not as much money as they would like. They frequently have no family, or have a diminished family. They have usually lost some of their friends.

Depressed people tend to see everything falling apart, including memory. But depression is not hopeless. Depression is a huge subject in itself and lies far beyond the scope of this book, but if you suffer from depression, you can get help from a competent therapist. That will improve your memory, and it will improve much, much more — such as making your world a more enjoyable place to live in.

Some kinds of physical deterioration clearly affect memory. As we grow older, many of us cannot see or hear as well as we could when we were young. This affects memory through the simple fact that we sometimes fail to see or hear whatever it is that people expect us to remember.

One Sunday when I took my son and daughter-in-law to brunch, my son nodded toward some people across the room and said, "There he is again."

"Who?" I asked, bewildered.

"Mr. Butterbaugh," my son said, somewhat testily because I didn't seem to be with it. "We saw him at the opera last night. Remember?"

I didn't remember him for two good reasons: In the confusion of people milling about the lobby of the opera house, and with my eyes not what they used to be, I had not been able to tell who my son was pointing at. And with all the noise, when my son mentioned his name, I did not hear it. So there was nothing for me to remember.

Does that reflect a failure of memory or a decrease in the ability to see and hear clearly in a confused mass of people? We must be careful not to blame all of our problems on memory. Strangely enough, many people do that. The reason may be that they think there is something disgraceful about having poor sight and hearing, whereas a poor memory is accepted. Bergen Evans said: "Many people seem to think that their humorous insistence on having an extraordinarily poor memory somehow confers a distinction upon them." If Evans is right, those people are wrong. Naturally you will have a poor memory if you blame all your shortcomings on it.

Sensitivity again

A big cause of the belief that memory weakens with age is, as I mentioned above, simply that older people are more sensitive to memory lapses than young people are. In a recent study, psychologists found "that older adults are more likely to be 'upset' when they experience memory failures, regardless of what is forgotten or its importance."

A friend of mine told me that his step-daughter had lost her driver's license. It didn't bother her a bit. He, being older, knew the problems it could cause. She took the position that it would show up eventually — why worry? He, knowing that eventually could be a long time, insisted that she go to the license bureau to get a new one. *He* worried about her forgetfulness even though she did not.

Older people notice their memory failures but overlook their successes. If someone asked you if you could memorize 50,000 words, you would probably balk. But the average educated older person knows about that many words. And that's quite a memory feat. True, we forget someone's name, and that embarrasses us, but think of all the names we remember.

The more accurately we can judge our own abilities, the more confidence we have in them. In another experiment, psychologist Perlmutter found that, "less educated subjects had greater expectation of memory loss than more educated subjects." Learning to evaluate our abilities realistically will reduce worry about memory loss.

Over-sensitivity to memory lapses can act like a self-fulfilling prophecy and lead to memory lapses. My reason for going into all this detail is to give you a basis for justifiable confidence in your memory. The greater your confidence, the better your memory — provided the confidence is based on fact.

Do we remember long gone events better than recent events?

A widely held belief that contributes to our down-grading our memories is that in our old age we remember things from our youth better than we remember things from the recent past. Although there is some truth to that belief, it requires a lot of qualification.

Try this on yourself: Remember what you had for breakfast this morning? Most of us do. Now try to remember what you had for breakfast on this date forty years ago.

I can hear you yelling, "Foul!" That's not what we mean when we say we can remember things from the past. I agree: that's not what we mean. O.K., what *do* we mean? Probably that we remember *important* things from the past. But that is too simple an answer for at least two reasons.

First, we remember *un*important things, too. I remember, when I was in summer camp as a ten-year-old, sitting on the wooden bench at the baseball diamond when a friend of my father whom I had never met, and who had moved out of town before I was born, came up and introduced himself to me. And I remember that it was a bright, sunny day. I can "see" the ball diamond and the blue sky. I can "see" him bending over to talk to me. But there was nothing important about the meeting. In fact, I never saw the man again. Why, out of the scores of things that happened to me as a child, do I remember that incident and not myriads of others?

Secondly, we forget important things. I was at large a party a few years ago. It was large enough that most of the people there did not know everyone else at the party. One elderly man, trying to be friendly, turned to the woman standing next to him and introduced himself.

"Oh, yes," she said. "I know you. I'm your first wife."

You don't believe that could happen? I was there.

We certainly do forget important things from our past.

Of course, we remember many important things. But the fact that we also forget important things tells us that importance does not guarantee that we will remember something. And certainly — as in my earlier example — *un*importance offers no guarantee that we will forget.

Salience

Perhaps things that stand out for some reason — things that are salient — are the ones that stick in memory. The sudden appearance of my father's friend made it salient to me. I had often heard my father speak of him, but I had never expected to meet him.

It seems to be true that the salience of an occurrence helps us remember it — the fact that it stands out from the humdrum series of our everyday experiences. Most of us remember our early days at work, but can we remember the forty-third day? The first day was different from every day after it. We had the emotional jolt of a new environment, new people working with us, a jumble of new duties to learn. We may remember it as only a jumble, with no clear details, but we remember it.

Think of the worker on an assembly line. He attaches the water pump to the automobile engine and tightens it up. It is an important job, but it never varies except for the few occasions when a part doesn't fit, or when a new model comes down the line. But the first day on the job was different. He may never have been in the automobile factory before. The size of the place alone is overwhelming. He must learn to perceive the order underlying what seems at first glance to be nothing but noise and confusion. So much is new and strange and intimidating. It is a memorable occasion, and he remembers it. What he remembers may be nothing more than the overwhelming noise and confusion — that is what impressed him most — but he remembers it. Does he remember the two hundred and ninety-second day on the job? Not very likely.

I can remember my first day at kindergarten — sixty-nine years ago. It was a real shock. No other day of school was like it. Several of the children cried. There may have been other days when one or even two children cried, but never again as many as that first day. No other day in school matched the emotional shock of that day. Needless to say, I can't remember the second day — or the forty-third day.

Think back to your early sexual experiences. Whether they were good or bad, they were exciting. But what about the ninety-eighth experience? It was too routine to remember. However pleasant it might have been, it was the same old thing.

Elbert Hubbard, whose books our parents read, told the story of a young man walking along a country road on a hot summer's day. He came across a horse shoe lying on the road and picked it up. We all know that a horse shoe means good luck. So the young man carried the horse shoe with him. Imagine his delight when he found a second horse shoe! Twice as much good luck! The more you find, the luckier you are!

Five minutes later, when he walked around a sharp curve in the road, he found in front of him an old wagon that had broken down. It was filled with old horse shoes, hundreds of them. Moral: one or two horse shoes are good luck, but a wagon load is junk. Similarly, one novel, outstanding, emotionally laden event may stick in our memory, but a wagon load of repetitive events is junk to be forgotten.

So it's true that we remember many events from our childhood, youth, and early adulthood, but the chances are that we remember them because they were outstanding — they were salient — not simply because they happened long ago.

The events we remember least well are generally those of the middle years of our lives. We remember our youth, and we remember very recent things. Many memory phenomena show this same tendency: Psychologists refer to primacy effects and recency effects. Subjects of experiments, when asked to memorize a list of words, usually remember the first few words and the last few words. We seem to do the same thing with our life as a whole; we remember the early years, and we remember the recent years.

The good old days

A final thought along these lines: We all remember the good old days, don't we? That should be a perfect example in which memories for old times are better than memories for recent events. But how good are those old memories? Were the old days really good? If you are as old as I am, the good old days meant the

Great Depression and World War II. Are *those* what we call *good!*

We can only think of those years as the good old days by forgetting how bad they were. Memory does that: we tend to forget unpleasant experiences. Mothers forget the pains of childbirth, and old soldiers dwell on the camaraderie of a life they hated when they were in the fox holes.

True, if we were very young during the depression, it was our parents who worried about being out of work, not being able to pay the bills, and how they would get us educated. But the war hit our generation directly. Thousands of our contemporaries are still limping around on artificial legs and using cleverly made steel hands that they acquired in those good old days. I prefer the bad new days, myself, and I consider myself fortunate that my memories no longer give me the feelings of fear and apprehension that I lived through at the time.

Are you losing your memory?

Before you decide that you are losing your memory, figure out for sure that you are. Most of us work on the basis of — "Darn it! I forgot my dentist appointment! I must be losing my memory." But that does not prove a thing. The chances are that forty years ago you forgot just as many things that were equally important.

The only way we can be sure about ourselves is to make careful measurements and records. Keep a record of your memory lapses. Get a special little notebook to use for that and for nothing else. Every time you forget something, make a note of it. Include the date, and write a brief description of what it was that you forgot. The questionnaire in Chapter 3 may give you some ideas for naming or classifying your memory lapses — and it may even remind you of some you forgot.

This record does two good things for you. First of all, you will probably discover that you do not forget as often as you thought you did. Secondly, it will tell you the kinds of things you are most likely to forget. That is important, because this book will explain different strategies for remembering different kinds of things. If you know what your own memory weaknesses are, you can select the strategies for that specific problem and work on them. This gives you a guided approach to memory improvement.

Do you believe it?

If you really believe that you are losing your memory, how come you are so stubborn about your favorite stories? Many years ago, when I was a lad of fifty or so, an elderly retired businessman told me at length about all the money he had made. He had given each of his children a million dollars. His former partner was in the conversation, and he burst out with, "But Joe, how could you? We never made that kind of money!"

Did Joe reconsider his statement? He was over eighty at the time — did he wonder if he was losing his memory? Not a bit of it. He knew he was right, and he stuck to his guns.

Memories are tricky at any age, but when we grow older we tend to think that our memory problems have just begun. The famous song writing team of Lerner and Loewe set it to music:

I Remember It Well

[Just before the song begins, Honoré tells Mamita: But I've never forgotten you. I remember that last night we were together as if it were yesterday.]

Honoré: We met at nine.
  Mamita: We met at eight.

Honoré: I was on time.
  Mamita: No, you were late.

Honoré: Ah, yes! I remember it well.

Honoré: We dined with friends.
  Mamita: We dined alone.

Honoré: A tenor sang.
  Mamita: A baritone.

Honoré: Ah, yes! I remember it well.

Honoré: That dazzling April moon!
  Mamita: There was none that night.

And the month was June.

Honoré: That's right! That's right!

Mamita: It warms my heart to know that you
        Remember still the way you do.

Honoré: Ah, yes! I remember it well.

Honoré: How often I've thought of that
        Friday ...
Mamita: Monday ...

Honoré: night.
        When we had our last rendezvous.
        And somehow I've foolishly
        wondered if you might
        By some chance be thinking of it too.

Honoré: That carriage ride ...
Mamita: You walked me home.

Honoré: You lost a glove.
Mamita: I lost a comb.

Honoré: Ah, yes! I remember it well.

Honoré: That brilliant sky ...
Mamita: We had some rain.

Honoré: Those Russian songs ...
Mamita: From sunny Spain ... !

Honoré: Ah, yes! I remember it well.

Honoré: You wore a gown of gold.
  Mamita: I was all in blue.

Honoré: Am I getting old?
  Mamita: Oh no! Not you!

  Mamita: How strong you were,
      How young and gay!
      A prince of love
      In every way . . . !

Honoré: Ah, yes! I remember it well.

*

And what, you may well ask, about finding my glasses?

I have not forgotten the glasses, but memory is such a wide subject, and is such a basic part of our lives, that there is much more to talk about than simply how to find your glasses.

I feel duty bound, however, at least to give you a tip at this point. One of the many devices I use — and you may be doing it yourself — entails my keeping all the old glasses my eyes have outgrown. I have a drawer full.

I keep my current pair of reading glasses with me at all times — except when I lose them. I keep the most recent outgrown pair on my breakfast table. If I misplace my current pair, I just get the pair from the breakfast table and use them. If I should misplace both of them (that has not happened so far), I would get an older pair from my drawer.

I don't worry about finding my current pair. They will show up. They always do.

But, you may say, that is not *remembering*. That's just admitting that you've forgotten, and you're working around it.

Okay, I have no objection to your calling it that. I don't care what you call it, as long as I have a pair of usable glasses when I want them.

My approach throughout this book is to suggest ways of getting the job done, whether it be by "memory" — biological memory — or some way that you might not call "memory" — an external memory aid. To me, improving one's memory means accomplishing what we want to do — calling someone by the right name, getting to the church on time, buying the groceries we need, increasing one's vocabulary, turning left at the correct intersection, or whatever. What does it matter how we do it — so long as it's legal and doesn't hurt anyone — if it gets the job done?

Chapter 2

Some Facts of (Older) Life

At their fiftieth college reunion, one man approached another and extended his hand. "My name's Harry Pott," he said, "do you remember yours?"

Two elderly women who had not seen each other for some time met by chance at the supermarket. After greeting each other, they decided to have lunch the following Saturday.

"I'll have to write that down," one of them said. "You know, my memory's getting so bad I have to write everything down or I never remember it."

"I do, too," the other replied. "You can't believe how bad my memory is. I can never remember whether it was you or your sister who died."

I'd like to condemn jokes like these because they help perpetuate the myth that memory falls apart as we grow older. I can't really condemn them, though, because they're too funny.

As long as we take them as jokes, I suppose there isn't too much harm in them. The problem arises when we begin to take them seriously.

Do we take them so seriously that when we get up on the morning of our seventieth birthday, we begin to forget things because we know we are now truly old? Maybe we should limp a little, too, and hesitate before we do or say anything.

Role playing

How are old people supposed to act? We all play the roles we believe that we belong in. When I was a child, I spake as a child. When I was a soldier, I dressed like a soldier, and I swaggered like a soldier. When I was a businessman, I dressed like a businessman; I took people out to lunch and cracked jokes and told them how good my product was. As a psychologist I weigh both sides of every question, look wise, and ponder before I speak. Now I'm an old man — I'm seventy-four. I've never been seventy-four before; it's a new experience. How am I supposed to play this new role?

If we believe that old people's memories decay, we are likely to include that as part of our role. If the role entails shunning memory tasks because we "know" they are now too hard for us, the self-fulfilling prophecy will come true. Memory skills become difficult to use if not practiced. Use it or lose it.

Sometimes the effect of role playing can be subtle. Friends tell us that taking a job is "too tough" or perhaps "unsuitable" for someone our age. No mention is made of memory, but if we do not take the job, or if we avoid taking a college course because we are "too old," our mental skills will get rusty. And that includes memory skills. Sitting in front of television will do nothing to help memory. Even worthwhile TV shows — and there are many of them — will do nothing for memory, because memory improvement requires activity and television is purely passive.

Role playing is tricky business. It can lead us into senility before our time. If we must play a role, let's play the role of the active, vigorous person who ignores the aches and pains and plows ahead, conquering each day as it comes, just as we did when we were thirty.

The little engine that could

When my children were young, one of the books they read at school was called *The Little Engine That Could*. If your children did not read it, they read something similar with the same moral. As I recall the story, it told about a little engine that had a hard time pulling its train up a hill — the job seemed impossible, but the little engine just kept telling itself that it could, it could, and in the end its efforts were crowned by success.

If that moral was good enough for our children, it is good enough for us. If there are things you want to remember, and they are important to you, then make the effort. You certainly won't remember them if you *don't* try — if you give up and decide that learning Spanish or learning to play the guitar or getting to your appointments on time is too difficult because of your age — then you have doomed yourself to failure. But brute strength and ignorance won't lead to success, either. It takes *intelligent* effort. The point of this book is to give you the information you need to make your effort intelligent. But only you can provide the effort — the effort that will make you the little engine that could.

Role models that encourage confidence

We have plenty of good role models to encourage us. The seventy-one-year-old Roman, Galba, over-threw the thirty-one year old Emperor Nero. Benjamin Franklin negotiated the peace treaty that ended our Revolutionary War when he was 75. Psychologist B. F. Skinner co-authored *Enjoy Old Age* (well worth reading) at the age of 78. In it, he mentions that "Michelangelo lived to be 89 and was painting to the end, Verdi wrote *Falstaff* at 80 . . . " Thomas Hardy wrote some of the greatest love poems in the English language after the age of 72. Leopold Stokowski signed a five-year contract to conduct a major symphony orchestra when he was 95.

Harvard Magazine for Jan/Feb, 1988, tells about Stephen Powelson, who memorized Homer's *Iliad* in the original Greek after he was sixty. Powelson studied Greek as an undergraduate at Harvard. When he was sixty, he found that he could still read classical Greek. He had not yet retired, but he set to work memorizing the entire book, which consists of 15,693 lines of poetry. By January of 1988, ten years later, he had mastered 22 of the 24 books, and expected to have the last two memorized by June. To get an idea of what this requires, the last two books alone include 498 proper names and 37 numerals. Powelson estimates that it would take seventeen to eighteen hours to recite the entire poem.

In an update in the September-October, 1991, issue, Powelson says: "I have now memorized the entire *Iliad*, except the last two thirds of Book two. The first third of that book and the ship and warrior catalogs in Book 2 have slipped from my memory from lack of review. I plan to complete the book and restore the lapsed parts in due course. Then I will scan the want ads for Homeric rhapsodes."

Note the importance of review. You will remember things by reviewing them over and over. I will emphasize the importance of review many times throughout this book.

Another example

To take a more modest example, look at my own case: I entered graduate school in psychology at the age of sixty-nine. My fellow students consisted of men and women in their mid- twenties to mid-thirties, carefully selected for their knowledge in the field. I have not only been able to keep up with them, but I have earned all A's so far, and I'm almost done.

My favorite bumper sticker reads: "Old age and deceit can overcome youth and skill." But I eschew such methods. There are many legitimate ways to compensate for whatever disabilities I may have developed. First of all, I used all the advantages I had. I was retired and living alone, so I had fewer demands on my time than my fellow students. I spent many Saturday nights studying, when most of my classmates were living it up. In addition, I had enough money to live modestly without holding a job, whereas most of my fellow students had to work as well as study.

Many of my contemporaries marvel that I can work so hard and do so well, but there is nothing marvelous about it. I do what I want most to do. I enjoy the work, so that working is a pleasure. Motivation counts for a lot in everything we do in life, and that applies to remembering the things we want to remember.

My interest in memory has grown as I have had to work my memory hard in school, and as I have specialized in the study of memory.

We should keep in mind the successes of old people like Franklin, Stokowski, and Powelson, not because we can all achieve at their level, but because it reassures us that age alone will not wipe us out as long as we are active — as long as we keep busy mentally and physically. In the first chapter, I mentioned that older people are more sensitive to memory problems than younger people. That sensitivity can be harmful to memory. Psychologist Hulicka found that " . . . older people tended to check more adjectives [on a memory questionnaire] . . . relating to fear, humiliation, frustration, worry, embarrassment, anxiety, and uneasiness, in contrast to just one or two by younger people." This observation led her to say, "Questions might be raised about the prevalence and intensity of fear of memory impairment, and when such fear exists, whether and how it affects behavior, general psychological well-being, and perhaps even memory itself. If anxiety can affect performance on laboratory tasks of little personal significance, it seems likely that fear of memory impairment could affect psychological well-being and general efficiency."

Dr. Hulicka confirms my belief in the need for confidence in our memory, but confidence based on fact. That's why we should take a closer look at what the psychologists who have studied the memories of older people have to say.

Slowing down

As mentioned in the first chapter, most psychologists find that memory is not as good in the later years as it was when we were young. But in what ways? Well, for one thing, most of them agree that it takes older people longer to remember things. In memory experiments where the subjects can memorize words or sentences at their own pace, older people spend more time, but they remember just as many words as young people do. In experiments where the subjects cannot move at their own pace, and words or sentences are flashed on a screen for a very brief time, older people do not remember as many of the words or sentences as young subjects do.

In other words, older people memorize more slowly, take longer to remember, and generally operate more slowly than younger people. That should come as no surprise. We walk more slowly, talk more slowly, eat more slowly. Our eyes take longer to focus and to adjust to changes in light. It generally takes us longer to react to any stimulus, mental or physical.

Reaction time

Reaction time has often been used as an argument to show that younger people can drive automobiles better than older people. But there is a serious question as to whether fast reaction time makes a better driver — and, of course, that depends on what we mean by "better." If we consider safety important, then fast reaction time does not seem to improve driving. British psychologist H. J. Eysenck looked at the question from a novel point of view:

> . . . the usual assumption that fast reaction times are a help in safe driving has not been verified on the whole. There are numerous investigations, all tending to show that the relationship between reaction times and the number of accidents suffered is practically non-existent. This may, at first sight, seem surprising, as one would expect that a person who can react quickly to a dangerous situation would be at an advantage, as compared with another one who was rather slower. There are many reasons why such an assumption would be unlikely to be true. In the first place, of course, the

driver is seldom confronted with a situation such as that represented by the typical reaction-time experiment. In the experiment, a lamp suddenly lights up and he has to press a bell-push as quickly as he can in response to this signal. He knows exactly what is going to happen and what kind of response is required of him, and, therefore, the actual reaction time is minimal, of the nature of about a fifth of a second. On the other hand, he does not know the precise moment when the light will light up. In the traffic situation the position is usually exactly the opposite. There is no sudden emergency which cannot be foreseen with any degree of precision, as is the case with the lighting-up of the lamp; the good driver is likely to have anticipated future developments from a general survey of the situation and from his experience of driving in situations of this kind. He will notice children playing with a ball on the sidewalk, and anticipate the possibility of the ball rolling out into the street, with a child running after it. This ability to anticipate events is far more important than the sheer reaction time to the child's actually emerging into the road, and is much more likely to lead to an avoiding reaction than would the simple reaction time, like stepping on the brake once the child had run out into the road. There is no reason to imagine that anticipation and reaction time have any relationship at all, and while undoubtedly in some, usually quite rare, circumstances reaction times might be important, in the great majority of cases anticipation is a factor which is very much more closely related to safe driving.

Another point which also deserves attention is that reaction times must always be related to other factors, such, for instance, as the speed at which the car is being driven. It is quite likely that a person who knows his reactions to be quick will take greater risks, in the knowledge that he can react more quickly than other people. In doing so, he may overstep the safety margin provided by his quicker reactions and, in actual fact, be a less safe driver than the person who has slow reaction times, knows that he is slow, and drives fully within the limitations set by this particular disability.

This passage illustrates the fact that even though the reaction times of older people have slowed down, they have fewer accidents than young people because they have compensated in many ways for their disability — and compensation is the key to living well when old.

That's important enough to say again: Compensation is the key to living well when old.

Slower can be better

One of the easiest ways to improve your memory is to slow down. When you rush out of the house to meet a friend or attend a meeting — that is when you forget to take the books or papers or whatever it was that you needed for the meeting. Take your time. Isn't it better to be a few minutes late than to arrive without the photographs or the book that was the purpose of meeting your friend in the first place? Consider two things: First, your chances of remembering are better if you take your time, and, second, is it *that* important if you arrive two minutes late?

The driving example illustrates both these points. Arriving at your destination without an accident is more important than setting a speed record in getting there. So, isn't it a good thing that older people drive more slowly and more carefully? I think it is. Older people have outlived the need to show off by fancy driving. They have learned that even if you get to your destination thirty-two seconds late, in the course of a long life that is not very important.

It often takes an older person longer to retrieve information from memory, but if the older person has learned to live with slower retrieval times and does not get flustered and embarrassed, what difference does it make? Keep in mind the old saying that haste makes waste. Remember that you will remember better if you take your time. That knowledge will ease any embarrassment you may otherwise feel.

An experiment by psychologists Burke, Worthley, and Martin drives this point home. They dealt with what is called the "tip of the tongue" phenomenon, or TOT. We all know what that is. When I was young, and I would reply to a question from my mother by saying, "I can't remember, but it's on the tip of my tongue," she would quip, "Stick out your tongue."

Burke, Worthley, and Martin took a more scientific approach. They had a group of young people (average age 20) and a group of old people (average age 70) keep track of every TOT episode they experienced during a month. They discovered two things.

First, they found that older people have fifty percent more tip-of-tongue experiences — half again as many — as young people. That agrees with what we already knew: older people take longer to remember things. The TOT experience is just part of the delay time till the memory comes to mind. We already knew that, but the TOT experiments confirm it.

Second, they found that when a memory stuck to their tongue, the young people eventually remembered it 92% of the time, but the older people remembered it 97% of the time. When we put the two facts together, we see that both groups remembered almost exactly as well (with the older group doing very slightly better) although the older people took a bit longer to retrieve the desired memory. The only difference seems to be a matter of time.

Take your time

I'm sure that you already got the message, but it is so important that I feel obliged to repeat it: Take your time!

That was good advice when we were young (and ignored it), and it is even better advice now that we are older and slower. I will give you all kinds of strategies for improving your memory, but every one of them will work better if you take your time and don't rush them. Haste makes waste. We all know that, but we tend to forget it just when it is most important for us to act on it.

I am making a big deal over this because it applies to everything I have to suggest throughout this book, and, as a matter of fact, to everything we do.

What memory experiments are like

Most memory experiments consist of learning lists of words or nonsense syllables or sometimes sentences and then taking memory tests. Some tests require the subjects to write down the items they learned; these are recall tests. Others present lists of items and ask the subjects to identify those that were on the original lists; these are recognition tests. As you can see, the procedures are artificial. They resemble the kinds of procedures that college students follow all the time, but they bear little resemblance to the normal activities of the everyday world we live in. It should not be surprising that young adults do better than old adults — the young adults that psychologists experiment on are almost always college students and the old adults rarely are.

Psychologist Perlmutter followed these procedures in a series of tests of young and old adults. But her series included not only lists of words, but lists of facts.

She found that, "Although older subjects performed significantly worse than younger subjects on word recall and recognition, they performed significantly better on fact recall and recognition."

Dr. Perlmutter commented: "Older subjects' better memory for facts should set their poorer memory for words in perspective. Although older subjects were evaluated as 'deteriorating' on typical laboratory tasks, they actually performed more competently than younger subjects on more relevant tasks . . . . The significance of list-learning word memory tasks should be questioned more extensively."

A question of motivation

My personal observations while taking and administering memory experiments, along with my studies of memory, suggest that older people simply can't work up enough motivation for remembering a meaningless list of words, nonsense syllables, or even sentences, to compete with college students who have to memorize such stuff all the time. Research psychologists are college professors, and college professors don't seem to realize that much of what they teach is considered meaningless by their students, who force themselves to memorize the material so that they can earn a college degree that will get them a better job. The first college course I took, when I returned to college after being out of school for thirty-nine years, was deductive logic. I had read enough on the subject to have an interest in it and to understand its value. Despite the early sessions in which the professor explained all that, several of my fellow students told me that they considered it all gibberish — meaningless stuff that was nothing more than an obstacle to be gotten over. Nevertheless, they did well enough to pass the course. They had accustomed themselves to learning gibberish — or what they considered gibberish. That had become their way of life. It is not our way of life in the workaday world.

Performing and observing memory experiments and the way young subjects behave during experiments led two psychologists to remark that the "only firm conclusion that can be made is the rather obvious one that far more factors are involved in everyday memory than those measured in the laboratory."

So, since the college students form the habit of learning material whether they consider it important or meaningless, it should come as no surprise that they perform better than older people on laboratory experiments. And it comes as no surprise that older people do better than young when it comes to what Perlmutter calls "more relevant tasks" — information that means something to them.

This is only a smattering of the large amount of evidence has accumulated to show that memory does not necessarily deteriorate to noticeably low levels with age. Psychologist Alan Baddeley tells us that the "young actually report more memory lapses than the old." Jeff Meer reported in *Psychology Today* that some kinds of knowledge, such as vocabulary, increase throughout life, and that if quickness is not considered a criterion, older people remember movies, sports information and current events better than the young.

Use it or lose it

More recent experiments, in which the psychologist uses tasks similar to the tasks we normally encounter in our daily lives, show that older persons continue to use both old and new knowledge effectively.

Reading offers an excellent example. People who read throughout their lives do not lose their reading skill. Better than that, people who read increase their vocabulary, which makes reading easier and faster, since it reduces the number of times the reader must stop to puzzle over unfamiliar words. In this way, reading skill will often increase with age, but that will only happen where there is continual reading practice — as with any other skill.

The problem of problem solving

The ability to solve problems, which is often used to test mental abilities, seems to decline with age. On the other hand, we become more proficient at problem finding, a talent that few of us have consciously thought about. To give you an idea of what it entails, consider the computer. Computers can solve many kinds of problems faster and more accurately than human beings; they are great problem solvers. But they cannot find problems to solve — human beings must determine what problems the computer will attack and must feed that information into the computer.

In addition to the increased talent for problem finding, we develop specialized skills as we mature. Engineers right out of college are not ready to design bridges or airplanes, although they may develop wonderful skills in one or the other as they mature. As one psychologist put it, "older persons become less skilled at general problem solving, but more skilled, sensitive, and adaptive within specialized areas." We lose very little of our memory for familiar things, and normally our fund of knowledge grows as we age, particularly within our field of work.

If you still have doubts about this, think of choosing a doctor. Do you prefer a doctor right out of medical school, who knows all the latest wrinkles, or an older doctor with years of experience and, one hopes, the knowledge and wisdom that go — or should go — with experience? My younger son spent the first month of his life in an incubator. We brought him home a strong, healthy infant. But he grew sickly and would not eat. We called the doctor, but found that he was out of town, so a young associate of his came out and examined the baby. He could find nothing, but the baby continued to sicken, so he took it back to the hospital. The baby flourished in the hospital, so we brought him home again, only to have the same experience.

Luckily, our regular doctor, a man in his seventies, came home and saw the baby.

"Celiac," the old man said.

I had never heard the word. (My dictionary tells me it is "a chronic nutritional disturbance in young children characterized by defective digestion and utilization of fats and by abdominal distention, diarrhea, and fatty stools.")

"But we tested him for that," the young associate protested, "and the tests were negative."

"Then the tests were wrong," the old man said. He ignored the tests, prescribed a diet of mashed-up bananas and no other food. The baby flourished. Today, thirty-eight years later, the "baby" stands six feet tall in his stocking feet, is in the pink of condition, and enjoys life.

I did not tell that story with the idea of putting down the young doctor. That has been done too many times, sometimes properly, but often when the young doctor is as competent or even more competent than his older colleagues. I told it simply to illustrate the fact that an old doctor *may* remember his professional stuff just as well as a younger doctor. It depends on the doctor, not on the age group he happens to fall into.

Scientific optimism

As psychological researchers develop increasingly more sensitive tests, the picture of memory aging improves.

We have more than one kind of memory. In fact, "memory" has been divided in many different ways. Just how we divide it depends upon the purpose we have in mind. A very common way of dividing memory is into "long-term" and "short-term" memory. That is a very old way. A very new way, which cuts across the long-term, short-term division, divides memory into three kinds: episodic, semantic, and implicit. Very recent work indicates that while episodic memory declines with age, semantic and implicit memories do not. They remain robust. Perhaps not entirely as robust as when we were young, but very, very close. In fact, some psychologists maintain that semantic memory improves with age.

Semantic memory refers to general knowledge and facts. The facts we come up with when we play Trivial Pursuits is a good example of semantic memory, and the facts we use — or used — on our job is an even better example.

Implicit memory refers to skills like riding a bicycle and swimming. We perform skills automatically — a notion that we will look into further in another chapter. Implicit memory does not decline with age. If you rode a bicycle when you were a child, you can ride now, if you want to. You may be a little wobbly at first, when you get on, but it will take only a very short time till you can ride with ease. And even if you are a little wobbly, that is nothing compared to the difficulty you had learning to ride when you were young. Remember how long it took, how many times you fell off? If you try it now, you may feel insecure, but you will not fall off.

Episodic memory — the only kind that seems definitely to decline with age — refers to specific events like the name of the lady you met yesterday at lunch, your spouse's birthday, your cousin's telephone number, your upcoming dentist appointment, and, of course, *where you put your glasses.*

Part of the reason for the decline of episodic memory with age comes from the fact that many older people tend to give up. (Remember the little engine that could?) Retired people often ease off on using their mind, including their memory. They don't exercise their mental faculties the way they did on the job before retirement.

But even the decline in episodic memory can be reduced — or it might be closer to the mark to say that we can compensate for it. There are all kinds of ways of compensating for the decline of episodic memory, and the way that helps most depends on just what it is you want to remember. The main thrust of this book is to provide you with tricks and techniques for compensating for episodic memory loss.

There is a wonderful gadget on the market that will help you remember where your glasses are. You've all seen it. It is a cord that fastens to both ends of the earpieces and goes around the back of your neck. When you take the glasses off, you let them hang. You always know where they are, because if they're not on your nose, they're hanging on your chest.

Women have taken to this device better than men, probably because men have more pockets than women. I always put my glasses in my shirt pocket when I take them off. I rarely put them on a table or desk, so I rarely lose them. Women rarely have shirt pockets, so they put their glasses on a table or desk and then forget where they are.

An alternative to the cord around the neck is the "glasses up" position, in which you put your glasses high on the head where they are out of the way but always available. As a bald man, I find this impracticable. I believe it takes a good head of hair to hold the glasses securely. It seems to me that even if you have a good head of hair, you will find the cord more convenient and reliable.

I've seen too many people searching for their glasses when the glasses were in the up position on their head all the time. So I recommend the cord without qualification for women. Because it has been used so widely among women, it has become associated with women's wear, and I believe that keeps many men from trying it. Some men use it, but I believe that the association with women's wear has frightened most men away from this very practical device.

Chapter 3

What Do You Want to Remember?

In reply to, "What do you want to remember?" it's easy to think, "Everything." But is that what you really want?

Do I really want to remember the exact spot where I parked my car every day of my life? If I could, would I want to sit in front of the fire on a cold winter's night, smoking my old meerschaum and reviewing in my mind's eye all those lovely old parking places?

As a matter of fact, we remember too much as we grow older. We remember too much of some things, too little of others.

We don't forget our stories, but we forget who we told them to. We remember all the trees, but we lose sight of the forest. What separates good speakers or writers from their inferiors is that the details they use bear on the point they are making.

You start out with, "Do you remember Fred Summerville?"

Your listener says, "No. I never knew anyone by that name."

That's your cue to change the subject, but instead you say, "You know, Fred and I were in Innsbruck — or was it Augsburg? No, I think it was Nuremburg — or maybe Frankfurt. Damn! I can't remember anything any more!"

Your problem is not that you can't remember. Your problem is that you don't realize that nobody cares. If you've never read Ring Lardner's short story, "The Golden Honeymoon," read it. In it, he laughs at an old man's over-active memory for irrelevant details. Here's a short excerpt to show you what I mean:

> We went to Trenton the night before and stayed at my daughter and son-in-law and we left Trenton the next afternoon at 3:23 p.m.
>
> This was the twelfth day of January. Mother set facing the front of the train, as it makes her giddy to ride backwards. I set facing her, which does not affect me. We reached North Philadelphia at 4:03 p.m. and we reached West Philadelphia at 4:14, but did not go into Broad Street. We reached Baltimore at 6:30 and Washington, D.C. at 7:25. Our train laid over in Washington two hours till another train come along to pick us up and I got out and strolled up the platform . . . .

Even without knowing the story, we can be sure that it makes no difference whether the train reached North Philadelphia at 4:02 or 4:03. In fact, the outcome of the story wouldn't change even if the narrator never told us that it stopped at North Philadelphia.

Although we may sometimes remember too much, we never remember everything. William James, one of America's greatest psychologists, pointed out: "If we remembered everything, we should on most occasions be as ill off as if we remembered nothing. It would take as long for us to recall a space of time as it took the original time to elapse, and we should never get ahead with our thinking."

Tristram Shandy by the eighteenth century writer, Laurence Sterne, is one of my favorite novels. In it Sterne makes the same point. The novel is ostensibly Tristram's autobiography. Tristram remembers *almost* everything — and includes it all in his book. The problem is — as he explains it — that with all that detail, it takes him three days to write the events that occurred on just one day of his life. Obviously, he can never finish the book. In fact, the more he writes, the farther behind he falls.

It's a good thing we *don't* remember everything.

Do we need to remember details?

Suppose you have invited a friend to dinner. He has never visited your house before, so he telephones you and asks you how to find it. You close your eyes to concentrate on your "picture" of the route from the bus stop to your house, and then you say: "Turn left from the bus stop and then take the third street to the right. My house is the fifth house on the right side of the street."

Those are simple, concise instructions, and your friend should have no trouble finding you. But your memory contains a great deal more information than you have given him. In fact, when you take the bus home yourself, you never use that information. You do not think, "Turn left; walk three blocks; turn right; count five houses." You could have given your friend the kind of information that comes to your mind when you visualize the route: "When you get off the bus, you will be on a broad, black-top road — Nelson Boulevard — with a great deal of traffic. There is a red brick Presbyterian church across the street, just a little to your right, with a yellow brick school — Nelson Elementary School — just beyond it. The huge old oak tree in front of the church is a well-known landmark. Turn left past the news stand and deli on the corner of Pine Street. Cross Pine, pass the drug store, the post office, and the large parking lot next to the post office. That will take you to Wilson Avenue, which is also a busy street with a bus route. Cross Wilson and continue on past the Sears Roebuck store and the Wilnel Theater to Margery Street. Turn right onto Margery Street.

"The first house, on the corner of Margery and Nelson is a large, white clapboard house of an indeterminate Victorian style with a wide verandah on two sides: facing Nelson and facing Margery. If the azaleas are in bloom, they are gorgeous. The second house is also white clapboard, but has a distinctive New England appearance with dark green shutters and a large, dark green front door precisely in the middle of the front of the house, and the doorway is flanked by two large evergreens. The third house is a brick colonial with a scrubby hedge across the front. The fourth is a brown shingle with green shingle roof, and the fifth, my house, is brick, painted white, with a slate roof. It has a round tower in the far front corner, giving it a French provincial air. The address is 2909."

If your friend wants to find your house with the least effort, he will read over your description carefully — assuming that he was able to write it all down as you spoke — and he will then reduce it to working instructions thus: "Turn left from the station and then take the third street to the right. Look for the fifth house on the right side of the street."

The details would only confuse him even if he could remember them.

Remember pi?

Most of us remember that we once learned something about pi — the number you get when you divide the circumference of a circle by its diameter. Rajan Srinivasen Mahadevan can remember pi to 31,811 decimal places. That put him in the Guinness Book of World Records.

Wouldn't it be wonderful to have a memory like that? Then you could remember everything! *Everything!* Or could you? It turns out that Rajan's memory for everyday things — names, faces, and words —

things like that — is no better than yours or mine. One of his best friends reports that, "He's unreliable, forgetful and annoying in lots of ways . . . He forgets our phone number constantly . . . "

Which would upset you more: to forget the value of pi entirely (and be the laughing stock of all your mathematician friends), or to discover that you forgot the tickets to the show when you are already miles from home and it is too late to turn back and get them?

When you think about improving your memory — just what is it you want to improve?

Photographic memory

It seems hard to believe that a photographic memory would not be a great help in getting through life, but it is not. About 7% of all children have photographic memories at age eleven, but they lose that ability as they grow older and develop more efficient memories. In my investigation of this fact, I picked up a bit of exotic trivia.

Psychologist George Stratton reported on a group of Jewish men in Poland called "Shass Pollaks" who had memorized the Talmud verbatim. The Talmud runs to thousands of pages, but the Shass Pollaks could recite every word. In fact, they were sometimes tested by being asked to tell, say, the third word in the eleventh line of page 873. They could do it. Nevertheless, none of them ever attained to any prominence in the scholarly world. When Judge Mayer Sulzberger of Philadelphia suggested to one of them "that he use his knowledge to some scientific or literary end, [he] was listened to with respect, but nevertheless received the impression that such proposals were deemed by his man to be nonsensical."

Some psychologists have found a higher incidence of photographic memory among retarded persons than among normal persons, suggesting that it is a more primitive form of memory. Alan Baddeley, who reports on this, concludes that photographic memory "seems to represent an intriguing but relatively unimportant byway on the road to understanding normal human memory."

What do you really want to remember?

The question is, then: What do you *really* want to remember? R. L. Kahn, concerned about problems of aging — not about memory improvement — wrote, ". . . the types of problem reported by older persons are primarily commonplace events, such as forgetting someone's name, forgetting what they went to the store for, or forgetting where they put something in the house. Because of the stereotypes about aging, older persons may take these everyday incidents, which would be ignored in the young, as indicating a pathological decline in memory."

There are other things we want to remember, too. Information we learned at school, current events, and, if we are still working, information needed to do our jobs. But since we can't remember everything, we must select the things we want to remember from the flood of information that pours over us every day.

And of course, different people have different needs and desires, so they will want to remember different things. Consequently, different ideas in this book will appeal to different readers. I expect that. I have tried to include as much as is practical for most people, and I assume that each reader will select what is important to him or her.

I have read many books on memory improvement, but not one of the authors has asked the question: What kinds of things do people want to remember better? More specifically, in our case, what is it that *older* people want to remember better so badly that they buy books on memory improvement?

Make up your mind

It is important to decide what kinds of things we want to remember, because remembering different kinds of things requires different kinds of memory skills. Strategies for remembering where we put our glasses are different from strategies for remembering the names of the important battles in the Civil War and the date of each. If you want to remember fifteen-digit numbers, you must master a skill that is different from the skill required to remember the names of people you meet socially. Some memory skills are easy to learn, but some are tough and take a lot of practice. In every case, you alone can decide whether the effort of mastering the skill is worth the promised results.

We must each clarify our field of interest so that we know what it is that we are after. The better we understand our goal, the better chance we have of reaching it. If we want to improve something, it will help us to know what that "something" is.

Since no one else has asked the question — what it is that people want to be able to remember better — I have asked it. I sent a questionnaire out to a hundred older people of my acquaintance, and I also had the participants in my memory improvement classes fill them out. I have also given the questionnaire to more than fifty college students at Cleveland State University. Here is the questionnaire:

Memory Questionnaire

The purpose of this questionnaire is to discover what things people want to be able to remember better. Things they would take a memory course to be able to remember them better.

Please check the *six* items you want to *remember better* so much that you would consider taking a memory course to improve your memory for them.

1. Personal data: own name, ss. no., address, tel. no.
2. Personal dates: anniversaries, birthdays of self and family
3. Reminiscences about past life, family members, friends
4. Personal schedule for work, school, etc.
5. Job duties, procedures, responsibilities
6. Routines of daily life (e.g. getting gas for car)
7. Shopping lists
8. Information needed for job, school
9. Appointments, date, time, and place

10. Things to do (e.g. attend to house repair, make telephone calls, etc.)
11. Where objects have been placed
12. Taking needed objects with one
13. Medication schedules
14. Names
15. Faces
16. Telephone numbers
17. Addresses
18. Road directions
19. Payments to make
20. Rules of conduct
21. Locations, places (e.g. where a particular store is, or a department in a store)
22. Responsibilities to others (promises, agreements)
23. Cultural and historical facts
24. Historical dates
25. Vocabulary
26. Numbers
27. Current events
28. Jokes
29. Trivia
30. Poems, parts for plays

One of the more interesting results of the questionnaire turned out to be the fact that the items checked most frequently by older people were not the same as the items checked most frequently by younger people. By far the most important things to remember for older people are names and the places where they put things. Younger people are more interested in those things that will further their career: information about school or jobs, and such things as vocabulary and cultural information, which is particularly helpful for students.

The questionnaire had a space marked "Other" which very few people used. But one lady in her late thirties phoned to explain why she had written "White lies" in that space.

She was sometimes embarrassed, she said, when walking down the street. She would meet a friend who would ask, "Are you feeling better?"

But she had not been ill. It helped, she said, if she could remember that the friend had asked her to lunch a week prior, and she had begged off with the white lie that she was not feeling well.

Let's return to the more serious questions – although if the statistics bore you, feel free to skim them – or skip to the next section. The items of most interest to older persons are listed below in the order of importance, based on the number of times people checked them off. I am using the results from 175 people over 60 years of age. Of the total number of checks, there were:

13.6% checks for Names

11.8% checks for Where objects have been placed (Where did I put my glasses?)

6.4% checks for Vocabulary

6.1% checks for Faces

5.7% checks for Cultural and historical facts

4.7% checks for Appointments, date, time, and place

You will notice a remarkable drop from the first and second items to the third item. Obviously older people consider names and where objects have been far more important to remember than anything else.

Comparable results from 28 people under 30 years of age are shown below.

10.2% checks for Vocabulary

8.4% checks for Information needed for job or school

7.2% checks for Cultural and historical facts

6.6% checks for Historical dates

6.0% checks for Where objects have been placed

6.0% checks for Responsibilities to others (promises, agreements, etc.)

The drop from first to last position here is not so steep, although the spread between each pair of the first four items is great enough to assure us that the ranking is correct. It is less clear-cut the farther down we go.

Some conclusions

The important thing to notice is how different the two lists are. Only two items appear on both lists: numbers 11 and 23. Number 11, Where objects have been placed, is right at the top for the over-60's, but it is fifth on the list for the under-30's. However, it looks like remembering where we put things is a problem for young and old alike.

Absent-mindedness is probably the chief reason we forget where we put things. I did not list absent mindedness in the questionnaire because it does not fit into the kinds of things I was listing; it is not something we want to remember better. It is a matter of prime importance, however, and I will discuss it along with the problem of remembering where we put things. It includes things like going into the basement and then, when we find ourself standing in the basement, wondering why we went there.

Vocabulary appears among the top six for young and old, showing that we never outgrow our need for more and better words. But it ranked number one for young people — who need to know words to get through college. The young gave it almost twice as many votes as the elderly.

Cultural and historical facts also seem to be a problem for both young and old, although slightly more important for the young.

The differences in the lists seem reasonable enough once we think about them, especially when we know more about the two groups that I questioned. The older group consisted of personal friends of mine and of students in some of the courses I have given for memory improvement for older people. Most of them are retired; the problems of mastering a job to earn a living are behind them. Most, if not all, are economically independent, and some are wealthy.

The younger group consisted of students at Cleveland State University. They consider school their chief occupation, although most CSU students work part time and some work full time in addition to their studies. Isn't it natural, then, that they rank vocabulary high on their list of things to learn? The second most important item for them was information needed for job, school. They are in school, aiming at a career in the work force. The third and fourth items in their list are cultural and historical facts and historical dates, all items of information that are needed to get through school.

Using the results

The importance of the results of the questionnaire lies in the hints it gives us for self-analysis. What is it that you want to be able to remember better? That is not as easy a question as it may seem at first blush. Think about it. Are you retired? Then information needed for job, school, etc., is not likely to be very important to you, unless you return to school, as I have done. In that case, it may be very important to you. Reviewing the items listed in the questionnaire and pondering the answers others have given can help you analyze your own priorities and choices among the kinds of things for which you want to improve your memory.

Do you want to improve your memory for names? Most older people consider that of greatest importance. Most younger people don't. The degree of importance you give to names will determine the amount of time and effort you want to expend learning how to improve your memory for them.

The rest of this book will be devoted to various strategies to help you remember various kinds of things. Everything listed on the questionnaire will be covered, and some additional things, too. But the questionnaire items are so important that this book has a special index that lists them for quick reference. They are also included in the general index that includes any other things you might want to look up.

In general, the things we want to remember can be put into three groups, which I call skills, facts, and intentions. My three groups are based on the work of British psychologist Peter Morris.

Three kinds of things

By skills, I mean such things as riding a bicycle, swimming, typing, and playing the piano. Remembering how to perform activities such as these is *not* the subject of this book. All of us have mastered some skills, and we have a pretty good idea of how to go about it. We usually learn from an instructor, who not only explains how we are to do the activity, but who also trains us and supervises our practicing. Father runs alongside junior on his bicycle, shouting instructions and warnings. After junior falls several times, he suddenly catches on — and off he goes. He will be able to ride a bike any time he wants to during the rest of his life.

Playing the piano is more complicated. It takes far more instruction and far more practice. We learn to ride our bike by sheer persistence: we take our spills over and over till we finally achieve the skill of balancing. Learning to play the piano requires that we learn the names of the notes, how chords are constructed, and many other *facts* — in addition to "skill" in the narrow sense. In other words, my three groups over-lap. As long as we know that, it should not bother us. There is nothing wrong with saying that playing the piano is a skill like playing mumbletypeg as long as we realize that it is a skill of a much higher order, requiring far more complex coordination and far more knowledge and thought.

One serious problem with these three groups is that memory itself has many of the characteristics of a skill, and some of the memory problems we face with facts and intentions entail particular skills.

If memory is a skill like tennis or golf, then we should be able to improve it by practice, and we can — in a way. But that way is not as simple as improving others skills. To explain this, I must review the dif-ference between biological memory and functional memory.

Biological and functional memory again

Biological memory refers to whatever it is in the brain that processes and stores memories. If the brain deteriorates with age, then biological memory will deteriorate with age.

Functional memory refers to the actual workings of memory. It includes the memories we dredge out of our mind, and it also includes the oven timer that reminds us that the roast is done. Obviously, the timer works just as well for an older person as for a younger one.

At the end of chapter 1, I suggested that you keep two pairs of glasses so that when you can't find one you can find the other. You can do that at any age — even if your biological memory has slipped. I know that many people would not call that a memory device at all, but I do. I consider it a form of functional memory. After all, it achieves the results you want from memory, and from my point of view, it is results that count. That is the position I take throughout this book.

We can improve our memory skill, then, by improving our functional memory. An example from William James illustrates what I mean. James said that practice does not improve memory. He had students practice memorizing poetry, and he found that practice did not improve their *ability* to memorize. But he was talking about biological memory, and that, since it is fixed by our physical bodies, cannot be improved with practice. However, James himself pointed out that we can improve our *methods* of memorizing — what today's psychologists call encoding. We can learn new strategies of encoding, and we can practice them.

For example, a student of James might have memorized the poems at first simply by reading them over and over. As long as he limited his practice to simple repetition, his ability to memorize would not change. But at some point he may have tried writing the poems out. The combination of repeated reading along with writing would improve his speed and accuracy of recalling the poems when tested. If the tests were oral, he might also have studied the poems by reading them aloud. This would improve his performance even more. In each case, it would be the change of strategy rather than simply continuing to repeat the poems that would make the difference. Thoughtful practice of this sort will very definitely improve functional memory.

The rest of the book deals with ways to remember facts and intentions, but I use both of these terms in a wider sense than usual. "Facts" covers not only such things as birthdays, the names of personal acquaintances and kings, historical dates, and telephone numbers, but also jokes, trivia, current events, poems, and road directions. "Intentions" covers all the kinds of things we intend to do, such as keeping appointments and promises, taking the birthday gift to Aunt Agatha, taking the right medicines at the right time, finding the deed to the house, and finding our glasses when we want them.

*

But have you found your glasses yet? If not, how in the world have you read this far?

Here's a puzzle for you. You say that you cannot find your glasses on Monday because you have forgotten where you put them. So you use another pair till you find them. Later, say on Tuesday, you remember what you did with them. You go to the place you remember putting them, and there they are. Now, is it correct to say that you had forgotten them on Monday? Were they not somewhere in your memory on Monday? If not, how did the knowledge of their location get into your memory on Tuesday?

Is it a matter of memory, or is it a matter of timing?

Chapter 4

Dredging Things Out of Memory

Remembering entails three processes: input, storage, and retrieval. Psychologists borrowed these terms from the world of computers, but they are beautifully descriptive.

Input

Input, as the word suggests, means putting something into memory. It is analogous to putting something into your pocket, but not exactly the same. If I put a dollar in my pocket, then I have a dollar in my pocket, but if I put the thought of a dollar into my memory, I do not have a dollar in my memory. As a matter of fact, I may not even have the thought of the dollar in my memory most of the time. It's not a thought unless I'm thinking about it, but I have a lot of things in my memory that I am not thinking about, so they can't be thoughts. They must be *something*, but no one knows what.

The closest we can come to understanding what that "something" might be is to call it a code. Somehow the brain takes information — the sight of the Empire State Building, for example — and transforms it into something that stays in the mind as long as we can remember what the Empire State Building looks like.

Nobody knows what the code is, but there must be some kind of code, so we can think of input as "encoding." I will use both terms. When I wish to emphasize the simple fact that something got into memory, I will use "input" — as a verb as well as a noun. When I wish to emphasize strategies for inputting that will help us remember the information later, I will use "encode."

Storage

The second memory process is storage. That is a mystery, too, although it is obvious that whatever we have in memory is stored there, and neuroscientists are beginning to find some answers to the mystery. Physiologists have assumed that the brain must change in some way — mechanically, chemically, electrically, or some combination of the three — when we learn things, and have searched for decades to find out exactly what changes. Only recently have they made any progress. New techniques, such as electron micrographs, have made this progress possible. But for our purposes it is enough to know that somehow, somewhere in the mind, our memories are in storage.

It seems that the way we store information depends upon how we put it into memory — how we input it — or, more precisely, how we encode it. So we will spend most of our time discussing encoding and very little on storage.

Those psychologists who believe that we remember everything forever are talking about storage. They believe that we store everything, whether we can retrieve it or not, and they draw an interesting comparison to a library. We can store thousands of books in a library, but that does not mean that we can find any particular book when we want it. If the system we use to store the books is not very good, we will have trouble finding our book. And even if the system is good, if we misfile a book when we put it away we are not likely to find it at all. (The analogy to memory would be poor encoding.)

Since everyone has heard of Freud (whether they understand him or not), we might take a look at one of his fundamental ideas. We are not aware of most of our memories most of the time. Freud would say that they are in our unconscious, and that is fair enough: There is nothing objectionable with that term as long as we understand what he means by it. Cognitive psychologists, who do the bulk of memory research, prefer to use the more neutral term "storage." They mean largely the same thing, although Freud's word lends itself better to his notion that many of our memories are repressed for one reason or another. Recovering repressed memories from the unconscious is a job for psychoanalysis, not for the garden variety of memory advisors like me. Fortunately, our memories for most of the things we want to remember are not repressed in the Freudian sense unless we somehow got them mixed up with heavy emotional burdens.

Retrieval

The third memory process is retrieval — dredging things out of memory. When we remember something, what we have done is to retrieve it from memory storage.

Although retrieval is obviously the third of the processes, I have two reasons for discussing it before I take up input and storage. First, retrieval is the pay-off. When we talk about remembering something, we usually mean that we have retrieved it from storage. Secondly, as I go through methods of retrieval, it will become obvious that if we want to improve our memories, we must learn to encode better. The trick to memory improvement lies in encoding, not in storage or retrieval, and there is no better way to learn that than to try to figure out how to improve retrieval.

Remembering where we put things

In the last chapter we saw that remembering names is the kind of thing that older people are most interested in improving. The strategies for remembering names can become very complex. They involve many techniques that will be easier to learn in connection with other kinds of things, so I will discuss the other things first; then, when we come to strategies for remembering names, you will be familiar with the various techniques that must be put together for names.

The second most important kind of thing to remember is where we put things. Finding things. Strategies for finding things are simpler than strategies for remembering names, but they call for some of the fundamental ideas of memory improvement. And of course they — like everything else — involve the three memory processes: input, storage, and retrieval. So we will begin by trying to remember where we put things — by trying to retrieve whatever we stored in our memory about where we put things.

Easier said than done. Is the information in storage at all? We assume that it is, although we might have failed to input it. In that case, there is no way to retrieve it. We can't retrieve something that isn't there.

A good way to begin a search is to look in the place where we *usually* put the thing we want — our glasses for example. There is nothing original about that. That's what we have always done. Unfortunately, that is about all there is to do. (And that is why encoding is so important.)

But we can also look in all the places that strike us as "logical" places to have put the glasses. The dresser, the piano, the top of the TV set.

If these strategies fail, then perhaps the most effective way to retrieve information is through reconstruction. Reconstruct what you were doing when you last used your glasses. Put yourself back in that situation;

reconstruct the context. Were you reading at the breakfast table? What did you do after breakfast? Did you go into the kitchen? The bathroom? Did you read in the bathroom? Where did you go then?

An old "absent-minded professor" story provides a perfect illustration of reconstruction:

An absent-minded professor was walking along the street one fine spring day when he encountered a student coming from the opposite direction.

"Excuse me," the professor said, "but am I walking north or south?"

"North, sir," the student said.

"Ah," the professor said aloud, but more to himself than to the student, "then I've already had my lunch."

It's a funny story, but it illustrates an effective way to retrieve information. If you walk south to get from your office to the restaurant where you usually have lunch, then, if you are walking north, you must already have eaten. The story is funny because very few of us forget that we've had lunch so soon after eating it.

The point is, though, that we can often remember things if we can reconstruct the event. Reconstruct the context: Where was I when I last had my glasses? Sometimes it helps to return to the last place we can remember using them. If we cannot actually return in person, we can always return in our imagination.

(Don't be upset if your glasses are always in the last place you look. That's where they *must* be, because once you find them you stop looking for them.)

You have probably used all of these methods at one time or another. They are not new. And they are not terribly effective. If you hoped to learn about a magic method that works every time, these suggestions can only disappoint you. But there are no magic methods, and there are no methods that work every time. This points once again to the importance of encoding. There *are* methods of encoding that may be new to you. They don't work every time either, although with practice you can get them to work very well. There is no perfect memory strategy. But encoding strategies work much better than retrieval strategies, and that is what makes encoding so important.

Encoding strategies and older people

In spite of the evidence that memory does not necessarily decline with age, the belief that it does is still widely held, even by psychologists. To explain memory decline in the face of the evidence, some psychologists maintain that older people do not use encoding strategies as often as younger people do.

There seems to be a lot of evidence showing this to be true. It seems odd, though, because the older people were young once, and they must have known and used the strategies. For some reason — and plausible reasons have been suggested — we tend to ignore the use of encoding strategies as we get older.

Ignoring them is a costly mistake. There is no reason why we older folks can *not* use all the strategies that younger people use — and use them just as efficiently. We *must* use them. Encoding strategies are the key to better memory.

More about reconstruction

Getting back to reconstruction, let's look at some of the more spectacular things that it can do for us. How would you reply to the question: "What were you doing on July 20, 1958?" Probably by throwing up your hands and saying, "There's no way I can remember that far back!"

But the chances are that you can give a better answer than that. I can, and if you follow my line of thought, you will be able to, too.

I begin by recalling that my children were ten and six in 1958. When they were that age, my wife and I took them to a cottage on the Michigan shore of Lake Michigan every summer for a vacation. My mother-in-law rented the cottage, and we stayed with her. Since I was working, I usually stayed for a week or two. My wife and children stayed a week or two longer. I am sure that we did that in July, and I am equally sure that we never spent the Fourth of July there. So the chances are very good that I was at Lake Michigan with my family on July 20, 1958. Or I might have been home without them.

Now, that does not tell exactly what I was doing on July 20, 1958, but it's a lot closer than giving up in despair and saying, "There's no way I can remember that far back." I can remember a lot of things that far back, and when I put them together I can come up with an idea of what I was doing that is a lot more accurate than a wild guess, even if it may not be right on the money.

What were you doing on November 22, 1963? You may draw the same blank as before unless you remember that President Kennedy was shot on that date. Providing that context almost automatically reconstructs your own activities on that day.

Try one more: When did the Cuban missile crisis take place? Assuming for the moment that I do not know the date of the Kennedy assassination, I would reconstruct my memory another way. I know that Harry Truman was elected in 1948 — that election year stands out in my memory. I know he only served one elected term, so Eisenhower had to be elected in 1952. Ike served two terms. Therefore Kennedy had to be elected in 1960. Kennedy was shot before the expiration of his first term. Therefore the missile crisis — I remember vividly watching him speak about it on TV — took place sometime between 1960 and 1964. I am fairly certain that it did not occur during the first year of his term, and that he did not live into the last year. So it was probably some time in 1962.

The correct date is October 1962. I didn't hit the bull's eye, but at least I hit the target. That may not exemplify perfect memory, but it shows how we can approximate knowledge by thinking about a matter and reconstructing it in our imagination.

Two kinds of events

We can divide events into two kinds: personal and impersonal. I have been discussing personal events, that is, events that happened to us, things that we did, or things that we want to think of in relation to our lives. We usually think of impersonal events as facts. The date of the Cuban missile crisis is a personal event if we think of it in terms of what we were doing at the time, or it is a fact if we are thinking of it as an event in history.

How can we retrieve strictly historical information? Information about events that occurred before we were born, and that we learned in school? For example: information about the War of 1812.

The first thing to do is to clarify the problem. Many people seem to think that unless they know where they learned a fact, they cannot be said to remember the fact itself. They want to remember, not only that John Quincy Adams was one of the members of the United States Peace Commission, but that they learned that from Miss Peabody in the eleventh grade at Cuyahoga Consolidated High School. Otherwise two terrible things might happen: Someone might challenge their veracity and they could not defend themselves; and, secondly, it might turn out that they learned nothing at all in Miss Peabody's class — all that time was wasted.

My position on this is simply that if you want to recall the fact, all you have to recall is the fact. You should forget where you learned it. If, however, you are a university professor writing a scholarly paper on the War of 1812, then you must be able to provide proofs and references for everything you say. Since most of us are not writing scholarly papers, why not settle for the facts and forget about the documentation?

If you bother to check my information, you will probably not find any mention of a body called the United States Peace Commission. At least neither the history book I consulted nor the Encyclopedia Britannica article on John Quincy Adams use that name. I must have made it up simply because the members of the delegation are sometimes referred to as "commissioners." But there is nothing strange — and certainly nothing "wrong" — with that. Our minds were created to store meaning — ideas — not words. We remember the gist of things; we seldom remember them verbatim.

So once again, I suggest that if our interest is in information, we should not expect to remember it verbatim — in the exact words that were used by the book or person from which we learned it. There are times when we do want to remember something verbatim: a part for a play or a poem we intend to recite. That requires a different kind of memory strategy. But when information is what we're after, let's not confuse the issue by groping for exact wording. Memory is naturally attuned to meaning.

How we can retrieve facts

With these qualifications in mind, how can we retrieve factual information? If the facts — about the War of 1812, for example — do not come to mind, try thinking of related things. Who was president at the time?

I have a vague memory of a movie that showed Dolly Madison fleeing the White House before the

British arrived to burn it. She had saved a portrait of George Washington, and off she went in some kind of buggy. For whatever that's worth, it tells me that James Madison was president.

Who was the big wheel in Europe at the time? My school teachers never mentioned that, but I learned later, from independent reading, that it was Napoleon. Napoleon was trying to bring all Europe under his control — as Hitler tried in our day. Despite all the romantic nonsense written about Napoleon, he was the bad guy of his time, and despite the bad press the British had in this country, they were the good guys. So we were on the side of the bad guys. Maybe that's why we were taught so little about the War of 1812. But once we know that, it's hard to forget it, because most of us develop an emotional involvement when we find that our country, which we love, was in the wrong.

Some interesting conclusions

A few important generalizations come out of all this. For one thing, it suggests that the more you already remember, the more new information you will be able to remember. My memory of an old movie makes it easy for me to remember that Madison was president during the war.

Similarly, we remember unusual things, striking things. If Napoleon had been just one more king or emperor, his name would not be so effective as a cue to remembering about the war. But he was an unusual man. He stands out. I called this quality "salience" in

Chapter 1. We remember things that are salient — that stand out.

So keep in mind that the more you know, the easier it will be to retrieve new material. Keep in mind that vivid, striking details will make facts stick in your mind.

And keep in mind that we remember meanings much more readily than we remember detailed wording or documentation telling us where we learned something. For the most part, the gist of the information is what we want, and that is what we remember most readily.

Finally, all memory is improved by reviewing the material. Rehearse the facts over and over and they will eventually stick.

Some other retrieval strategies

There are other retrieval strategies, most of which you already know and practice, but I will review them to refresh your memory.

If you want to remember a word or a name or a concept (which you would remember as a word), one common strategy is to run through the alphabet. Does it begin with "a"? With "b"? The initial letter of the word or name sometimes acts as a cue.

Think of a related word or concept. If you are trying to remember the word "retrieval," you might begin by running through the alphabet or you might find it simpler to think of related words. You know it is related to "remember," "recall," and "recognize." Perhaps one of these words will cue the word "retrieval" for you.

(Later on, I will discuss tricks such as thinking of "remember," "recall," and "recognize" as the "three R's." Since the expression "three R's" is very familiar to most people, it can be used as a cue to bring to mind the three words we want — and they will bring "retrieval" to mind.)

Think of the last time you used the word. Reconstruct the time and place and perhaps the situation. Reconstruct the situation in which you learned it or in which you normally use it. Think of everything you can *about* the word. One such thing — or several of them together — may act as a cue.

Sometimes you may want to remember items on a list, but you neglected to use an encoding strategy to fix the list in your mind. Someone challenges you to name the provinces of Canada. How can you retrieve the names — assuming you ever knew them?

As with words, you can run through the alphabet. You begin by trying to think of all the provinces that begin with "A." Then "B," and so forth.

A strategy that works better for me — although it only works with geographical entities like provinces, states, cities, etc. — is to visualize the map. I usually work from west to east, just the way we read. That usually cues in some of the provinces, or whatever I am searching for. I find that if I repeat the procedure a few times, I remember more of the names I am after, each time I repeat the list. If the list is long — all of the countries in Europe, for example — I may lose a few when I repeat them, but that seldom happens, and the gains outnumber the losses.

Ask a friend to help

We all do it: when we're trying to think of something, and we believe a friend knows what it is, we ask for help. The same thing applies to business associates, and certainly to the secretary who never forgets anything.

A tip for remembering: Tell your friend whatever it is you want to remember. Even if your friend is not in sight when you want to retrieve the information, the mere fact that you have put the information into words will help you remember it later.

After all: what are friends for?

Take it easy

Another generalization that comes out of thinking about retrieval is that we should not get up tight. Memories come back more readily when we are relaxed than when we are tense. Of course, simply telling people who are nervous to relax is futile; they are not nervous by choice. Perhaps a better way to approach it is to suggest that you do not take things so seriously. When my father was in his eighties, I remember that when he would forget something in the middle of a conversation, he would shrug and say, "What difference does it make?"

It seldom made any great difference. I don't remember any occasion where he caused the world to come to an end. His forgetfulness did not start wars or floods or earthquakes. By realizing and accepting that, he made his life and that of his relatives and friends more pleasant.

So relax. If the information does not want to come out of your memory storage now, it will later. If there is a good reason why you can't wait, stretch, take a few deep breaths, and try again. (I mean that literally: Stretching and deep breathing often help.)

The incubation period

It sometimes helps to turn away from a memory task entirely. You do not just relax, you forget the problem altogether. Later, when you try to bring to mind the item of information you forget, it may come as though of its own accord.

The period during which you turn away from the task and do other things is called the incubation period. It often works for memory retrieval, and it often works when you are trying to solve a tough problem. No one knows exactly how it works, but at least three suggestions have been made. It may be simply a matter of rest; you have tired your mind trying to find the memory or solve the problem, and what you need is complete rest. It may be that your mind has been running in a groove, like a phonograph record; turning away from the memory task lets you start over in a new groove when you turn back to it. It may be that while you are doing something else, your unconscious mind is struggling with the problem. And of course it may be a combination of all three. In any event, if all else fails, drop the attempt to dig up the memory, turn to something else, and if it is important to you, go back to the problem another time.

Cues

Perhaps the final generalization we can make about retrieval is that it depends upon cues. Reconstructing a situation will act as a cue to bring information out of memory. But where do the cues come from? Cues are bits of information that are in memory. But how did they get there?

Cues get into memory the same way other information gets in: through the input process. The effectiveness of cues depend on how they are encoded in memory. In the story about the absent-minded professor, he had evidently "inputted" the information that he usually walked north after having lunch. Consequently, the information that he was walking north acted as a cue to the information that he had already had his lunch.

Obviously, then, retrieval depends upon encoding. Had the professor not encoded lunch together with walking north, he would not have been able to retrieve one fact from the other. So if we learn to encode information more effectively, we will improve our chances for retrieval. And that is what memory improvement is all about. We will spend most of the rest of this book discussing encoding strategies that will help us retrieve information when we want it. And those strategies work by supplying us with cues to bring the desired information back.

Absent-mindedness

The problems of retrieval bring us quite naturally to the problem of absent-mindedness. Many people would simply call our professor absent minded and let it go at that. Fair enough — as far as it goes. But the idea of reconstruction is too good to overlook. And too valuable.

And a generalization that should delight all of us who are absent-minded comes out of the story. Although not all professors are absent-minded, and most absent-minded people are not professors, nevertheless, there is a germ of truth in the notion of the absent-minded professor. Research has shown that absent-mindedness goes with higher educational levels. So when you find yourself absent-mindedly doing something foolish, you can regain some self assurance from the fact — and it is a fact — that your high educational level bollixed you up.

Absent-mindedness is often a matter of priorities. Is it more important that our professor clarify the intricacies of nuclear physics for his students or that he remember that he just ate his lunch? I often find myself forgetting where I have put things when I am engrossed in deciphering a psychological problem. Although searching for a misplaced paper irritates me, I consider the psychological problem more important.

A scientist became so engrossed in his work that one morning he took two baths, one after the other, without realizing it.

Absent-mindedness can plague us in many ways. We have all had the experience of walking into a room and forgetting why we went there. That is troublesome, but don't make the mistake of thinking that it is a result of age. I was reading about this problem at a coffee house several months ago when a young friend joined me. I told him what I was reading and why.

"I walked into the bathroom this morning," he said, "and couldn't figure out why I was there. And I'm thirty-four."

Automatic processing

Sometimes we confuse automatic processing with absent-mindedness. Automatic processing refers to activities that we do without much thought. Driving a car is a good example. Haven't you sometimes found that you have been driving for several minutes but cannot remember doing it? That occurs to good drivers when they have been driving well and have encountered no problems. If a truck makes a sudden dash out of a side street, your mind shifts from automatic to conscious without your doing anything. You find yourself very much aware of where you are and what you are doing. That sudden change highlights the fact that you were previously unaware of what you were doing.

But why should your memory store information about your driving if you were doing a good job and the drive was uneventful? What purpose would it serve?

Automatic processing can sometimes get us into trouble — usually when the automatic process is interrupted. If someone comes to the door just as I am about to shave, I may forget to shave that day. The visitor interrupted my routine, and I picked it up a step beyond where I left off. When I was working, I always drove to work via the same route. Sometimes on a Saturday, when I planned to go shopping, I would be absorbed in thought and suddenly discover that instead of going to the store, I was headed toward my office — which suggests that even automatic processes require some thought.

These are petty annoyances. The advantages of automatic processes far outweigh them. Think what it would mean if walking were not an automatic process. We would have to think, "Now I put my right foot forward and shift my weight to it from the left foot. Now that my weight is on my right foot, I must put my left foot forward and shift my weight onto *it*." And so on.

When you were learning to ride a bicycle, you had to think of everything you did, every muscular movement. (You didn't think of *everything*, of course; it just seemed that way.) The result? You fell down. Gradually some of the movements became automatic: you could do them without thinking. Eventually that led to being able to ride. Once you learned to ride a bike, you never thought about the many delicate movements that you had to make to keep your balance.

Never? Well, not quite. Automatic actions of this sort take some thinking (as I mentioned before), but not much. Even walking is not completely automatic — even if you are on a flat, clear stretch of sidewalk. You can test this with a simple experiment. The next time you are walking with someone, ask them to subtract 48 from 64 mentally. For most people, the subtraction takes all their thinking capacity for a moment because they have to borrow in order to subtract 8 from 4. During that moment, they usually stop walking. Why? Walking is automatic, but not completely. It requires a little thought, but the arithmetic problem temporarily used *all* of our friend's thinking capacity. There was none left to think about walking.

Practice makes perfect

It takes a lot of practice to make a process automatic. An infant learning to walk must try over and over before it can walk with ease. Back in the days when you and I learned to drive — with manual gear shifts — we jerked and stalled many times before we mastered the process. The typewriter is even more demanding; it takes a lot of practice before you can achieve the degree of expertise that a man I once worked for demanded of his typists: they had to be able to type and look out the window at the same time.

More demanding skills call for a combination of automaticity and conscious thought and effort. Musicians, for example, practice throughout their careers. The pianist must be able to strike the right key without thinking about it and must be able to run up and down scales automatically. This frees the musician to concentrate on the more sophisticated aspects of musical art. Playing a piece of music well requires the proper balance between automatic processing and conscious concentration on artistic values. A piece that is played automatically sound mechanical.

Then there are tasks that improve with practice even though they never become automatic. College courses are easier for college seniors than they are for the retired person who returns to school after being away for forty years, because the college senior is in practice for them. The "returnee" can catch up quickly by intelligent practice. "Intelligent," in this case, means following study procedures that have been found most effective, and which are explained in any of the many excellent "how to study" books.

Memory improvement is another task that improves with practice but which never becomes automatic. It, too, must be practiced "intelligently," and the purpose of this book is to give you the guidance needed to make your practice intelligent.

*

It is not hard to see how automatic processing can contribute to frustration when we do something automatically, then try to retrieve a memory of the event. Just as we sit down to reconcile our bank statement with our check stubs, the telephone rings. We put down our glasses as we go to the phone. After we complete the telephone conversation, we return to the job of reconciling the bank statement. But where did we put our glasses? We automatically put them down when we went to the phone. Because the action was automatic, we did not think about it.

We could look at the same event and say that it was an instance of absent-mindedness. The name does not matter, and, in fact, both names fit equally. "Absent-mindedness" and "automaticity" both imply that you "did not think about it." And that is exactly what happened. When you act automatically, when you act absent-mindedly, it is because you did not think about what you were doing. That is the key to avoiding absent-mindedness.

Think about it.

Chapter 5

Two Magic Words and the Secret of Success

There is no magic short-cut to better memory. If you want to improve your memory, you will have to work on it, and the harder you work, the better your memory will become. Then what are the two magic words? And what do they do?

Two magic words

The two magic words are: *"Pay attention."*

What they do is answer all of the memory problems we considered in the last chapter — finding where you put something — absent-mindedness — and much, much more.

Think of the three memory processes: Input, storage, retrieval.

If you skip "input" and don't put something into memory because you were not paying attention, there will be nothing there to retrieve.

The key to controlling input is attending to the thing you want to remember. Pay attention. Our greatest source of failure in trying to remember names is not hearing the name in the first place. When we are introduced to someone, we are so busy thinking about what that person and other people around us are talking about — or we are so busy thinking about ourselves and the impression we are making — that we never hear the name. We did not pay attention to the name, so it never got into our minds to begin with. How can we possibly remember it?

There is a tremendous difference between the magic of our magic words and the magic of the stage magician or the magic of movies and TV. The magic we read about in romances can do anything for us. The two magic words just get us started. We still have work to do even when the magic words do their work.

We even have to work to pay attention in the first place. It will help if we tell ourselves to pay attention and make an effort, but it takes more than that. What can we do?

As long as we are awake, we are paying attention to *something*. The trick, then, is to pay attention to the right things. Another way of saying that is that we must avoid distractions.

It is a good working rule to assume that we can only attend to one thing at a time. That may not be strictly true, but if you manage to attend to two things at the same time, both of them will suffer to some extent.

Distractions

A very common distraction is thinking about ourselves instead of thinking about the job at hand. We've all found ourselves in the situation where we are talking with someone, and we see a glaze come over our friend's eyes, and we know that they are not thinking, about what we are saying, but about what they are going to say as soon as the opportunity arises. And we've all done that ourselves, too.

As long as I am thinking about what I am going to reply, I am not attending to what you are saying, and I am quite likely to miss the point of what you are saying. And of course I will be unable to remember what it is you said, because I never got it into my mind in the first place. No input, no storage. No storage, no retrieval.

Mood

Sigmund Freud made a valuable contribution to psychology when he pointed out that emotions affect everything that goes through our minds — including our memories. An almost forgotten humorist once wrote, "Nobuddy ever forgets where he buried a hatchet." That joke is true to the extent that anger is usually an intense emotion, so that even when we make up, a trace of that emotion is likely to preserve the memory of the quarrel, while we forget other events in which we had less emotional involvement.

Emotions and moods are hard to work with in the psychological laboratory, but most psychologists agree that strong negative emotions generally reduce our ability to remember things other than what is directly concerned with that emotion. This probably comes about because strong negative emotions interfere with our paying attention to anything other than the cause of the emotion.

Similarly, depression depresses memory — although I have made it sound simpler than it is. There seems to be no question that depression makes people complain about memory loss, but when those people are tested, they do as well as people who are not depressed. I wonder if the catch here isn't that depression distracts us from paying attention to what is going on around us, but does not actually affect our ability to remember when we are faced with a memory test. Some psychologists have found a somewhat complicated relationship between depression and memory loss: There is ". . . an interesting relationship between mood state and varied or constant condition during learning. The neutral mood subjects in the varied condition showed the best recall, whereas the depressed mood subjects in the constant condition showed virtually no recall." Depression also seems to depress intelligence — which is not surprising because memory and intelligence are closely related.

Obviously, the solution to this problems is to put ourselves into a more cheerful frame of mind. Easier said than done? Yes, particularly in cases of severe depression. Persons suffering from severe depression should seek the help of a licensed therapist, and as the depression is relieved, memory will improve. But in the garden variety of depression — a blue mood — and other ordinary moods, there are ways we can perk ourselves up. Simply being aware of the potential problem can help. Maintaining good health is an important way toward more positive moods. And concentrating on anything *but* ourselves and our personal problems helps.

Health

One way to preserve memory is to preserve health.

The importance of achieving and maintaining good health cannot be exaggerated. It frees us from one cause for thinking too much about ourselves — about our aches and pains. It makes life more pleasant, leading to the kinds of moods that enhance memory rather than depressing it.

On the other side of the coin: one serious kind of distraction is sickness and physical pain. Last Christmas I had a toothache, and I can testify that memory collapses under pain. How can one think about anything else?

There are no magic drugs

I have read about drugs and even diets that are supposed to improve one's memory. I don't believe it. If you have a disease that is known to affect memory, your physician may be able to prescribe a drug or a diet that will help you, depending upon the disease. But don't prescribe for yourself, and don't accept the kind of shotgun prescriptions you may find in books or magazines.

Since poor health and pain can weaken memory, if we want a stronger memory, one thing we should do is take care of our health. Eat a balanced diet, get plenty of exercise, and see your physician for any specific problems you may have. And I might add that if you take any illegal drugs, or if you drink beyond moderation, either stop at once or give up any idea about improving your memory. Even some prescription drugs can have adverse effects, and you should discuss this possibility with your doctor. With your doctor's help you can weigh the good effects of the medicine — which might be essential to your health — against the bad.

Hypnosis and truth serums

Every once in a while the news media run a story about a crime that was solved by hypnosis. A witness cannot remember what happened, although he was right on the spot. Under hypnosis, he remembers everything, and his information leads the police directly to the scene of the crime.

A similar scenario tells about a patient who cannot remember some traumatic event that crippled him mentally or physically or both. Under hypnosis the memory comes back, a cure is effected, and the patient lives happily ever after.

These events no doubt occur. But they do not occur every time. Psychologist Elizabeth Loftus reports that " . . . although hypnosis is held up by many to be the magic cure for getting at deeply buried memories, this isn't necessarily the case. Even when hypnosis does work to revive a memory that is temporarily blocked, it does not involve any awesome, mysterious power. Rather it seems that hypnosis encourages a person to relax, to cooperate, and to concentrate. In this state, people feel free to talk. What they say is on occasion a new important fact, but on other occasions nothing useful is said. All too often, totally false information comes out."

The story is similar, but even less promising, for truth serums. Among other discouraging facts, investigators have found that normal persons can lie, and can maintain their lie, even when treated with a truth serum.

In any event, such techniques as hypnosis or truth serums, even to the extent that they work, are totally impractical for you and me to use to improve our memories. We can hardly visit a hypnotist to help us find our car keys, or take a shot when we want to remember a luncheon date.

How to avoid distractions

Returning to more specific ways of improving your ability to pay attention: Take an interest in whatever it is you want to remember instead of passively hoping that whatever it is will sink into your memory by itself. If the subject matter of a conversation is of interest to us, that is no great problem. If it is not of interest, we should look for some aspect of it that is of interest. We can usually find something of interest if we search for it. And usually that interesting angle or fact can be used to build a more general interest in the subject.

Conversations are often lively enough to hold our attention, but most of us have a tendency to let our minds wander when we are reading — particularly when we are reading something difficult. In the middle of reading Baddeley's *Your Memory: a user's guide* we remember that we need a loaf of bread. Then, instead of concentrating on the book, we half think about what we are reading and half think about remembering to buy the bread.

The way to avoid this distraction is to keep a pad and pencil next to your book while you read. When a distracting thought enters your head, write it down. That will enable you to put it out of your mind when you turn back to the book.

Focusing attention

Writing has the additional advantage of focusing attention. You focus your attention on the note when you write it, then, even though you "forget" the note when you turn back to your reading, you will find that the need for that loaf of bread is fixed in your memory better than if you had simply tried to hold it in memory as you continued to read.

Since concentration means focusing attention on the job at hand, avoid a stimulating environment. Someone suggested that when you are reading or writing, the best view out your window would be a solid brick wall. If you look out over an airport or a lake, you will spend a certain amount of time watching airplanes take off or boats sail by. Some people seem to be able to work with a radio on. I am sure it is an inefficient way to work, unless the process of tuning out the sound somehow shuts out everything else except the job at hand. Certainly exciting music or speech will distract you.

Work in a familiar place. Set aside one or two places in your house or apartment for reading and desk work. Unfamiliar settings and unfamiliar events will pull your attention away from your work.

Can you force yourself to concentrate? Sometimes — to some extent. Sometimes when I am sitting in a psychology class, I find that my mind is wandering. I ask myself: what am I here for? I can daydream at home. I have only one chance to hear the lecture and the discussion; if I miss that, I have missed my entire purpose in going to school. That line of thought usually works. I am usually able to get back to paying attention.

Finally, relax. If you are tense or worried, you will have a hard time concentrating. But if you are tense and worried, how can you relax? By facing the source of your worry and working it through. That is seldom easy, and it usually takes time, but, as far as I know, it is the only way.

Form good memory habits

Habit is another form of magic. If we can form habits of concentration, then we don't have to think about concentrating (on reading a book, for instance), and we don't have to work at it. If the habit is in-grained, we just concentrate. It's automatic.

The obvious thing, then, is to form good memory habits.

Easier said than done. Our fantastically wonderful electronic entertainment centers — radio and television — train us to *not* pay attention. They work very hard to teach us *bad* memory habits. I have heard of a rule (which may or may not be true) that in writing TV and radio stories, everything is repeated three times so that the listener will become aware of it. This assumes that the listener is not paying attention, but it also trains the listener to ignore two-thirds of what is said.

Don't you keep the radio and/or television going even when you are not listening? You tune out the parts you aren't interested in. You get into the habit of tuning out speech that you are not interested in, and that habit carries over to things that you do want to hear.

So the weakening of the ability to pay attention is not necessarily a matter of age. It is in large part the cost of watching TV and listening to the radio.

Q: How, then, can we learn the habit of attention?

A: By practice. The way we learn all habits.

How to do it

Begin with something simple, like paying attention to where you put your glasses. If you do not wear glasses, use your car keys, or whatever it is that you sometimes misplace. But let's take glasses as the example.

When you take your glasses off, think about what you are doing. Tell yourself where you are putting them. Say it out loud. "I'm putting my glasses on the sink." If you do that, you'll remember where you put them.

After you've been successful for a while, you'll decide to short-cut the procedure and just put them down without saying out loud what you are doing. That is *not* the way to form a habit. Keep up the procedure until you are absolutely certain that you will *never* forget where you put them. That will take a long time. Years. But if you keep it up, you will form a good habit, and you will cut out a source of frustration, and you will save yourself a lot of wasted time.

After you have begun to feel successful with one good memory habit, start working on another. Work on whatever you consider next in importance. Don't try to remember things that are not important to you. That not only wastes time and effort but may be counterproductive. Our minds developed as tools to help us cope with the world around us, not as toys for our amusement. There is nothing wrong with using them as toys for amusement, but when we are trying to develop habits that will help us cope better with life, we should concentrate on the important things.

We do not remember everything; memory is selective. The image of things that we see and hear, and the thought of things that we learn only go into memory storage if we attend to them. The way that they go into storage will determine how easy it will be to recall them. So now let's take a closer look at the way things get stored.

Storage

One of the greatest blessings of age is the huge accumulation of knowledge stored in memory. It is not an unmixed blessing. Sometimes we remember too much — and bore our friends. Sometimes we confuse one memory with another. Sometimes we remember things we would rather forget. But, since learning builds on prior knowledge, the more we know, the more we will be able to add to our stock of knowledge.

When we come across a new piece of information, we relate it to what we already know. Only then can we say we understand it. The other side of the coin, of course, is that if we cannot relate it to what we already know, we do not understand it.

Many psychologists see the memory system as a vast network of information, with every piece of information interconnected to every other either directly or, for the most part, indirectly.

How networks work

Psychologists got the idea of a vast network of information by from the analogy of a physical network like a fishing net or a hair net. If you will visualize a fishing net or a tennis net, you will see cords crossing at various intervals. In network theory (which is what we are talking about) each crossing, where you see a knot, is called a "node." Every node represents a concept. And what is a concept? Most of us have a general idea that it is an idea — and we are almost exactly on target. A "concept" usually includes the notion that it is formed by thinking of instances of something: we get the concept of "animal" by thinking about horses, sheep, goats, etc. In addition, "concept" suggests what the thing ought to be. An animal ought to be living — or to have lived in the past — and ought to be mortal, etc. And finally, concepts can usually be represented by a word.

The nodes in the network — the concepts or words — are interconnected by relations. For example: a dog is an animal. In some network theories, we would say that dog and animal are connected by an "isa" relation: a dog "isa" animal. That is true of all dogs. But all animals are not dogs, so the relation has a direction: from "animal" to "dog." And there are different kinds of relations. Dog and fur are connected by a "has" relation.

Since we have thousands of concepts in our memory, the network is far too big for anyone to describe except in outline. It is complicated by the fact that one word often represents several concepts, many of them related, but some unrelated. Wing is related to bird, but also to airplane, and there are some similarities in the two relationships and some dis-similarities.

Furthermore, there are at least two kinds of nodes. We have a node for dogs, and we have a node for Fido, a node for Rover, a node for Tray, and so forth.

A characteristic of all network theories is that remembering something means searching through the pathways (the cords or wires that connect the nodes) from one piece of knowledge to another. In searching, we travel — mentally, of course — along the pathways or relations.

Association of ideas

Network theory may sound like no more than the old "association of ideas" that everyone is familiar with. "Association of ideas" has had a long history in psychology. In fact, networks are not really different from associations. The relationships are associations, but they are very complex associations.

My purpose in digressing into this abstruse subject is to show how our fund of knowledge makes it easier to absorb and remember new information. Suppose we were to show a picture of a penguin to someone who had never seen or heard of a penguin before. That person might well ask what a penguin is. When we say it is a bird, that immediately calls to mind that it is a warm-blooded animal, that it has feathers, two wings, two feet, and that it flies. All this related information about the penguin stored in the person's network, will make it easier for our friend to remember what the word "penguin" means.

But, you will say, penguins don't fly. True. That's one more complication for our network. Assuming that our friend had never before heard of a bird that could not fly, she will add a new node to her network: birds that cannot fly. (And since we have no single word for that concept, you can see one difference between words and concepts.) Imagine the problem we would have if our friend had never heard of birds! That, of course, is the problem that small children have when they first learn to talk.

Compare the position of an old person who has a vast network of knowledge with an infant just learning to talk. Can you explain to the child what a penguin is? Children go through a stage where all animals with four legs are dogs; if they can't tell the difference between a dog and a cat, can you explain to them what a giant panda is? How old must they be before you can teach them the meaning of concepts like "England," and "long division"? Before you can teach them that cold is not different from heat but is simply a low degree of heat? That the difference between men and women is deeper than differences in clothing and hair styles?

As we mature, we build specialized knowledge about the field in which we work, either as our regular job or as a field of great interest to us. This knowledge continues to increase as long as we are active in our work. Each of us has developed a specialized area of his or her network, containing thousands of pieces of knowledge that we understand because each piece has many relationships with each other piece.

As we grow older, we seem to have increasing difficulty making new connections outside our area of expertise, but we have little trouble adding nodes and connections within that area. And that is how we resolve the paradox that the more you know, the more easily you can add new information to your store of knowledge. If you are not sure why that is a paradox to begin with, consider the old idea of memory as a storage bin. If that were true, it would seem that the more we had in the bin, the less we would be able to add, whereas the fact is that the more that is in the bin, the *more* we can add. The modern concept of memory as a network of concepts more closely fits the fact that each person's memory seems capable of holding an infinite amount of knowledge.

The secret of success

Although network theory is new, the idea of multiple associations was understood long ago. A hundred years ago, William James, one of America's greatest psychologists, put it this way:

> ... *the more other facts a fact is associated with in the mind, the better possession of it our memory retains.* Each of its assrciates becomes a hook to which it hangs, a means to fish it up by when sunk beneath the surface. Together, they form a network of attachments by which it is woven into the entire tissue of our thought. The "secret of good memory" is thus the secret of forming diverse and multiple associations with every fact we care to retain. But this forming of associations with a fact, what is it but thinking about the fact as much as possible? Briefly, then, of two men with the same outward experiences and

the same amount of mere native tenacity, the one who thinks over his experiences most, and weaves them into systematic relations with each other, will be the one with the best memory. e.g. the athlete who remains a dunce at his books will astonish you by his knowledge of men's "records" in various feats and games and will be a walking dictionary of sporting statistics. The merchant remembers prices, the politician other politicians' speeches and votes . . .

Almost a hundred years before James, in the days when a simpler notion of association prevailed, James Mill wrote:

"What is the contrivance to which we have recourse for preserving the memory — that is, for making sure that it will be called into existence when it is our wish that it should? All men invariably employ the same expedient. They endeavor to form an association between the idea of the thing to be remembered and some sensation, or some idea, which they know beforehand will occur at or near the time when they wish the remembrance to be in their minds. If this association is formed and the association or idea with which it has been formed occurs, the sensation, or idea, calls up the remembrance, and the object of him who formed the associa-

tion is attained. To use a vulgar instance: a man receives a commission
from his friend, and, that he may not
forget it, ties a knot in his handkerchief.
How is this fact to be explained? First
of all, the idea of the commission is
associated with the making of the knot.
Next, the handkerchief is a thing which
it is known beforehand will be frequently seen and of course at no great distance of time from the occasion on
which the memory is desired. The
handkerchief being seen, the knot is
seen, and this sensation recalls the idea
of the commission, between which and
itself the association had been purpose-
ly formed."

We will use the notion of association a great deal,
and there is nothing wrong with thinking of it as the
old, simple association between two ideas. Sometimes, though, it will help if we keep in mind the more
complicated notion of networks. As always, my advice
is: use whatever device works best for you.

Why all the theory?
Since the purpose of this book is to help you improve your memory, I have included quite a bit of
information about psychology in general in order to
establish more nodes and relations that will help tie
together the specific memory helps that are offered.
Without some knowledge about how the mind works,
memory aids become tricks that may be helpful to

those who use them, but, because they take time to learn and effort to use, they are likely to be discarded before they are mastered.

A fund of knowledge brings another benefit in the form of motivation. If you want to master a new subject, say astronomy, push yourself to learn some easy information about it — a few elementary facts, if you are a beginner. The more you learn, the more interest you will take in the subject, making additional learning easier and, usually, more enjoyable. If you have not already discovered this for yourself, ask artists about their art or businesspersons about their businesses, and you will find them delighted to talk about the things they know. You can almost *feel* their interest leading them to learn more and more. (CAUTION: Be careful about asking the physician about medicine or the lawyer about the law unless you do not mind getting billed for your curiosity.)

A practical application: locations

You don't buy hats very often, so you always forget where they are located in your favorite department store. Why not associate them with a department you *do* remember? "Hats and coats" — where are they in relation to the coat department?

Can't remember where Joe Dork lives? Try associating his name with the name of a nearby street that you do know. If he lives near a bowling alley, think of him as a bowler even if he isn't. Associations work just as well based on fantasy as on fact.

A practical review

In the earlier chapters, my advice about finding your glasses concerned retrieval, but why not use what we learned in this chapter about encoding?

1. The magic words: When you put your glasses down, pay attention to where you put them.

2. The secret of success: Make some association between the glasses or where you put them with something else that you are likely to think of when you look for them. You put them on the TV? Visualize the TV with a happy face that wears glasses. Or if one of your favorite TV characters wears glasses, think of him or her wearing *your* glasses. Or think of yourself putting your glasses on to watch TV. Make *some* kind of association.

Remember, in the old days, when Dad drove across a railroad track, we would see the sign that said, "Stop, Look, and Listen"? That pretty well summarizes the whole procedure. Take your time. When you put your glasses down — or anything else that you hope to find later on — stop for a moment, look at where you are putting them, and listen to yourself say, "I'm putting my glasses on the TV, and I'll find them on the happy face of the TV, when I want them."

Chapter 6

Strategies

When we talked about the ways to find things — like reading glasses — in Chapter 4, we assumed the glasses had been put aside without any particular thought. We were considering the problem of retrieval: how to retrieve the memory of where we put our glasses. If we want to improve our memory, though, we must learn ways of getting information into our minds in a way that will make retrieval easy. So we come back to encoding — the *way* we get information into storage.

Encoding

Network theory suggests the direction we must take. We want to make the connections between the nodes (pieces of knowledge) as strong as possible, so that one idea brings related ideas to mind. And we want to develop as many connections as we can, so that every idea brings to mind many associated ideas.

We can also think of encoding in terms of cues. One idea acts as a cue to bring another idea to mind. If I put my glasses down on the TV, then, when I want them, seeing the TV set may act as a cue to remind me where the glasses are. We associate the cue with the glasses so that seeing the cue reminds us of the glasses.

Encoding strategies

We want to learn strategies that we can use to attack memory problems. For a working definition of "memory strategy" that will suit our needs, we can say that a memory strategy is "a deliberate and planful operation to enhance memory."

Since our definition calls for a *deliberate* operation, it should come as no surprise that we must begin by paying attention to what we are doing. We must exert some effort. And as with most activities in life, the more effort we expend, the better our results will be. If you find yourself struggling to memorize something, console yourself with the thought that the more effort you put into the job, the stronger the memory will be as a result.

Please note two important points before we get into strategies: First, strategies are particularly important for older persons. Second, strategies are not theoretical.

As I mentioned in Chapter 4, psychologists have found that even if older persons have the same memory abilities as younger persons, they often do not perform memory tasks as well as younger persons. How can that be? Because, although they know many memory strategies, they fail to use them. Instead of attacking memory tasks with the skills they have acquired over the years, they seem to rely on habit (not all memory habits are good) or experience or perhaps just dumb luck. So you should read the following sections on strategies carefully. You will find most of them — perhaps all of them — familiar. But review them. Think about them. And *use* them.

The second point: The strategies are not theoretical. They consist of ways of attacking memory tasks that psychologists have observed people using. Psychologists have merely spelled out the various techniques people use in real life. And they have found that these techniques work when they are properly applied.

So begin using them right now. Select the one that intrigues you most, and use it every chance you get till it becomes second nature. When you reach that point, concentrate on one of the other strategies till you have mastered that one.

Maintenance rehearsal

Although the term "encoding strategies" may be new to you, you have used encoding strategies all your life. The simplest strategy is called "maintenance rehearsal" — a long name for a technique you began using in kindergarten if not sooner. When you wanted to memorize a nursery rhyme, you repeated it over and over. That is all there is to "maintenance rehearsal."

Another example occurs when we look up a telephone number. Between the time we read the number and the time we dial it, we repeat it over and over in our minds. You can see from this where the name came from: we maintain the number in our minds by rehearsing it.

Maintenance rehearsal works. We all know that. According to network theory, it works by strengthening pathways. If we are talking about nursery rhymes, the nursery rhyme section of our memory network is activated; that is, we become sensitized to anything having to do with nursery rhymes. Then if someone says, "Little Jackie," the name "Horner" instantly comes to mind because we have heard it so many times. In the case of the telephone number, "4" leads to "5" which leads to "1," and so on. The first words of the nursery rhyme act as cues for the words that follow. The number "4" cues "5."

We usually begin to learn our address, telephone number, and social security through maintenance rehearsal — repeating them over and over — although we may use more sophisticated techniques also. We have each heard our names so many times that there is little chance of forgetting them. Maintenance rehearsal works.

Maintenance rehearsal is the only strategy there is for some kinds of memory work, but there are better strategies for most of the things we want to remember. Maintenance rehearsal is not very efficient, so that when we can find other techniques, we should use them.

Elaborative rehearsal

A far more efficient technique is called "elaborative rehearsal." Once again we have a long, technical term for an old idea: thinking about whatever it is you want to remember. William James mentioned it in the passage I quoted earlier: "The 'secret of good memory' is thus the secret of forming diverse and multiple associations with every fact we care to retain. But this forming of associations with a fact, what is it but thinking about the fact as much as possible?"

It is often easy to "think about" whatever it is we want to remember. A baseball fan who wants to remember so-and-so's batting average will think about the averages of other ball players without even trying. He will talk about the averages with his friends. All this will help fix the numbers in his memory.

But how will he remember the notion of "elaborative rehearsal"? If we assume that to be a new concept to him, we can see that he might have trouble. Well, to begin with, he might re-read the last couple of paragraphs. He might think about his own way of remembering batting averages and think about how it exemplifies the notion of elaborative rehearsal. He might ponder the meanings of the words "elaborative" and "rehearsal." What associations does the word "elaborative" bring to mind? It surely brings to mind the word "elaborate" — both as a verb and an adjective. As a verb it refers to giving a subject fuller treatment and adding details. As an adjective — "an elaborate description" — it suggests that we have expanded the description through carefully added details and more complete treatment. Also, we talk about making elaborate plans or doing something with elaborate care. Perhaps you can think of other ways of using the word. Try it. Just making the attempt, whether you succeed or not, will help fix the notion of "elaborative" in your memory.

Do the same thing with "rehearsal." Imagine taking part in the rehearsal of a play. You go over and over the play, speaking the parts and acting out whatever behavior the parts call for. The more completely you rehearse, the more elaborate the rehearsal becomes — you include every action, every facial expression.

An illustration

If you thought about the last two paragraphs as you read them, then you performed an elaborative rehearsal on the notion of "elaborative rehearsal." An illustration from psychologist Leonard Stern shows the difference between the two kinds of rehearsal, and clarifies their meaning at the same time:

> . . .imagine that two people, person A and person B, have just been introduced to someone named Arnold Brown. Contrast the strategies that A and B might adopt in an attempt to remember the name:
> Person A: Arnold Brown; Arnold Brown; Arnold Brown; Arnold Brown...
> Person B: Arnold Brown; let's see, Arnold can be a person's first or last name, as in the name Benedict Arnold;

Brown can also be a color name; Arnold
Brown; this person's initials are the first
two letters of the alphabet and they are
in alphabetical order ...

And an illustration from psychologist Alan Baddeley:

...if you are trying to associate the
words *man* and *watch* a simple sentence
like "the man dropped the watch" is less
likely to lead to good learning than a
more elaborate one like "the old man
hobbled rheumatically across the courtyard and dropped the gold watch down
the castle well." Generally, putting a lot
of effort into encoding leads to better
recall ...

Person A used maintenance rehearsal; Person B
used elaborative rehearsal. He (or she) thought about
the name and thought about its association with other
information that she (or he) already knew. The association of new information with old information is
the secret of success in memory.

Association again

Association is so important to memory that I must
go into it again. Association can be called a memory
strategy, but one that underlies all memory strategies.

Nine years ago, when I found myself living alone for
the first time in my sixty-five years, I decided that I
would have to make a conscious effort to keep up my
living standards. For one thing, I would shave every

day, whether I went out or not, and for another, I would make my bed every day, whether I had visitors or not. I planned to remember both of these things by associating them: When I made my bed, I would immediately shave, or, if I shaved first, then I would immediately make my bed.

If I walked past the bedroom and noticed that the bed had not been made, then I knew that I had not shaved either, and I would do both tasks. If I happened to run my hand over my chin and felt a stubble, then I knew that I had not made my bed, and I would do both tasks.

Sounds silly, doesn't it. But the fact is that both tasks got done and I can remember only one exception. My sister had visited me from Richmond. On her last morning, we talked over the breakfast table till it was time for her to leave. Then, as soon as she was gone, I hurried off to a luncheon date.

When my friend and I were talking at lunch, I happened to run my hand over my chin and was embarrassed to realize that I had left the house without shaving — and without making the bed. When I explained this to my friend, he almost fell off his chair laughing.

An occasional goof does not mean that association does not work. It only means that association is not perfect. My trouble was that I had been in too great a rush, and that is always bad for memory.

Some rules of association

Philosophers and psychologists have worked out some rules of association. An ancient list includes: 1) contiguity or togetherness, 2) similarity, and 3) contrast. Contiguity simply means that one thing reminds us of another if the two things occurred together in our experience. Making my bed reminds me to shave because I always do them together. Similarity and contrast suggest ways that we can make associations: look for similarities or contrasts. Note when you put your blue-rimmed glasses on a blue table: similarity. Note when you put your black-rimmed glasses on a white table: contrast.

More recent writers have added many rules, but only a few of them aid memory improvement. Cause and effect can be helpful. If we understand how one event causes another, then one will remind us of the other. The rule of frequency tells us that the more often two things occur together — or the more frequently we think of them together — the more readily one will remind us of the other.

A more important rule for our purpose is the rule of vividness. A vivid association helps memory far more than a weak association. That is why many memory advisors urge us to make bizarre associations. If you want to remember Mrs. Short's name, "see" her as three feet tall even if she is a woman of medium height. You can let your imagination run riot as long as the association actually connects the things you want to remember.

Of course you must exercise some judgment. When you park in one of those huge parking lots at a shopping mall, you must associate the location of your car with a permanent landmark. If you use the big dump truck parked near your car, it might not be there when you return, so that your association will do you no good.

Organization

Organizing information usually makes it easier to remember. As an illustration, try this experiment: Take a quick look at this string of 12 letters and see how easy — or hard — it is to memorize them in order:

A I O Z T N G R N A O I

After you have pondered that a while, try the same experiment on this string of 12 letters:

O R G A N I Z A T I O N

Unless you have a very unusual mind indeed, you will find the second string of letters far easier to memorize than the first. And yet, both strings contain exactly the same letters.

You already know why the second string is easier to remember, but I will discuss several reasons. The first, of course, is organization. The first string was displayed in random order; the second string took the same letters and organized them into a word. Even if you had never heard the word before, you would be able to pronounce it because it conforms to the pattern of English words. But since you had heard of the word and you know what it means, you can remember it very easily.

I have run into many people who pride themselves on being disorganized. Most of them consider themselves artistic types. Maybe they are. The objection to being disorganized is that it puts an unnecessary burden on memory.

If you want to improve your memory, get organized.

Organize your life

You must be worried to some extent about your memory or you would not be reading this book. Well, the best way to compensate for any biological deterioration that might affect your memory is to improve the organization of your life. Take the time to be more deliberate, more methodical. You will find more specific suggestions as you read on.

An example from everyday life will show one of the many ways that we use organization. And you will notice that the organization helps more than just memory. Suppose you have to run four errands. You want to remember all four. The first thing most of us would do would be to organize the four in the order in which we want to do them. I will pass the bank on my way to the laundry, so I will begin to organize my list by putting the bank deposit at the top. The laundry is about the same distance beyond the bank as the shoe repair shop, but the supermarket is close to the shoe shop on the way home. So it would be best to make the laundry number two, the shoe repair shop number three, and the supermarket number four. This is a commonsense way of organizing my four errands, and the organization will help me remember them.

More examples

Libraries are often used as an analogy to show the importance of organization. Imagine trying to find a book in a library where 100,000 books have been stored helter-skelter. Without organization, libraries of more than a couple hundred books would be of very little use. Obviously a library is not memory, but organized memories are far easier to retrieve than unorganized memories, because organization is a form of meaning, and our minds work best with meanings.

The organization of books in a library suggests other obvious kinds of organization. In a business office, correspondence is usually filed in the alphabetical order of the correspondents' names. Invoices are often filed in the alphabetical order of the customers' names and cross-filed in numerical order. Sometimes correspondence with salespeople is filed by territory using some kind of geographical principle of organization.

We all organize things by class or category. We put salespeople in one category and clerks in another. That seems to be the way we think: animals are animals, vegetables are vegetables, and minerals are minerals. And because that's the way we think, we remember things better if we organize them by categories.

Do you still prefer disorganization? Then think of what it would be like to look up someone in the telephone book if the names were listed at random.

If you think about the examples, you will see that organization is a kind of association. In the errands example, I associated four items in order; going to the bank brought to mind the associated idea of going to the laundry. In the library, all the psychology books are stored in the same section; they are associated "geographically." If you want to find a book by B. F. Skinner (one of the most important names in recent psychology), you would look in the psychology section of the library. If you want to find a book by William James you might have a little more trouble, because he wrote important books in philosophy as well as in psychology. Luckily, librarians offer us either card files or computers in which the books have been organized by author, subject, and title, so that we can find them easily.

A note on theory

Americans, they tell me, are practical people. And, they also tell me, that is why they don't like theory.

BUT. Theory, in many cases, is the best way we have to organize information. Theory is an explanatory scheme. It shows us the relations among isolated facts. It shows us their associations.

An example from astronomy illustrates my point. Ancient observers collected thousands of facts about the heavenly bodies, their positions, and their movements. They wove many of these facts into theories that helped them predict tides, seasons, and other phenomena that they could use, for instance, to aid agriculture. The Egyptian, Ptolemy, constructed a theory that wove almost all of the facts and earlier theories together in one vast theory that seemed to explain everything. By relating almost all astronomical information, Ptolemy gave meaning to thousands of otherwise isolated and meaningless facts.

As the centuries rolled on, astronomers found so many additional facts that the Ptolemaic theory became clumsy. Copernicus worked out a theory that associated the facts in a way that was easier to work with. Was Ptolemy's theory false and Copernicus's theory true? In a sense both were true and in another sense both were false. The important thing is that Copernicus's theory organized astronomical facts better than Ptolemy's. That is what good theories do.

Theories and networks

When I explained the three memory processes, I was reciting a theory of memory. It is a very useful theory, because it enables us to understand what goes on in memory and consequently to use our knowledge to improve our memory.

Perhaps you have caught on to where I am going. Theories are networks of associations, just as the memories in mental storage are networks of associations. Looking at James's advice in a slightly different way, we can see that when we want to learn some facts, we can learn them more easily and remember them better if they fit into a theory — if we can relate them to other facts and ideas that we know.

It would be hard to remember what a carburetor is if we did not know anything about automobiles or automobile engines. The more we know about how an engine works, the more we find ourselves knowing about carburetors. The automobile is a structure; each part fits into its place in the structure. A theory is a structure into which related ideas and facts fit. Knowing the theory helps us understand and remember the facts and ideas that it incorporates.

Other strategies

We can use many other techniques to aid our memories. We can think of them as additional strategies, or we can think of them as additional techniques of elaborative rehearsal. It really does not matter as long as we understand them and use them.

One common technique has been called "divide and conquer." When our high school teacher assigned Hamlet's "To be or not to be" speech for us to memorize, we did not try to memorize the entire speech at one crack. We divided it into smaller pieces. We worked on the first line, then the second line, and so forth. At some point we worked on several lines together, grouping more and more as we conquered the smaller pieces till we finally could recite the speech as a whole.

Any extensive piece of information can be divided into smaller pieces. The smaller pieces are easier to remember, so we work on them until we have mastered them.

Chunking

"Chunking" is a funny name for a process we all use, although we may not be aware that we use it. It refers to grouping things together in units that are easier to remember. A few examples will make it clear.

The telephone company chunks our telephone numbers. My old number was 9910306, which is hard to read, to say nothing of being hard to remember. Why? Because with all the digits run together, each digit is equal to every other digit, so that each one can be considered to be a chunk. Seven chunks. But the telephone company broke the number into two chunks. Like this: 991-0306. The first chunk, 991, has only three digits, so it's much easier to remember. The second chunk, 0306, has four, but we tend to break even that into two chunks: 03 and 06.

The magic number seven

Psychologist G. A. Miller discovered, many years ago, that we can hold about seven chunks in short-term memory. The seven digit number can be remembered, but fewer chunks make it even easier to remember. The letter string AIOZTNGRNAOI is hard to remember because each letter, having no obvious relation to the other letters, is a chunk. Twelve chunks exceed the capacity of short term memory. But when the letters are reorganized into the word OR-GANIZATION, we see it as one chunk. And that makes remembering it duck soup.

As you can see, there are no hard and fast rules about chunks. What is 12 chunks looked at one way becomes one chunk looked at another. That is probably why Professor Miller used the word "chunk" instead of coining a four-syllable word derived from the Greek, as with most technical terms. "Chunk" *is* a technical term, but not a tough one.

Look for an easy way to chunk this 12-letter string:

IBMCBSPHDFDR

If you break that 12-letter string into four 3-letter chunks the letters will make some kind of sense. Not much. But at least they will be familiar to you.

In the section on organization, I mentioned organizing things by category. We often do that when we chunk. I can illustrate that by assuming that you want to memorize a list. Take this list:

> bush, snake, chair, tree, petunia,
> wolf, lamp, cat, table

It is easier to remember these nine things if you group them by categories, thus:

Animals	Plants	Furniture
snake	bush	chair
wolf	tree	lamp
cat	petunia	table

You can remember the three categories easier than the nine separate things. Each category is one thing, so you are only remembering three things — less than seven. The things in each category — also less than seven — will usually come back to you by association.

If you will think back on the section about "divide and conquer" you will realize that it is simply another way of speaking about chunking. It will remind us that we can divide things up into chunks, or we can collect separate items into chunks. Chunking is a very flexible, very useful memory tool.

Understanding

Most of the facts, concepts, and complex ideas that we want to remember have meaning. Our minds work most naturally with meanings, so that if we can grasp the meaning of those facts, concepts, or complex ideas, we will be well on our way to remembering them. Understanding is the most powerful way of keeping things in memory.

Perhaps the main reason we found ORGANIZA-TION easier to read and to remember than AIOZTNGRNAOI is because the word "organization" means something to us. The example also illustrates how organization and meaning go hand in hand. The second string used meaning as its principle of organization.

Learning is mostly a matter of understanding and remembering. We can hardly say that we have learned something unless we understand it. We sometimes say that we have learned something in the past but no longer remember it, but when we reflect on what we have learned, we can see that understanding and memory fit together.

Understanding is so important to memory that I will discuss it at greater length in Chapter 9 on remembering things that make sense.

But some things that we want to remember just don't make much sense. Most numbers don't, and that is one reason why it is so hard for most of us to remember numbers — and I suspect that that is an important reason why many of us have so much trouble learning math. Names don't make much sense, either, and, again, we have trouble remembering names.

When we are faced with the need to remember information that makes little sense, we use strategies called "mnemonics." Mnemonics are devices — or tricks — that impose some kind of meaning on information that is pretty much devoid of meaning. We will spend some time studying them later in the book.

Imagery

I have discussed the other strategies largely in terms of meaning. Imagery is different. Although it can be meaningful, it need not be. If you want to remember what your friend's house looks like, a pure visual image will help more than trying to figure out some kind of meaning in the architecture of the house. Most of our imagery is visual. We can "see" the faces of our friends if we close our eyes and call them up. Because vision is so important to us — we think of most things in terms of their looks — visual imagery is the most important kind of imagery. All books on memory improvement emphasize the use of visual imagery, and I will, too.

Most people have no trouble seeing images in their mind's eye. If someone asks you how many windows are in your living room, the chances are that you will close your eyes, "see" the living room, and count the windows. Most people know from experience that if they can see an image clearly, they can remember a lot about the image that they see. Even though, as I mentioned earlier, a photographic memory is not as efficient as a memory that works with meanings, images can give valuable help to memory. They are so valuable that if you are one of those people who does have trouble making images, you will do well to practice doing it.

Imagery supports other strategies, and you should use it as much as possible to support other strategies. In the quotation from Baddeley early in this chapter, he points out that a good way to associate the words *man* and *watch* is through elaborative rehearsal: think of the sentence: "The old man hobbled rheumatically across the courtyard and dropped the gold watch down the castle well." That sentence sets a scene that is easy to visualize, and if you combine the image with the bare sentence, it will vastly increase your chances of remembering the association.

Conclusion: wherever you can, use imagery in addition to other strategies.

Using imagery

After you have organized your shopping trip to the bank, laundry, shoe maker, and supermarket, close your eyes and see yourself driving to each of them in order. If you see each place clearly, you will remember all four errands when the time comes to make the trip. The image must be sharp and clear. You must see each place the way it looks when you drive up to it. Imagery is used in many memory tasks. If we want to remember someone we meet, the best way to remember the face is to make an image of it in our mind. The best way to remember the name is to associate it in some way with the image of the face. I will mention various ways of doing this in Chapter 13.

When you realize that your cross-country short cut has led you into a maze of back roads and you stop to ask how to get to Pittsburgh, visualize the directions that the lady gives you. Make a mental image of the right turn and then the left turn, the red barn and the old house with the roof blown off. They won't look like your image, but seeing them will cue the image which, in turn, will cue the instruction to turn left.

Psychologists often use the word "image" as a verb. It means the same thing as "imagine," but we use it to stress the notion of making an image in your mind. Most images are visual, but we make images with our other senses, too.

Imaging with our other senses

Hearing is our second most important sense. Aural images can be useful. I have never thought of myself as good at memorizing poetry or a part for a play. I find that it helps me if I listen to a record of a poem; then, when I try to recite it, I can "hear" the poem as I go. Musicians often use this method — along with others — to memorize music. They "hear" the music in their mind as they play, and that helps them remember the thousands of notes that make up a lengthy piece.

We can use our other senses, too. We can remember the odor and the taste of our Thanksgiving turkey, and we can remember the feel of marble and of sandpaper, and how it feels to walk and to run. In most cases it is hard to use these senses, although they can be helpful in strengthening a visual image.

We will do even better if we can combine more than one kind of imagery. If you think you may forget that it is strawberries you want to borrow from a friend, combine images of the way they look, smell and taste to fix them in your mind.

Similarly, combining imagery with meaning helps memory. If you want to remember what your friend's house looks like, visual imagery helps more than the meaning of the architecture — if there is such a thing as "meaning" of architecture. But use both. If the house is Tudor, knowing that and thinking about it when you think about the house, will help fix the appearance of the house in your mind. Is the arch over the front door really Tudor? Did genuine Tudor houses have storm windows? Attached garages? Can you see Henry VIII standing in front of the house trying to figure out what the electric wires are for? If you can see him, you will remember the house. Probably forever.

When we use imagery to help our memory, we are also using association. We often use organization, too.

In fact, when we use strategies, we seldom use them pure. And we remember best when we use every strategy that we can apply to the task at hand.

How to strengthen your images

The stronger the image, the more reliable your memory will be. Here are some tips for making the strongest images possible:

1. Pick out the most important aspects of the material you want to remember and exaggerate them.
   a. Pick out the salient features.
   b. Use the technique of cartoons and caricatures.
2. Make your image concrete. Something you can see, hear, feel, taste, and smell. Use as many senses as you can.
3. Association entails a relationship between two things. Be sure you include both of those things in the image.
   a. The two things must be related in the image.
   b. Whenever possible, have the two things interact with one another.
4. Make your image as vivid as possible.
   a. Vividness means clarity. Your image must be so clear that you have no trouble seeing every important feature.
   b. Bizarre, ridiculous, impossible images are great.
   c. Use motion whenever you can. Moving objects stand out.

5. Make the image unique, that is, avoid using the same image for more than one thing, otherwise you can easily confuse one with the other when you try to recall them.
6. Make your image yourself and make it personal. The images I have described are illustrations. Your own image will mean more to you. If you can include yourself in the image, that will strengthen it.

One reason older persons forget

I said it before, and I'll say it again: One of the chief reasons that older people do not remember as well as younger people is that they do not bother to use the memory strategies that they know.

After a successful career as a machinist, merchant, letter carrier, housewife, musician, or whatever, many people seem to believe that their expertise on the job will carry over into everything they do. Sorry, but that's not so. The letter carrier may not have exerted great effort to learn the names and addresses on his route (or perhaps he did), but he spent forty years working with them before he retired. Now, if he wants to learn something in less than forty years, he must exert enough effort to make up for the shorter span of time. And of course that goes for all occupation including the learned professions.

And that brings to mind a problem with this book — or any book on memory improvement. The book can tell you what do to, but it can't make you do it. You must not only know what the memory strategies are, but you must practice them until you use them automatically.

Use this book for reference. Read it through, but keep it on hand, and refer to it from time to time. Concentrate on the strategy that appeals to you most until it becomes second nature. Your memory will improve tremendously. When you have conquered one strategy, refer back to the book and select another one to work on. Read about it, so that you can attack it intelligently. Don't depend upon your memory from having read the book a year earlier, because you are bound to forget some of the details.

Memory is a skill. It is something like playing the piano. (But not exactly.) There are plenty of books that tell you how to play the piano, but even if you read every one of them and understand them perfectly, you will not be able to play until you sit down at the keyboard and work at it. Practice. The same thing holds true of memory. You can read and understand everything in this book without any improvement in your memory. You must work at it. Practice.

Memory is part of thought. To improve it, you've got to think about it. You've got to practice, and you've got to practice intelligently. The purpose of the book is to guide you, so that your practice will be as intelligent as possible.

*

Where are those glasses? If you have forgotten what we said about reconstruction, this is a good time to review it (pages 77-78, 80-81). Everything in the book must be reviewed, because memory can only be improved by reviewing the information we want to remember.

We discussed reconstruction in Chapter 4, and we also discussed automatic processing there. The chances are that you can't find your glasses because you put them down automatically — without thinking. No conscious encoding, and certainly no encoding strategy.

So let's try to reconstruct the event. Where were you when you last remember having them? What were you doing at the time? If you can't remember what you were *actually* doing, what do you *usually* do? What did you do next? Or: what do you *usually* do next? Follow your progress until, hopefully, the memory of your putting them down on the kitchen table jumps into conscious memory.

Or try running through your day. Did you have the glasses at breakfast? I always do, because I always read at breakfast, and I can't read without glasses. Many of us make a pit stop after breakfast. Did you have your glasses then? I always do, because I always read in the biffy. (It's quiet, and no one disturbs me.) What then? Ah! Changed purses (men: changed jackets) before leaving the house? Then take a look in the purse (jacket) you left behind.

It may not always be as easy as this to reconstruct your day, but try it. It may work.

And if it doesn't, what have you lost by trying?

Chapter 7

How to Find Things

Scenario: When you bring in the mail, you find that your bank statement has arrived, and you decide to reconcile it with your check stubs. As you begin to walk to your desk, the telephone rings. An important call. You talk for five minutes or more. Then you start to your desk to reconcile the statement. But where is it? Where did you put it when the phone rang?

Novel situations

I call that a novel situation, even though it happens to us many times in our lives. It is novel because each time it is different. If, when the phone rang, we always put whatever we had in hand in the same place — say in an "In" box on our desk — then it would be a routine situation: Every time the phone rang we would go through the same routine, and we would have no trouble finding the bank statement.

A novel situation is new and different. At the parking mall, we always park in a different place, so we can have trouble finding the car when we want to go home.

We all know the frustration of trying to find important documents, and in Chapter 4 we looked into ways of finding them. No way of finding them worked very well. Far better to encode the information so that retrieval will be easy.

How can we improve our encoding? Take the example of the bank statement: We get the mail, find our bank statement, and decide to reconcile it with our check stubs. The telephone rings. We answer it, talk for a while, and then cannot find the bank statement. We cannot remember what we did with it when the phone rang because we did not encode the act of putting it down. How can we avoid this situation?

The most important thing we can do is to slow down. What usually happens when the phone rings is that we feel rushed, so that we do not notice where we put the statement. Take your time. The phone will continue to ring. The additional time will be only a matter of seconds; if the call is not important enough for the caller to wait three seconds, is it so important that you must rush to the phone?

Take enough time to think about what you are doing. Think: I am putting the bank statement on the TV. Why on the TV? Think of the reason, and you will remember where the bank statement is. Did you put it there simply because you happened to be next to the TV when the phone rang? That's O.K. — if that is really the reason. Perhaps you put it there because you normally put nothing there, so that you are more likely to notice it when you want it. That's a better reason.

Tell yourself what you are doing, and say it out loud. "I am putting the bank statement on the TV because I am sure to notice it there when I come back into the room." Sound silly? Of course. But it will insure your finding the bank statement. It will obviate the frustration that comes from being unable to find the statement.

Make it a habit

On the surface, there seems to be a catch to this well-meaning advice: How can we remember to follow it? If we can't remember where we put the bank statement, how can we be expected to remember to slow down and to say aloud where we are putting it? The answer is the same as the answer to all of the suggestions in all books on memory improvement: Practice. Form the habit of doing things the right way.

You have reached the age where it is natural to slow down, and people expect you to slow down. So do it. Make it your way of life. From an early age, we were told to make haste slowly. Most of us recognized the advice as good, but we hustled through life anyway, making mistakes that we could have avoided. It's time, now, to do things right. It would drive us crazy to give up our automobiles and travel as slowly as Benjamin Franklin and Thomas Jefferson had to. Think of all the time they wasted! But perhaps if we could slow down to their speed we could accomplish as much as they did.

When you slow down and think about where you put your bank statement, you will make a mental note of its location. Make some kind of association. In giving yourself a reason for putting the bank statement on the TV you are making an association between the statement and the TV. The TV will then act as a cue; when you see the TV, you will think of the bank statement.

When you park at the shopping mall, you most likely go through exactly that procedure: You find a landmark near your car and associate it with your car. Many large parking lots have numbers or letters on the lamp posts for exactly that purpose. That permits you to say the number or letter out loud to fix it in your mind. If you must use a landmark such as a clump of trees in the distance, close your eyes and "see" your car in relation to those trees. Use imagery to reinforce the association. When you are halfway to the mall entrance, look back at your car to see it and the landmark as you will see them when you return. Remember, the more different ways of associating the car with landmarks, the less trouble you will have finding it later.

Say it out loud

I have recommended saying out loud what you want to remember. That is something that should be stressed. If someone overhears you, they may think you are a little touched. But you will find your car — or whatever it is that you were fixing in your mind. Whoever laughs has failed to understand the power of one's own voice.

If, when you sit down to tackle a difficult reading assignment, you say, "I want to understand this, and I am going to master it," you will find it easier to accomplish. Ask your friend to remind you to buy spaghetti; she will forget, but you will remember because you exerted the effort to say it out loud, and you heard yourself say it.

Try it. The next time you drive on a foggy day and turn your lights on, say — and say it OUT LOUD — "I have turned my headlights on. When I stop the motor, I will turn them off."

Multi-modal strategies

Psychologists use the grandiose term "multi-modal strategies" to refer to using more than one action or sense to help remember something. The more modes you use, the better your chance of successful remembering. When you turn on your headlights on a foggy day, you should not only *think* about the need to turn them off when you park the car (one mode), and say out loud that you will turn them off (another mode), but also form an image of yourself turning them off (a third mode). "See" yourself doing it.

It is usually impractical to write yourself a note to say where you put the bank statement or that you must turn off your headlights, but if you did, you would remember better, even if you never looked at the note. It *is* practical to write a note reminding yourself where you parked you car, especially if you park in a lot where you get a ticket. Jot a note on the ticket indicating where the car is. The chances are that you will find the car without ever looking at the note. Just writing it down (another mode) will fix it in your memory.

To sum up: In a novel situation, we forget where we put things because we were not thinking about what we were doing. We were absent-minded; that is, our mind was not on the act of putting the bank statement on the TV, it was absent — it was thinking about answering the telephone.

Absent-mindedness is the perfect example of failure to encode. We were thinking about something else, so nothing got into memory to remind us where we put the object we must now search for. And this emphasizes the fact that memory is a form of thinking. When we put the bank statement down, we were not thinking about what we were doing. The solution is obvious: think about what you are doing if you want to remember it.

Pay attention

I've said it before, and I'll say it again: Pay attention. But attention is a limited resource. If we think about answering the phone, we may not have enough attention capacity left to think about the bank statement, too. So think about the bank statement. We all tend to think about the phone, because it is ringing, and the loud ring demands that we give it all our attention. It insists that we forget about the bank statement. All the more reason to think about the bank statement. Experience has shown us that we are quite likely to forget where we put the bank statement, but there is no way we will forget the telephone with its insistent ringing. So train yourself not to panic when the phone rings. Always take your time getting to it, whether you have a document in your hand or not. Make it a habit to be deliberate in your response to the phone. Make a mental note (and say it out loud) of where you are and what you are doing. Then answer the phone. You won't forget *it*, and it will still be ringing when you get to it.

You should react in a similar way when you are face to face with someone. For example, you have the bank statement in your hand when someone enters the room — your spouse, a child, or a friend — and asks you a question. Excuse yourself politely to finish your job — taking the bank statement to your desk (or completing whatever task you were in the middle of). Then return to the person who interrupted. Naturally, you should return as soon as possible, but never with undue haste. The ancient saying is true: Haste makes waste.

Remember that attention is a limited resource. Don't squander it by paying attention to the wrong things.

A digression

While we are on the subject of training yourself to pay attention, I must repeat and elaborate on the theme: Don't pay attention to the wrong things!

Most memory improvement books are good. For the most part they offer good advice. But not always. Several of them suggest that you can improve your ability to pay attention by paying attention to *every-thing*. And they even advise you to practice doing it!

Here's a quotation from a recent memory improvement book:

> With a photo of trees, notice the shape and color of the leaves, the number and orientation of the branches, the appearance of clouds in the sky, and the details of shadows cast by the trees. Now open the book and find two details you missed before. Continue checking the picture for missed details until you are convinced that you have noticed everything.
>
> Ask yourself questions about your everyday actions. Which hand do you use to turn on the light switch in the bathroom? to remove your glasses? to pick up your purse or wallet? Do you take the same route to work each day? Describe that route. How do you place your glasses when you put them down? Do you get dressed in the same order each day? Try to list that order.

But that will never do! The human mind is naturally selective in its work. It does *not* notice all the sights and sounds that impinge on our eyes and ears because not everything is important to us. What we should practice is paying attention to the things that *are* important to us, and the more important something is, the more intense our attention should be.

Take the suggestion of describing your route to work (if you are not retired). What you *should* remember is where to turn and which direction to turn. The furniture store in the middle of the block that you have passed a thousand times without noticing should not be noticed till the day comes when you want to buy some furniture. Time enough to notice it then.

If you wish to enhance your enjoyment of the visual arts, then it may be well to study photographs in the way the quotation suggests, although a far better way would be to take some drawing or painting lessons.

An illustration

Let me illustrate the point from my own personal experience. My favorite subject in college was physics, which I took in my sophomore year. I never worked so hard on any other subject during my college days. I studied every detail of the subject because it was of interest to me, and I considered it important to know everything I could about it. During Christmas vacation that year, I went to a party where we played a parlor game that required us to study a picture for a set length of time, after which we took a test to see who could remember the greatest number of items in the picture. That is exactly the test the writer of the quotation suggests. Well, the reason that I remember the party so well is that I won the game. I remembered far more items than anyone else.

The reason for my success was *not* that I had practiced remembering everything I looked at. Not by any means. The reason was that I had discovered a technique for remembering those things that I decided were worth remembering. The technique — and it is ancient, although I thought I had discovered it — is nothing more or less than elaborative rehearsal, which I discussed in Chapter 6 on strategies. Very simply, elaborative rehearsal means thinking about what you want to remember, rather than merely saying it over and over.

When faced with the picture game, how did I think about it so that I could remember it? There was nothing mysterious about it. I simply said to myself: "There is a squirrel in the lower left-hand corner behind the tree. A swing hangs from the tree, and there is a little girl swinging from it. Etc." I begin at the left and looked at every item in the picture. As I did, I told myself what I was seeing and related that item to whatever it was near.

What I had learned from my college work was to organize my thinking — to be systematic. I systematically began at the left and moved slowly across the picture, so that I saw every detail. By naming each detail to myself and relating it to the other details, I fixed them in my mind. And I got a feeling of accomplishment from the game that I truly enjoyed.

Studying unimportant things is dull, unrewarding work that is more likely to make *you* dull than to sharpen your powers of attention. Take it seriously, and you will become a perfect bore to your friends. Studying important things is interesting and can be fun. And perhaps the most important skill we can learn is that of being intelligently selective. We may laugh at the absent-minded professor who cannot remember whether he has had his lunch, but we admire his ability to explain the recondite teachings of Albert Einstein in a way that brings enlightenment to his students. He does not observe or remember everything; he remembers the important things.

Go, and do thou likewise.

Another note on absent-mindedness

Finally, to avoid the absent-minded act where you find yourself reaching into the medicine cabinet and not being able to remember why you are even in the bathroom at all, follow the procedure we've been talking about. When you decide you need an aspirin, say out loud, "I'm going into the bathroom to get an aspirin." When you get there and reach into the medicine cabinet, you will pick up the bottle of aspirin.

Routine situations

Every time you want to drive your car you must remember where you put your car keys. If you need reading glasses, then every time you want to read you must remember where you put them. Most people, by the time they reach my age, have figured out how they can keep such things as car keys and reading glasses where they can find them. We all know the trite but true solution: A place for everything and everything in its place.

There is really nothing to add to this perfect piece of advice except some details about how to carry it out. The "place" should be logical in the sense that you would ordinarily think of looking there for the object. Men will usually look for their car keys in their pants pocket. At night they will keep them in their pocket if they plan to wear the same clothes the next day, or they will put them on the dresser, where they will be handy. Women will keep them in their handbag — but which handbag? When they take their keys out, a good place to put them is on a table or in a drawer near the place they keep their handbags. The important thing is to select one and only one place to keep them.

A logical place for everything

A logical or reasonable place to keep many objects is near the point of use. If you keep your gloves in the coat closet, they will be easy to find when you put on your coat. I always read at breakfast, so I keep a pair of reading glasses at the breakfast table. I keep a pencil there, too. You might want to have a "pencil drawer" in any room where you are likely to need to write. Loose change can be kept where you keep your handbag or your wallet.

Do you take off your rings or your watch when you wash dishes? If so, put an attractive hook on the wall alongside the sink at eye level so you can store the ring or watch on it. This will do several things for you: It will always be there within easy reach, so you need not look for a place to put your ring or watch; it will keep the items safe and dry; and because you always put them in the same place, you will always know exactly where they are.

We all know these things; the problem is doing them. Once again, the only effective solution is habit. Make it a habit always to put your car keys in the same place. Select a bowl on the hall table or a drawer in the table as the one and only place to keep them. Never deviate. Then they will be there when you look for them.

Simple as this advice is, it is surprising how few people follow it. If you are truly concerned with maintaining your memory as you grow older and sincerely wish to do something about it, follow these two simple strategies: 1. A place for everything and everything in its place, and 2. Make that a habit. If you do, your memory will serve you even better than it did when you were young.

Habit and routine

A routine situation is one that recurs. That allows us to develop habits to handle those situations. We *always* need our keys to drive the car; therefore we can utilize habits that make it easy to find the car keys.

Since routine situations are easier to control than novel situations it makes sense to turn novel situations into routine situations. Then we can utilize the good habits that help us handle routine events. We can set aside a place on the dining room table where we *always* put mail or papers or anything else that we want to put down temporarily when we are in that part of the house. If we build up a habit, then, when the phone rings, that will be the place they end up.

Going to the theater during a vacation trip is a novel situation. Where do you put the theater tickets so that they will be in your hand when you approach the theater? A handbag or jacket pocket is not so good, because you make take a different handbag or wear a different jacket. Why not form the habit of always keeping tickets in the same place — the top dresser drawer of the motel room, or an envelope in your suitcase, or on the TV held down by something heavy like the Gideon Bible? Whatever place you choose, be sure that you will find the same place in every motel room you stay at.

Vacation trips and traveling generally present many novel situations — that's why we travel; we enjoy new sights and unusual experiences. But the novelty upsets our routines, and that often upsets our habits.

A novel situation

A friend of mine was driving to a football game in Pittsburgh, but he took a wrong turn somewhere and found himself in Coraopolis. He pulled into a gas station to ask directions. As he was getting out of his car, the attendant approach him.

"Lost, aren't you," the attendant said, smiling.

The Ohio license on the car made it obvious that it was out-of-state, but — "How did you know I was lost?" my friend asked.

"What would you be doing in Coraopolis if you weren't lost?" the attendant — obviously not a home-town booster — replied. (I've been there myself *on purpose* and found it a pleasant little town.)

The situation was evidently routine for the station attendant, but it was a novel situation for my friend, and the attendant's remarks truly surprised him. Surprised him enough to upset the best of habits. After he received his instructions and returned to his car, he found that he had inadvertently locked the door with the motor running and his keys inside.

And a lesson to be learned from it

Usually, as in this case, the attendant knows how to open a locked car — a sad reflection on automobile locks. But what if this had happened where no such help was at hand? It has happened to me once or twice, and I now carry an extra key in my billfold. The idea is, of course, the same as the one I suggested about keeping an extra pair of reading glasses. I never go anywhere without my billfold, so I always have the extra key with me. A pocketbook presents a more difficult problem, but if a woman uses a money purse of some kind, which she puts into whatever pocketbook she intends to carry, that purse is the place to keep the extra key.

Permanent situations

The word "permanent" in this phrase is somewhat like the same word in the phrase "permanent wave." It means for a long time, but not forever. Some examples will make it clear: the title to your car, which you need only once a year or when you sell the car; your passport, which you need only when you travel abroad; your ice skates and skis, which you need only in winter

— if you are foolhardy enough to skate or ski at your age. (Incidentally, I did both last winter, and I live to tell the tale.)

As with car keys and reading glasses, permanent storage should be logical. Valuable papers like stock certificates go into your safe deposit box. If you keep a lot of documents at home, get a file cabinet. Organize shelves and storage rooms so you can find things.

I encountered an extreme example of organized storage when I was in the army. The food storage warehouse had to be inventoried once each month. To keep everyone honest, regulations required that an officer who normally had nothing to do with the warehouse must supervise the inventory, and it had to be a different officer every month. That meant that a complete stranger, usually someone who had never been in the warehouse before, had to be able to find every one of the thousands of items in storage. How did he do it?

Very simply. All it took was a tremendous amount of excess storage room. Everything was stored in alphabetical order. Beans came before carrots. Coffee came before tea, but was nowhere near the tea. So did sugar. From the point of view of using the food, or of food groups, the system made no sense, and you will never see a supermarket arranged that way. But from the point of view of completing the inventory in a day or two instead of taking all month, it was the most efficient organization you could imagine.

Moral: Organization should fit your needs. Sometimes keeping things near the point of use helps, although that is more likely to apply to routine storage than permanent.

The important thing is that wherever you put things, that should be the logical place to look when you want them. Keep in mind the story of the man who hid some valuable papers in the oven when he went out of town with his wife. His problem was that he did not tell her where he had stored them, so when they came home, she lit the oven to make dinner, and the papers burned up.

A great idea

A friend of mine gave me a great idea for finding documents and other things in permanent storage. At her suggestion, I bought a telephone index — the kind that has the alphabet printed vertically along one side and has a sliding pointer you move so that it points to the letter you want. Then, when you press a bar at the bottom of the device, it opens to the page with that letter. You can buy a telephone index of this sort at any stationery store. The name for a gadget — any gadget — that is used in this way is a "document locator."

The procedure for using the index calls for making a note in it for all the important documents and other items that I have stored. I listed my will on the "W" page, my passport on the "P" page and so on. I listed my automobile title on the "T" page for "title," but I cross-referenced it on the "A" page for "automobile."

Ice skates are listed on the "I" page and cross-referenced them on the "S" page. I head every note with the name of the document or item, then state briefly where it is.

I date every entry in my index, because I know that some time I will change the location of something, or even get rid of something, and forget to change the note in the index. Let's say I forgot that I gave my ice skates away, and I search for them in vain. I look in my index and find that I keep (kept) them on the bottom shelf in the garage at the far right. They are not there. But my note is dated 4/3/79. That's so long ago that it will jog my memory with the realization that I must have got rid of them. It doesn't take long to make the note, and it takes almost no time to date it. The note can save you hours of frustrated searching, and it will work even better if, when you get rid of something like the ice skates, you make a note of that right under the original note that told where you used to store them.

This is one place where I make a point of writing my notes in pencil. When I get rid of something, I should erase the entry. Even if I do, the date of each entry may be useful for some purpose, and it is easy enough to fill in. It might also be useful, when getting rid of something, to add a note to that effect rather than erasing the entry. That would eliminate the possibility of forgetting that the skates were given to the Salvation Army and wondering why the entry is no longer there. Or wondering if the entry had ever been made.

I do *not* list such things as car keys or glasses in this index, because I use them every day. The index is for the kind of thing that I want to find very seldom. For "permanent" storage.

I include in the index everything that I keep in my safe deposit box. That way I do not have to search through it for papers that are kept at home and vice versa. I keep my investment documents at my broker's. My index includes notes to that effect.

An alternative method

You can do the same thing with a set of 3 x 5 index cards as you can do with the telephone index. You can buy a pack of 3 x 5 cards at most drug stores or any stationery store. You should also buy a file box for them. Use one card for each item and one for each cross reference.

Although the 3 x 5 cards work just as well as the telephone index, I prefer the telephone index for several reasons. Unless you are careful, the cards can be separated or some may be lost. You will take the cards out of the box to work on them, and it is easy to mislay one. The card box is not as compact as the telephone index. Finally — and this is probably my main reason — the telephone index is more fun.

On the other hand

If you list everything that I recommend in the next section, you may find it more convenient to use a loose-leaf notebook. You may need the space to list such things as credit card companies and numbers. The loose-leaf feature makes it more convenient to work on each individual page. It also allows you to use a word processor, which I like because it is so easy to make changes such as adding or deleting a credit card or changing an address.

So I suggest developing your document locator the way I did. I began with a telephone index. As I accumulated more and more information, so that it became difficult to write it all into the index, I switched to a loose-leaf notebook. The point is that instead of making a federal project out of it, I found it easier to jot down information as it came to mind or as I ran across it when going through papers and files. The important thing is to have a specific place to jot down the information as you wish, so that it will be centralized when you want to work on it.

What to list

In case you are not sure exactly what kind of information should go into your telephone index list, 3 x 5 card file, or loose-leaf notebook, here is a list that will most likely remind you of some important items that you might not think of otherwise.

  A. Personal information

    1. Be sure to include your own name and legal address and your social security number

    2. Social Security card

    3. Birth certificate

    4. Veteran's discharge certificate and/or branch and period of military service

    5. Passport

    6. Safe-deposit box and key

      a. List of contents.

       b. Names of other people who have access to it

B. Important people — include addresses and
   telephone numbers

  1. Parents, brothers and sisters, children

  2. Attorney

  3. Physician

  4. Spouse (or former spouse)
     a. Place of divorce; divorce papers

  6. Person to whom you have given a power of
     attorney

C. Financial information

  1. Include an estimate of your income and
     general standard of living for the past few years.

  2. Major assets
     a. Title to house
     b. Title to automobile
     c. Appraisals of valuables

  3. Bank accounts

  4. Investments
     a. Stocks and bonds
     b. Real estate
     c. Financial planner, tax adviser, broker

  5. Insurance
     a. Companies and agents
     b. Policy numbers
     c. Include health, life, auto, homeowners/
       renters, and any employee benefit or pension
       plans

  6. Income tax and gift tax returns for the past
     three years

  7. Credit accounts with addresses and account

numbers

8. Complete information about personal loans you owe or are owed (including loans to children)

D. Final things

1. Living will, if you have one. (Your physician, attorney, and next of kin should have copies.)

2. Will and any trust instruments you may have

3. Executors, trustees

4. Beneficiaries

5. Property not disposed of in will and your wishes for its distribution

6. Funeral arrangements you would like, and preparations you have already made

7. People to be notified of your death.

Two birds with one stone

The primary purpose of the document locator is to make it easy for you to find documents when you need them. But it can serve another purpose, too. When the time comes that your children or your executor must find those documents, the locator will make their job easier. So tell your children that you have a document locator, and tell them where it is. You will be making things easier for them at a difficult time of their lives. They will appreciate it.

You may also find your document locator a convenient place to let your heirs know who is to get what; who gets Grampy's gold watch, who gets Mother's sampler, etc.

Finding things

Back to encoding: After we encode the location of things we put down or put away, the trick is to find them when we want them. If the location has been encoded well, that will usually be no problem. But none of us is perfect; there will still be problems. So it will be well to review the techniques of retrieval that we discussed in Chapter 4.

If the location does not pop into your mind, take your time. Relax. It will usually come. Look in the logical places, including, of course, the usual place. Reconstruct your activities leading up to the time when — as well as you can remember — you put the item down or put it in storage.

Then be sure to use this experience to reinforce your determination to practice the encoding strategies that will make it easier the next time.

∗

Before closing this chapter, I'll give you my final tip on how to find your glasses.

How many times did your son or daughter, when they were young children, come to you because he or she could not find some toy or, more often, something you had asked them to get for you? You told them to go back and look more carefully. It is there, you said, just look harder.

It's an everyday story with parents and children.

My tip is simply this: Practice what you preach. Look more carefully. Look again. Look harder.

If that was really good advice for the children — if it was not just a way to shut them up or a way to express your irritation — then it is good advice for you.

If at first you don't succeed, then, as the old saying says, try again.

Chapter 8

Good Intentions

Here's a great place to keep your car keys — but first let's go through another scenario.

A seventy-year-old man who lives alone has a date for the opera. Carmen. He picks up his date and begins the drive into town. Halfway there a terrible thought strikes him: Did he turn off the gas stove?

What can he do? Turn back and miss half the first act? He goes on.

The opera is terrible. The Habanera goes:

I left it on   I turned it off   I left it on, oh no I turned it off

And the toreador song:

It was not a very good opera.

When I presented this scenario to one of my classes in memory improvement, a woman made a suggestion that I think is a dandy. She said that she always keeps her car keys on her stove. Naturally, when she goes out, she knows whether the stove is on or off.

Two things impressed me about this woman. The first was that she had a great idea.

She does have to remember something, though: to keep the keys on the stove. What if she forgets, and leaves them in her coat pocket? Several things: She may have trouble finding them — or she may remember coming home in a hurry, stuffing them in a pocket, and running to answer the phone. But what about the stove? Well, the only way she discovered that the keys were not on the stove was by looking at the stove, so the keys — even when she misplaces them — serve the purpose of reminding her to check to stove.

The second thing that impressed me about the woman was her embarrassment in sharing her nifty idea with us. She apologized for having such a weak memory that she had to use an expedient like this, when she had every right to brag about her intelligence in thinking it up.

External memory aids

Keeping automobile keys on the stove is an external memory aid (or strategy). It is outside the mind. Internal aids are such things as forming a mental association between the act of opening the door and thinking of the stove. Both kinds of rehearsal — maintenance, where you repeat something over and over, and elaborative, where you think about the thing — are internal strategies. So are the strategies for planning to find things: paying attention, saying out loud what we are doing, and practicing. When we practice, we internalize a routine so that it becomes a habit.

In ordinary conversation, we tend to think of memory in terms of internal strategies, and we tend to think of external aids as tricks. But what difference does it make — a memory aid or a trick — as long as it gets the stove turned off and you *know* that it is off after you have left the house? I strongly recommend both internal and external aids. Use whichever works best to enable you to do what you intend to do at the time you wish to do it.

The notion of external strategies is not new. Putting an extra pair of glasses on the breakfast table is an external strategy. So is the telephone index used to keep track of documents and things that we seldom need to look for.

I do not use the key-on-stove strategy because I have formed a different habit for keeping track of my keys. I always keep my keys in my pants pocket. That gives me one place to keep them whether I am at home or anyplace else. As to remembering to turn off the stove, I have a different external strategy that I strongly recommend. A checklist.

Checklists

Several years ago, when I first began to live alone, I found that I was forgetting to do things before I left the house. I would come home and find my stereo turned on or my telephone answering machine turned off. Finally I made up a checklist. I wrote down all the things that should be checked before leaving the house. I kept the list on my dresser and carried it from room to room. And I changed it from time to time as I noticed things that I had overlooked when I first wrote up the list. Every once in a while I would get cocky and decide that it was too much trouble. After all, I'd been using the list for a couple of years. I didn't need it any more.

That's when I would come home and find the tea kettle bone dry and red hot, with the burner blazing under it.

I now keep the checklist taped to my back door — the door I normally use when leaving the apartment. Instead of carrying it through the house, I look it over. If the list suggests that I may have overlooked something, I go back and check it.

Every once in a while I shift the position of the list. If I don't, it eventually blends into the background and I ignore it. Moving it to a new place calls my attention to it. I also change the list itself, eliminating things that are no longer appropriate and adding new things I should check. Sometimes I can change the order of the list slightly, as long as it conforms to the way I will actually go about checking. For example: since my typewriter and computer are in the same room, I can put either one before the other on the list; but since I begin my check at the far end of my apartment, I always put the computer and typewriter before the stove because I come to the computer-typewriter room before I come to the kitchen.

Does the checklist indicate that I am getting dotty? Not at all. Commercial and military airplane pilots use checklists. They are people who are selected for their mental alertness and fine physical condition, yet they depend on checklists. So why shouldn't you and I?

I also use a checklist when I pack to go out of town. I have worked up a checklist over the years that reminds me of all the things I should take on a trip. I put the list alongside my suitcase, and I pack in the order of the list, so that I am sure to get everything.

I call this checklist my travel inventory, and I never leave home without it — without checking it. I often take a copy with me so that I can make changes as I discover that it would have been good to have included something I never thought of before. The list will become more helpful over the years if it is corrected from time to time based on experience.

The world's greatest memory aid

Writing.

Ancient Chinese proverb: The weakest ink is stronger than the strongest memory.

What is writing *but* a memory aid?

So use it.

Working on this book has made me sensitive to the way people use strategies. About a year ago, I had lunch at a restaurant with seven friends. I had never been in that particular restaurant before. The waitress intrigued me by the fact that she did not write down the orders; she listened intently and kept everything in her mind. I noticed it with the first order she took, and from then on I watched her closely. She stared hard at the customer, and you could see that she was concentrating on what he said. No pad. No pencil. I got a kick out of that.

Then she brought in our lunches and — would you believe it? — she had *every order wrong!* Not a single one right! A perfect zero!

(She did bring two correct orders, but she gave them to the wrong people.)

I did not say anything to her — she had enough trouble with eight complaints — but I could not help wondering why she did not just write the orders down when she got them. Even if she did not know how to write (the only explanation I can think of), she could have made marks that would have acted as cues to jog her memory.

Even the simplest mark is stronger than the strongest memory.

Intentions

We are constantly planning things that we intend to do some time in the future — a minute, an hour, a day, a year. They range from getting an aspirin from the bathroom to meeting a friend for a movie on the thirteenth of next month. Unless we have a fit of absent-mindedness, we will remember to get the aspirin when we step into the bathroom. But keeping appointments is another thing. Internal strategies can correct absent mindedness. External strategies do the job for intentions such as keeping appointments.

When you make an appointment, don't depend upon "remembering" it — in the conventional sense of keeping it in your mind. Write it down. There are many tricks of memorization ("mnemonics" again) that can be used to remember appointments, and in many cases they will work if properly applied. But why bother? It's easier and more certain if you write it down.

By the time people reach my age, most of them have developed the habit of keeping some kind of date book. I keep three, and I use them all.

Date books and calendars

My fundamental date book is a month-on-a-page calendar. It shows dates far enough in advance to make planning easy. I make up a week-at-a-time sheet from that. The week-at-a-time sheet includes more detail, and I sometimes include shopping lists on it. This may seem like unnecessary duplication. It does duplicate the month-on-a-page calendar, but I find it convenient — probably because I use my word processor to keep it up to date. The word processor permits me to make changes every day without having to re-write anything. It also permits me to carry the sheet with me; if I lose it, the information is in the word processor, so that I simply update the information and print a new sheet.

If you think the week-on-a-page requires too much work, you may want to use a one or two day note to carry with you. You want something that you can carry with you so that you can double check the exact time of an appointment, and so that you do not forget to stop at the shoe repair shop on the way home. But you must use it every day, or you will not have it with you on the day you need it most. (Once again: form good habits. That's more than half the battle.)

The third date book that I use is a year-on-a-page sheet. I usually make several trips a year, and I use the year-on-a- page sheet to keep track of them. I am sure that I could plan trips without it, but seeing everything at one glance makes it easier to avoid conflicts. Of course, if you do not travel very much, this sheet may not do much for you.

I felt that my three date books were justified when I found a bound calendar in a book store that included all three. Mine are separate, but I have found a source for a month-on-a-page calendar that includes three years. I like to plan ahead.

I keep my month-on-a-page calendars in a three-ring, loose leaf binder. I usually have to remove the binding the calendars come in and punch the pages. That gives me a somewhat bigger book with a hard binding that I find convenient. At the end of each month, I remove the page for that month and put it at the back of the book. Then, if I want to know when I did something in the recent past, I can turn to the back of the book to find out.

Some added benefits

I belong to a dining club where all expenses are billed and the members pay by check. The club does not give members a copy of the bill at the time of the dinner, so how do you check the bill when it comes in the mail a week or so later? Well, I make a note of the dinner on my calendar when I make my reservation. That reminds me when I am scheduled to go there. When the bill comes in, I look back at my calendar, because the bill shows the date of the dinner. I pencil in a brief note when I pay the bill. If the club should make an error and send me a second bill for the same evening, I will discover that when I check the calendar. You can adapt this procedure to all kinds of temporary records where you want to be able to confirm a date in the past.

I usually pay bills as they come in, but I often put big bills aside till they are actually due. Then, so that I don't overlook them, I mark them on my month-on-a-page calendar. I also mark the dates that income tax estimates come due. We *should* remember important dates like that, especially since they are the same every year, but there is always a chance of forgetting, and since forgetting can cause real headaches, why not take a minute to write the dates down each year?

In addition, the loose leaf form of my calendar enables me to add plastic pages in the form of sleeves that will hold notes of any size up to and including the standard eight and a half by eleven sheet of paper. These plastic sleeves, called "page protectors," can be obtained at stationery stores. I keep one behind the page for the current month, and I put in it notices of meetings, invitations, and sometimes tickets for special events.

Subscriptions and contributions

Some organizations like to send their bills out so early that you pay for the same subscription twice in the same year — or the same membership or contribution. I prevent this by keeping a notebook in my desk drawer in which I enter payments for subscriptions, insurance, and anything else that recurs regularly. I date the payment, show the amount, and jot down the date the next payment will be due.

The notebook can serve a double purpose if you itemize your contributions for income tax purposes. Keep contributions on a separate sheet, and at the end of the year you will have them all listed.

Written reminders

We all write ourselves notes, because that is the best way to remember to do things we intend to do. The trick, of course, is to find the note when it is needed.

Put the note where you are bound to see it in time to act on it. I often use the bathroom mirror because I know that I will see it at least once every day when I shave. The little note pads with temporary adhesive are wonderful for the mirror and for almost all the other places where we are likely to put our notes.

People often put notes on the refrigerator, and you can buy magnetic holders for just that purpose. An urgent note on the coffee pot will remind you of something you want to do before beginning breakfast, and that idea can be extended to anything else that you use — other utensils, tools, appliances.

I often use the note pad with temporary adhesive to put notes on the dashboard of my car to remind me to do something or go someplace. And sometimes to remind myself to buy gas before I run out.

Looking back to the month-on-a-page calendar for a moment, I sometimes put a note with temporary adhesive on a page or on the loose leaf cover. I do that only for very, very special reasons: when I have an unusual bill to pay or a very, very special event that I do not want to risk missing. I think of this as a back-up strategy. Sometimes — very rarely — I write two notes about the same thing. I may put one on my mirror and one on the breakfast table. There is no point in using this device very often, because the calendar itself or the original note takes care of most reminders, but the fact that I seldom use it makes it stand out when I do — when there is something I simply cannot afford to overlook.

We can't afford to overlook emergency telephone numbers. You probably keep a list of them — the police and fire departments, your doctor — somewhere near your telephone. If you don't have them near your phone, it is a good idea to put them there. The 911 number has eliminated the need for much of this, but there are usually a few numbers you will want to have at hand in an emergency.

More notes — and lists

When you are going to leave the house and absolutely *must* remember to do something when you leave, a note stuck to the door will help, and a big note — on a full sheet of paper — on the floor in front of the door will remind you.

Use lists. Checklists handle routines. A form of checklist is the list of errands you must take care of during the day. Most people use shopping lists, and I highly recommend them. I do not understand why so many memory books explain ways that you can remember a shopping list when it is so easy to write it down. And it has the added advantage that you can make up the list by adding items every time you find yourself running low in the kitchen. When you take the last stick of butter out of the refrigerator, you add butter to the list.

While you are at it, make a note to return those empty bottles for refund. You can write your note on the shopping list or on a separate slip of paper that you clip to the list. And you can clip your shopping coupons to the list, too. Might as well make the whole job as easy and foolproof as you can.

Shop the easy way

The best way to write the list is to put the items on the list in the same order that you will encounter them in the store. Then you can easily check off the items as you select them from shelves. Most of us are familiar enough with our supermarket to be able to list things in store order from memory, but if you really want to be organized, you can make up a form from the signs in the store listing the items in each aisle. For example, I would list the first two aisles in Dave's, where I shop, like this:

Aisle 1 a	Aisle 1 b
Fruit juice	Dairy
Oil/shortening	Milk
Ketchup/mustard	Eggs

Aisle 2 a	Aisle 2 b
Soups	Spices
Canned vegetables	Baking needs
Gravy mix	Canned fruit

And of course you would list all the aisles in the store. In this photocopying age, it is easy to make up a form and use a copy for each shopping trip. Or it may be simpler just to keep the form handy to the pad on which you write down your list, using the form for reference.

But no one is perfect. I sometimes find myself near the supermarket with some extra time but with my shopping list at home. If I go into the store, I usually remember everything on the list. I did not try to memorize the list, but the act of writing it down fixed it in my mind. (I don't always remember everything on the list, but I remember most things.)

Writing does many things for us in addition to giving us a permanent record to which we can refer at any time. It focuses our attention — so it is one way to use the magic words: "Pay attention." That is one reason why we can often remember a shopping list — or any other writing — without referring back to it.

Another reason is that writing reinforces the memory. If we read that 300,000 people die each year from smoking-related causes, and we want to remember that figure, writing it down will reinforce it in our memory. It contributes to multi-modal reinforcement: We see the statistic in the paper; we think about it; we use muscles in our wrist and hand to write it down; and we see what we have written. Each mode reinforces the others. And if we tell the information to someone, that will reinforce it even more.

Birthdays

Many people I know make a list of all the birthdays they want to remember during the year. Some make a note on their calendars. I use a mixed system: I have a list of all the birthdays I should remember, and I put the particularly important ones on my calendar. Use whatever method you find easy and effective, but whatever you do, write the dates down somewhere. And of course you should do the same with anniversaries and any other special, recurring dates.

General external aids

We use many external aids in addition to writing. Some are general in the sense that they remind us that we want to remember something, but unlike a note they do not tell us what it is that we want to remember. An alarm clock does not tell us to get up. It signals the time of day (or night) — but we know what that means!

I have an alarm wrist watch that I use to remind me of all kinds of things. If I have an appointment to be downtown at 10:00, and I estimate that it will take me twenty minutes to pull myself together and drive there, I set my wrist alarm for 9:40. When it goes off, I know what it means. The wash cycle I use on my washing machine takes thirty minutes. When I start the machine, I set my wrist alarm. Then I can read or write or do anything else with a clear mind. I do not have to think about the laundry. When the alarm goes off, I know what it means. I have never confused getting the laundry with driving downtown.

Kitchen timers can be used for similar purposes in addition to their primary purpose of timing jobs in the kitchen itself. Even a regular alarm clock can be drafted for other reminder purposes.

The alarm watch has an advantage over the kitchen timer: It is always with me because I need it to keep track of the time. I may go into another room or even leave the house so that I will not hear the kitchen timer. But the alarm watch is always there.

General aids of this sort can be used when there is little danger of forgetting what the task is once the alarm reminds us that we have a task to do. That is what the string around the finger is for — although I have never been able to figure out how to tie a string around my finger. I need two hands to do it. But a rubber band serves the same purpose. Similar devices are putting your wrist watch on the wrong arm or turning your ring wrong side out. They remind you to do something but do not tell you what it is.

Do you ever turn your parking lights on when it is foggy out and then forget to turn them off when you get to your destination? Next time, when you turn them on, put something on the dashboard — a box of Kleenex or your gloves or anything you can easily reach. If the dashboard will not hold it, throw it on the floor — anyplace that is unusual and that you will notice as you leave the car.

What do you do when you think of something in the middle of the night, but you don't want to get up and write yourself a note? Some people reach over and tip the lamp shade. When you get up and see the shade tipped, you first wonder why it's tipped; then you remember that it is supposed to remind you of something; and then you will usually remember what it is you wanted to remember.

Since I am not sure I would even notice that the shade is tipped, I suggest a more obvious device: throw the Kleenex box on the floor. It serves the same purpose. You will know that something is wrong when you get up and see it. In most cases you will quickly rebuild the connection between the Kleenex box out of place and the thing you wanted to remember. Not always, but in most cases.

Specific external aids

Ever wake up in the middle of the night and realize that you must mail a check to IRS the next day? You'd better be more specific than tipping the lamp shade or throwing the Kleenex on the floor. Those are effective devices, but they are not perfect, and you cannot afford to miss this one. You could write yourself a note, but what if this happens to be the one day out in a hundred that you fail to see the note when you get up? Still, you don't want to disturb your sleep any more than necessary.

You've got to get up. No choice. Get your check book and put it on the breakfast table. You can go back to a sound sleep then, confident that you will not only be reminded to do something, but the reminder will tell you what it is you want to do.

Some people keep a pad and pencil next to their beds to write down those flashes of genius that come to all of us in the middle of the night. I prefer a small, hand-held tape recorder. The recorder permits me to make a record of my thoughts with minimum arousal from sleep. I don't have to turn the light on, and I don't have to worry about not being able to read my own handwriting in the morning.

(There was the scientist who awoke in the middle of the night with the discovery of the cure for cancer. Careful not to awaken his wife, he wrote his idea on the pad that he always kept next to his bed. When he got up in the morning, he took up the pad and read: "Think in different categories.")

Another external aid that you can use night or day — usually during the day — consists of putting things in unusual places. Actually, the IRS check is an example of this. If you have an important letter to answer, but cannot answer it at once, put it in an unusual place, where you will see it, and where you know it should not ordinarily be. Try the breakfast table instead of your desk.

If you normally have lunch at a restaurant but for some reason decide to take your lunch to work, put the brown bag on your breakfast table to remind you of it in the morning. If you must change a washer in the bathroom, the pipe wrench on the kitchen table will remind you to do the job.

This reverses the old adage of having a place for everything and everything in its place. That is why it stands out and reminds you to do something out of the ordinary. You should always keep your tape measure in the same place, *except* when you have agreed to measure a friend's furniture to see if it will fit into an apartment she is considering. Put the tape measure on the bathroom sink or the kitchen sink, wherever you will be sure to see it.

A nifty internal strategy

Most of the strategies for remembering things we intend to do are external, but there is one very effective internal strategy that I have been using for fifty years. I visualize what it is that I intend to do, and, when the time comes, I automatically remember to do it.

An example may help: A few weeks ago, I had a portable radio in the trunk of my car. It was out of sight, so when I came home, I would go into the apartment without it. But one night I remembered it as I was driving home. I could have put the Kleenex on the dashboard, which would have given me a general external aid, but instead I used my visualization strategy. I imagined myself driving into the garage, getting out of the car, opening the trunk, and taking the radio out.

When I say that I imagined the scene, I must stress that I "saw" it. I visualized it so vividly that I could see every move that I made. I saw the garage wall, and I saw the beam of light from my headlights move across the wall as I pulled into my parking space. I could feel myself pull up the handle that releases the cover of the trunk. I could feel the handle of the car door as I opened it. I saw myself get out of the car, and I saw the Chevy that is always parked next to my Dodge. I saw myself walk to the back of the car, and I saw the row of cars opposite mine in the garage. I saw the door to the apartment building, which is on the wall opposite the wall my car faces when parked. I saw and felt myself raise the cover of the trunk, reach in, and pick up the radio.

Traffic problems called my attention away from the image, and I am not sure whether I thought any more about it till I got into the garage. But when I got there and pulled into my parking place, I went through exactly the same actions I had visualized in the image. If you try it, and if you construct an image that you can actually "see," it will work for you. All strategies improve with practice, including this one, but this one also requires vividness of the image, which most of us can accomplish even at the first try — if we try hard enough.

Visualizing directions

Last summer when I was returning from a trip to Canada, I got off the freeway to have lunch at a motel. I noticed quite a bit of road work in the vicinity, so when I was leaving, I asked the lady at the motel desk how to get back onto the freeway. As she gave me the instructions, I visualized them as best I could. In this case, since I had never seen the streets she mentioned, I could only guess at their appearance, but I could visualize myself coming to a corner and turning right. I concentrated so hard on visualizing the instructions that I did not think about them or I would have realized that if you make four right hand turns, you will end up back where you started. And that is exactly what happened. She had said "right" at two turns that should have been "left." But at least the memory part of the task worked.

That experience was unusual, and it was her mistake, not mine. Whenever you ask road directions you run the risk of getting erroneous instructions. But if they are all you have, you will have to use them.

The best strategy is to write directions down. But when you stop along the highway to ask directions, it is often difficult to write: you have nothing at hand to write with. In that case, try to visualize yourself following them as you receive them, and you will have a better chance of getting them straight. This internal strategy will not work as well with road instructions as it will for familiar activities for the reason I mentioned above: since the roads are strange, you cannot visualize them except in vague, general images. It is the clear, specific image that works best.

An external-internal strategy

This is one we've all used: When you want to be sure to do something, ask someone to remind you. If they do, that's an external aid that worked. If they don't, the act of asking reinforces your memory, so that it is an internal aid.

Remembering to take things with you

External aids work better than anything else to remind us to take things with us when we leave the house, office, or anyplace else. Most of us have learned to write ourselves notes to remind us to take the dry cleaning or the gift for cousin Mabel with us. If you think you may overlook the note, put cousin Mabel's gift on the floor in front of the door, where you must almost stumble over it to leave the house. But avoid putting it where you or someone else may actually stumble over it. Sometimes you can hang it from the door knob.

You can hang your umbrella on the door knob on those days that start out with a clear blue sky but when the weatherman has announced rain for later in the day. If you want to wear your rubbers, too, the umbrella can be used as a cue. Use the internal strategy of visualizing yourself seeing the umbrella, getting the rubbers out, and putting them on. This follows the general rule of using more than one strategy wherever that is possible. In this case you are combining the external strategy of the umbrella with the internal strategy of the image.

A memory place

Establish a "memory place" near the door. The memory place can be a table or a cabinet used for temporary storage of things you plan to take with you at a later time. My breakfast table is in a wide back hall through which I pass when leaving the apartment. If I have mail to take out or a book I want to take with me, I put them on a part of the table that I do not use for eating.

The idea is that every time you think of something you want to take someplace, you put it in the memory place. You accumulate everything in one place, and since it is always the same place, and since it is convenient to the door, your chances of remembering everything you want are almost perfect.

There have been times when my accumulation has grown to confusing magnitudes because I accumulated things for several days' work. In that case, I make separate piles, and I label each pile with the day that I will want it. I am going to the library on Tuesday, so I put the books to be returned in one pile with a temporary-adhesive note on top reading, "Tuesday." I stick a similar note, reading "Wednesday," on cousin Mabel's present.

Even though you have your memory place near the door, you might want to add a note to your checklist to check the memory place before you leave home.

If your memory place becomes unsightly, you might consider using a cabinet instead of a table. The problem here is that it is much easier to forget things that are out of sight than those that obtrude themselves upon you. But if you list the cabinet on your checklist or if you form so strong a habit that you never fail to look in it before you leave — even when you "know" there is nothing in it — it will work.

One warning: Never dump on the memory place. Never put anything there that you do not intend to take out of the house. Otherwise the memory place will become just another storage place, and it will lose its effectiveness as a special storage-reminder. It must be a specifically set-aside place. Sacrosanct.

Remembering to take medicine

According to the questionnaire (Chapter 3), remembering to take medicine is not a high priority problem, but several people checked it off. The easiest solution to remembering to take medicine is external. Drug stores sell special medicine containers that are marked to indicate when the medicine should be taken.

I am on an "aspirin every other day" regimen. If I had to take an aspirin every day, that would be easy. But taking one every other day means remembering whether today is the day — or was it yesterday? I have a container with the trade name, "Seven Day Pill

Reminder." It has seven small compartments, each labeled with a letter signifying the day of the week. The letters are in Braille as well as regular print. Once a week or more — I usually do it more often than once a week — I fill every other compartment with an aspirin. I keep the container on the sink in my bathroom, so that it is always in plain sight.

Many variations of this container are on the market. Some are marked for several medicines to be taken in one day. Whatever your needs, your druggist will be able to get a container that will make it easy for you to remember to take the right medication at the right time.

Have I already taken my pill?

When my father was eighty, he woke up in the middle of the night, wondered if he had taken his pill, and decided he had not. So he got up, went to the bathroom, slipped on the floor, hit his head, and ended up getting three operations.

If the pill is not too important, forget about it till morning when you can think straight. If you use a "pill reminder," you can check it to see if you've taken the pill. You might make it easier to check by leaving the top up on the compartment where you had the pill for that day. Some of these devices have indicators to show that you have taken the pill. Whatever routine you work out to remind yourself to take the pill and also that you have taken it, make that routine habitual. Do it the same way every time, so you'll be sure to get it right.

Some rules for external aids

Psychologist J. E. Harris has put together some rules that summarize much of what I have said. His list can help you improve the kinds of aids you use. Here they are:

1. The cue should be given as close as possible before the time when the action is required. It may be no good reminding someone as he leaves in the morning to buy some bread on his way home.

2. An active cue is better than a passive cue. Notes and calendars are passive; if we forget to look at them, they won't do us any good. (So develop an inflexible habit of looking at your calendar every day.)

3. A specific reminder is better than a general one. A rubber band around the finger only reminds the user that he or she is supposed to remember something, but not what that something is.

4. A portable aid is more useful than one that is difficult or impossible to carry around.

5. An aid is more valuable if you use it for more than one thing. I mentioned the fact that I carry an alarm watch. It is always with me. If I used a kitchen timer for the same purpose, the chances are that I would forget to take it with me when I needed it most.

6. An aid is more valuable if it can store more than one cue. If my watch had more than one alarm, I could use it to remind me of more than one thing.

7. The aid should be easy to use.

Chapter 9

Information That Makes Sense

Much of the information that we want to remember makes sense. This chapter will discuss ways of remembering that kind of information. A great deal of the information we want to remember does not make much sense. That kind of information will be discussed in later chapters.

Organization

Information that makes sense is organized in some way. Organizing something means putting its parts into relation with each other so they work together or fit together into a form or structure, usually in accordance with some plan or system. The two letter strings from Chapter 6 are a good example. The first string was not organized:

A I O Z T N G R N A O I

The second string was organized:

ORGANIZATION

The human mind is attuned to meaning; therefore the best way to organize information we want to remember is by meaning. That, in turn, requires that we understand what the information means. Understanding a piece of information involves fitting it into the network of knowledge already in our minds.

We understand that a chickadee is a bird when we fit it into our network, which already contains the information that a bird is an animal (has skin, can move around, eats, breathes, etc.) and that it has wings, has feathers, and can fly. The chickadee fits nicely into our existing memory storage network. But when we first learn about the ostrich we may have a little more difficulty because it can't fly, and our previous understanding of birds included the belief that they can fly. In that case, we have to adjust the information already in our network to admit some birds that cannot fly.

Once we fit an item of information into our network, we, as adults, will have many connections to hold it in place because we already have so much information in our networks. A very young child — under five — is just developing its network. It can make only a few connections with new information. As a result, very young children have very poor memories.

Meaning and understanding

Using or grasping the meaning of a piece of information involves understanding it. Understanding meanings is vitally important to us because it is our link to the world around us.

Several years ago, a Señor Martini boarded an airplane in Buenos Aires bound for Miami. Señor Martini flew first class, and the flight attendants did everything they could to make his trip comfortable. When one of the attendants asked Señor Martini if he wanted anything, he thought she was asking his name, so he replied, "Martini" — and he promptly got one. As soon as he finished it, the flight attendant, realizing that there was a language barrier, simply asked, "Martini?" Señor Martini, thinking she was asking if that was his name, said, "Si." They repeated this performance every time Señor Martini emptied his glass.

When the plane arrived at its final destination in New York, they discovered that Señor Martini had not disembarked in Miami, which had been his destination. He had been in no condition to disembark. He had not even known that they were in Miami. The airline sent him back to Miami on another plane.

And all because of a simple misunderstanding.

Understanding and memory

Psychologists generally agree that understanding information is essential to remembering it. Three hundred years ago, the philosopher Spinoza said: "The more intelligible a thing is, the more easily it is retained in the memory, and contrariwise, the less intelligible it is, the more easily we forget it." And more recently a psychologist has said, "When the underlying logic and structure of what is to be learned is understood, recall is far easier." For that reason, this chapter will stress understanding.

Understanding means linking new information to old. That should be a familiar idea to us by now. When we use association to remember something, we link new information to old. We all know that Columbus sailed the ocean blue in 1492. We can easily remember that the Jews were expelled from Spain in 1492 by associating the two events. The old information brings the new information to mind by association. We understand it.

Making sure we understand

When we come to more complex ideas, how can we be sure that we understand them? By asking ourselves the following questions. If we understand the idea, we will be able to answer at least some (but probably not all) of these seven questions:

1. Can you explain the new idea in your own words?
2. Can you give examples of it?
3. Can you recognize it when you encounter it in different guises and different circumstances?
4. Do you see the connections between the new information and information that you already know?
5. Can you make use of the information in various ways?
6. Can you foresee some of the consequences of the idea?
7. Can you state the opposite of the idea? Or an idea so different that the contrast is obvious?

192.

Using the seven points: an example

We can see how the seven points work by going through an example in detail. Chapter 11 covers a topic called "mnemonics." Understanding what "mnemonics" means will make that chapter easier to read. So I will use the notion of mnemonics to explain some of the seven points, and I will use other examples to explain the rest of them.

The term **mnemonic** (the first m is silent: ne-mahn'-ick) means "to help the memory." It always refers to *an active, strategic kind of learning device or method, a rehearsal strategy,* if you will. Formal mnemonic devices rely on a set of memory aids established in advance, and they usually call for considerable practice in which you mesh the information you want to remember with the set of memory aids you already know.

One way of remembering this definition is to memorize it in the sense of saying it over and over until you can repeat it. That is the hard way. The way I recommend is first to understand it; then memorize the ideas in it by repeating them over and over in your own words — although you will find that after you have worked through the understanding process you may not have to "memorize" the definition at all. You will not be able to repeat it in the same words — which is unimportant — but you will be able to state the idea in your own words.

Let's go through the seven points one at a time:

1. Can you explain the new idea in your own words?

Since this definition is complicated, a good way to attack it is to outline it.

A. Basic definition (first sentence of the definition)
   1. A means (a tool — something we use)
   2. Helps memory (its purpose)
B. An active process
C. Uses memory aids established in advance
   1. Aids are established before we encounter the information we want to remember
   2. Learning the aids requires practice
D. Mesh the information you want to remember with the set of memory aids

The outline expresses the same idea as the original definition, but in different (our own) words. It has the added advantage of exposing the structure of the definition. We can see how each part of the definition fits into the whole.

2. Can you give examples of it?

We can start by giving a few straightforward examples, but that is not enough. If you were trying to understand the word "organization," you might begin with examples like an alphabetized file and a salespersons file organized by territory. But add some variety to your examples. Think of histories and biographies that are organized chronologically, and think of organizing things using the familiar animal, vegetable, and mineral scheme. Think of the organization of books by subject matter in a library. And finally, think of negative as well as positive examples. Imagine a telephone book that is not organized alphabetically. Think of the two strings of letters at the beginning of this chapter: one is organized; the other is not.

3. Can you recognize it when you encounter it in different guises and different circumstances?

Let's begin with something more familiar than mnemonics. When we first learned to do multiplication, we memorized the multiplication tables by rote. Eventually we learned to multiply numbers like 24 x 60. Did we understand multiplication? Only if we could solve "word problems" (or "story problems") like: What is the area of a table that is 24 inches wide and 60 inches long? Here we have the same multiplication problem, but in a different guise.

An example of a familiar mnemonic is the jingle we use for remembering the number of days in the month: "Thirty days hath September, etc. . . ." Knowing that this is a mnemonic, we can recognize that "In fourteen hundred and ninety-two, Columbus sailed the ocean blue" is a mnemonic, too.

But what about the trick of recalling the names of the Great Lakes from the word "homes"? The names are Huron, Ontario, Michigan, Erie, and Superior. That is not a jingle, but if we understand the definition of "mnemonics," we should recognize this as one. And we should recognize advertising jingles as mnemonics framed by advertisers to keep their products and services jingling through our minds.

4. Do you see the connections between the new information and information you already know?

Your first reading of the definition of "mnemonics" may have puzzled you because it was new information, but I am sure that you had no trouble with the outline because all of the ideas in the outline were familiar. The new information is largely in the name, "mnemonics." The ideas it expresses were already known, making the connections easy to see.

5. Can you make use of the information in various ways?

You may understand the concept well enough by this time to use it in discussions of memory — and I might add that outside of discussions of memory, the notion of mnemonics has little or no use at all. As to using mnemonics themselves, you will read about several mnemonic techniques in Chapter 11. Some of them will be familiar, and you already know how to use them. As you recognize them, your understanding of "mnemonics" will increase. You may wish to master one or more of the new mnemonic strategies, which will increase your understanding even more.

6. Can you foresee consequences of the idea? I hope that you can foresee that mnemonics will help you improve your memory. Most of us have used the mnemonic device of "Thirty days hath September" many times; knowing that this is a mnemonic device should lead us to realize that other mnemonic devices can be equally useful.

7. Can you state the opposite of the idea? Or an idea so different that the contrast is obvious?

In the strict sense, mnemonics has no opposite, although, in a loose sense, rote learning can be thought of as opposite. Mnemonics is a way of imposing organization on disorganized, meaningless information. Rote learning does not change the material in any way. In rote learning we simply repeat the information over and over until we can remember it. Rote learning works, and sometimes it is the only way we can memorize something. But it is tougher than using mnemonics and usually much more tedious to use.

Mnemonics: a review

Although you probably learned a lot about mnemonics, the purpose of this discussion was to illustrate how we can analyze any meaningful piece of information so that we can be sure we understand it. And I hope it illustrates my belief that if you go through the analysis carefully, you will have learned the subject of the analysis so well that you can remember it without having to repeat the words over and over as in the learning-by-rote approach.

That does not mean that the information will be available for recall any time you want it in the future. If you want to keep the information on tap, you must review it occasionally.

An easy way to review is to look over the outline. Outlines take time to make, but if you intend to review the information, they will cut down your review time. They highlight the important points. If you review an outline of an analysis like the one on mnemonics, then your memory will usually fill in the details that the outline omits.

If you do not make an outline, at least you should verbalize the outstanding features. Name things. Names and labels help us remember.

During the George Bush-Michael Dukakis campaign for president, Mr. Bush labeled Mr. Dukakis a liberal. Whether the label is true or false, fair or unfair, does not matter for the point I wish to make. The important thing for us is that people remembered it. Giving something a name or a label helps hold it in the memory.

(Make a note that this is another strategy: Name things. Label things. Keep this in mind when we take up vocabulary in the next chapter.)

Remembering lectures and conversations

In order to remember the points that a lecturer makes — or that someone with whom you are conversing makes — the best first step is to understand what they have to say. After all, if you don't understand, what is there to remember?

If you don't understand, ask questions. Many lectures are informal enough to permit questions during the lecture itself. Many formal lectures include question periods. And of course if you are conversing with someone, it is usually assumed that questions are in order.

In conversations and in some lecture situations such as a lecture in a college course, assert your own opinions. If you are taking a course, the teacher will often ask questions of the class. Answer them. If you get the answer right, you will get a boost that will engrave the answer in your mind. If you get the answer wrong, the embarrassment will engrave the answer in your mind. So either way you come out ahead.

Reading to remember

People read for all kinds of reasons from an attempt to avoid boredom to a wish to understand nuclear physics. Suit your reading to your purpose.

Many years ago I took a speed reading course. Everyone in the course expressed concern over failing to remember if they read too fast. One day the teacher asked how many of us had read the evening newspaper the night before. Every hand went up. She then asked if someone would tell the class what had been in the paper. No one volunteered. She went on to ask what difference it made how fast or slowly we read if we did not remember what we read anyway.

So I read my newspapers fast. When someone asks me about the news, I can often tell them what I have read. I remember enough to satisfy myself.

Fast reading has the advantage that it concentrates attention on what you are reading. Slow reading allows time for your mind to wander. Read at the fastest speed that allows you to understand what you are reading.

We should read at our very fastest speed when we are looking for some brief, specific information. If you want to find the year of George Washington's birth, you look it up in the dictionary. If you want to find the year he built Fort Necessity, you may have to skim through a biography — either a book or an encyclopedia article. But skim. Don't waste time poring through the entire biography if you only want that one fact.

Before you start

Before you settle in for some serious reading, find a place that is free from distractions. Put a pad and pencil within reach to write down anything you think of while you are reading, so that you will not divide your attention between the book and your stray thoughts. Before you begin, try to decide how much time you will spend reading. Agree with yourself that you will spend that time reading and doing nothing else.

The SQ3R reading technique

I returned to college after I retired because I was disappointed in my ability to read. I did not understand what I read as thoroughly as I wished, and I was not retaining enough of it. The two go together, of course. Better understanding; better retention. Although I had reached sixty at the time, I was sure that my age had nothing to do with it, and I have since read that psychologists are coming around to the belief that older people can comprehend what they read just as well as younger people. The discipline of college courses has enabled me to improve my reading tremendously. On the whole, I understand what I read, and I retain it well enough to be in the top 5% in all of my classes.

I will explain in detail a reading method that will enable anyone to do as well as I have done or better. It is designed for reading textbooks, but it can be adapted to any kind of nonfiction from newspapers through magazines to calculus textbooks. It is called the SQ3R method. The abbreviation stands for Survey, Question, Read, Recite, and Review. This method may not appeal to you, but unless you know what it is, you will not be in a position to decide whether you want to use it or not.

Survey

The Survey stage gives you an overview of the material you wish to read. Say that it is a textbook on psychology, and you plan to read the first chapter. Since it is a new book, go through the entire book, reading the chapter titles. Textbook chapters are usually divided into sections, and you may want to look at some of the section headings, too. Look at the pictures and read the captions of the pictures that catch your attention. You are not reading at this point, but getting into a receptive frame of mind.

The survey will activate related knowledge that you already possess in the network of your memory storage. You are activating the pathways that connect the many ideas that you already know and that are relevant to the contents of the book. This makes it easier to absorb new information into the network.

Look over Chapter One, the one you are about to study, the same way. Read all of the section headings. Look at the pictures. Glance through the summary at the end of the chapter. The survey will give you a framework on which to build the knowledge you will gain from the book. It will be a flimsy framework at first, but it will grow in strength as you progress through the SQ3R procedure.

The survey also acts as a warm-up for your more concentrated reading that will follow. It is a good idea to make a mini-survey each time you begin a reading session, even though you may then be in a later stage of the SQ3R procedure. A brief survey will remind you of what has gone before and where you are now in the reading.

Question

Why are you reading the book? What do you hope to get out of the book? Be honest with yourself when you answer. Are you taking a course that requires you to read it, and you would never read it otherwise? Have your friends read it, and you are merely trying to keep up with the Joneses? These can be perfectly good reasons, but only if you face them and admit them to yourself. You should be able to answer these questions, even though your answers may change as you learn more about the subject from your reading.

The survey of the book should put other questions in your mind that you can *not* answer. Why do they have a chapter on the physiological bases of perception? What do they mean by creative problem solving? Will the chapter on altered states of consciousness tell me what I want to know about drug addiction?

The most important questions you can ask are those about the subject matter of the book. You should find enough information in your survey to raise fairly detailed questions in your mind about the information the book contains. Textbooks usually have a list of questions at the end of each chapter. It is not a bad idea to glance through them when you make your survey, but you should certainly read them now. They are your best guide for reading the chapter.

Read

Now read the chapter through from start to finish — the way you usually read a book. But this should be a more active process than usual because of the questions you have asked. Be alert for the answers to the specific questions about the chapter. Refer to the questions from time to time to refresh your memory.

Recite

Re-read the chapter, testing yourself as you go. Can you answer the questions at the end of the chapter without referring to the book? This is the time to try. But check the book to be sure you answered them correctly — and to find the answers you cannot remember.

State the important ideas in your own words. Apply the other six points about understanding that we discussed above to be sure you understand the material.

Outline the text. This can be a separate written outline, or you can underline or high-light the important sentences and phrases in the book. If you use underlining or high-lighting, do it selectively. If you underline everything, you might as well underline nothing. It is impossible to remember everything in a book. Therefore, you must evaluate the material and concentrate on remembering the most important information.

If you write a separate outline, construct a hierarchy of themes. The book itself will help you, because you can use the section headings for your main points, and many books have subheads for the second tier of points. Look for the relationships between topics at the different levels.

Review

You may want to review the chapter at once, but if you do, be sure to review it again at a later time. Several short review sessions will help your memory far more than one long session. This is an important principle, called "distributed learning," that applies to all learning and memorizing.

The review repeats the survey, except that you now know what is in the chapter. Skim through it, slowing down at the points you had trouble with when you were answering the questions.

Concentrate on the most important information. That is the information that you underlined in the book or included in your outline of the book.

Further reviews from time to time will refresh your memory. It all depends on how long you want to remember the information. If you want it to be a permanent part of your memory, you must review it every once in a while — probably forever.

The reason all teachers advise against cramming — studying like crazy the night before an examination instead of studying regularly every day — is because cramming is the least efficient way to study. The most efficient way to put information into your memory is by distributed learning.

Making the system yours

People who use the SQ3R technique usually modify it to suit their own needs and abilities. The best way to go about it is to use the technique as I have presented it, then modify it if you find that you do better by emphasizing some parts and perhaps cutting other parts down — or even out.

You will almost certainly want to loosen up the technique when you read non-fiction that is not as heavy duty as the usual textbook. If you read biography or history for fun, you will increase your fun by using the SQ3R system, but not so rigorously. You should still skim the book when you first get it, and you should certainly ask yourself why you are reading it and what you hope to get out of it.

After you make the survey and ask yourself some questions — not as detailed as the questions you ask of a textbook — you will read the book through. Then, depending upon how much you want to remember, you can go through the recite and review stages. You are not so likely to make an outline, but if you own the book you might want to high-light some of the important passages so that you can find them for review later. (Please don't do that with library books. What little you gain will be vastly offset by the fact that you have ruined the book for all future readers.)

It is often helpful to make notes of the names of important people, important dates, and important facts. I use a slip of paper in my own books as a bookmark on which I scribble that kind of information. Some people use 3 x 5 cards with notes or even with a two or three sentence summary of the book.

Reading fiction

We don't read novels the way we read non-fiction. And we certainly don't survey a murder mystery — which would tell us who done it before we even started. No, read a work of fiction straight through; that's the way the author intended it to be read. You may want to make notes. With those complicated Russian novels, I use my bookmark to write the names of the characters, the page on which they first appear, and sometimes a word or two of identification.

If you want to be able to remember a work of fiction, summarize it in a very few sentences on a 3 x 5 card. The card is easy to file, and it will limit your summary to a reasonable length.

Remembering the events of the day

Thurlow Weed was a powerful New York State politician of the last century. He owned and edited one of the most influential anti-slavery newspapers in the country, and he became one of Abraham Lincoln's staunch supporters throughout the Civil War. Our present interest in him lies in the method he developed for improving his memory. This is what he said about it:

"My memory was a sieve. I could remember nothing. Dates, names, appointments, faces — everything escaped me. I said to my wife, 'Catherine, I shall never make a successful politician, for I cannot remember, and that is a prime necessity of politicians.' My wife told me I must train my memory. So when I came home that night, I sat down alone and spent fifteen minutes trying silently to recall with accuracy the principal events of the day. I could remember but little at first; now I remember that I could not then recall what I had for breakfast. After a few days' practice I found I could recall more. Events came back to me more minutely, more accurately, and more vividly than at first. After a fortnight or so of this, Catherine said, 'Why don't you relate to me the events of the day, instead of recalling them to yourself? It would be interesting, and my interest in it would be a stimulus to you.' Having great respect for my wife's opinion, I began a habit of oral confession, as it were, which was continued for almost fifty years. Every night, the last thing before retiring, I told her everything I could remember that had happened to me or about me during the day. I generally recalled the dishes I had had for breakfast, dinner, and tea; the people I had seen and what they had said; the editorials I had written for my paper, giving her a brief abstract of them. I mentioned all the letters I had sent and received, and the very language used, as nearly as possible; when I had walked or ridden — I told her everything that had come within my observation. I found I could say my lessons better and better every year, and instead of the practice growing irksome, it became a pleasure to go over again the events of the day. I am indebted to this discipline for a memory of somewhat unusual tenacity, and I recommend the practice to all who wish to store up facts, or expect to have much to do with influencing men."

Weed's method works for more than the kinds of facts he referred to. You can use it with anything you want to remember. When you read a book, discuss it with your friends. If you can, get a friend to read the same book at the same time. Better still, join a discussion group. You will get more out of the book if you can discuss it with a group, because they will open your eyes to things you missed in the book, and they will challenge your ideas about the book. And you will remember what you read because you have expressed your ideas about it and heard theirs.

Among the advantages to taking college courses is the fact that it forces you to express yourself both in examinations and in written assignments. Performance — expressing yourself orally and in writing, and thinking — these activities will improve your memory.

Everything you want to remember must be reviewed. There is no other way. The point of this section is this: Active review, in which you personally involve yourself and express yourself, is the best way. If you want to remember the definition of "mnemonics," explain it to a friend or write a paper about it (even if you have no other use for the paper) or ask someone to quiz you on it, or argue about it with someone who disagrees with your definition.

The more energy you expend, the more active you are, the better you will remember.

Chapter 10

Word Perfect Memory

This above all: to thine own self be true,
And it must follow, as the night the day,
Thou canst not then be false to any man.

Those lines from *Hamlet* make perfect sense. They are expressed in blank verse and in archaic language — we do not say "thine" or "canst" — but otherwise they are straightforward. Perhaps in our day, we would put it like this:

The most important thing in life is to be true to yourself, because if you are, then you cannot be false to anyone.

If the two sentences have the same meaning — and for all practical purposes they do — then why, if you are rehearsing for the part of Polonius in *Hamlet*, must you be sure to say it the first way and not the second?

One answer that is over-simple but true is that if you are learning a part of a play, you will be expected to get it word perfect. But why? Because the original language is better for the purpose of the play than your language is likely to be. For example, Shakespeare's language speaks to our emotions in a way that my paraphrase misses entirely. The rhythm of the poetry affects our feelings as well as our thoughts. If we want the full effect of a poem or play, we must memorize the work verbatim.

Our minds are built to work with meanings. In most situations in life, the exact wording of an idea is not important; it is the idea that counts. But we all occasionally find ourselves in situations where we must be word perfect. The obvious example is when we learn a part for a play, or when we want to memorize a poem. We may want to be able to quote a poem or a saying in a speech. We could read the quotation from notes, but we know it will be far more effective if we look at the audience when we say it. Although few of the people who answered my questionnaire indicated an interest in memorizing poetry or parts for play, a large percentage indicated an interest in remembering jokes, and that entails some word perfect memorizing. Vocabulary appears to be important to people of all ages, and of course you cannot increase your vocabulary unless you get the words right. So I will take up all these matters in this chapter.

Even though acting in a play is not a wide-spread matter of interest, it illustrates most effectively the problems involved in learning anything so that we become word perfect. Consequently, I will discuss learning a part in some detail. What I say about it applies to many other kinds of learning "by heart."

Memorizing a part for a play

At one time educators believed that repetitive practice of one thing will improve our ability to memorize anything else we may wish to memorize. For instance, they thought that memorizing passages of poetry would improve the ability to memorize anything — like, for example, the axioms of geometry. It didn't work. We might think that practice of that kind works, because we know that professional actors can memorize long parts with greater ease than you and I can manage. William James cleared this up years ago:

> I have carefully questioned several mature actors on the point, and all have denied that the practice of learning parts has made any such difference as is alleged. What it has done for them is to improve their power of *studying* a part systematically. Their mind is now full of precedents in the way of intonation, emphasis, gesticulation; the new words awaken distinct suggestions and decisions; are caught up, in fact, into a preexisting network . . . although the mere native tenacity is not a whit improved, and is usually, in fact, impaired by age.

James anticipated some of the points that psychologists have "discovered" since his time, such as networks and multi-modal strategies. I would add two factors that also contribute to effective learning: one, which James mentions elsewhere, is keeping mentally active, and the other is confidence. Experienced actors learn new parts all the time, which keeps them mentally active, and they are confident that they can memorize parts like Medea and Hamlet, while you and I are likely to be so frightened at the prospect that we doom ourselves to failure. (Stress and fear suppress memory, probably by diverting our attention away from the information we want to remember and directing it to the personal trouble that has brought on the stress or fear.)

Although I have done no acting myself, like James I have talked to actors about the strategies they use. Having read this far in the book, you will not be surprised by their strategies.

If you want to memorize a part, begin by understanding the play; then understand your part. Meaning acts as the cement that binds the words together and binds your memories of the words. Understanding the meaning will not give you the exact wording, but it will give you the structure, so that each scene leads naturally to the scene that follows it. And in general, each speech leads naturally to the speech that follows it. Everything fits into the structure.

Hamlet, however, illustrates a common problem. When the critics disagree on the meaning of a play, how can you discover the true meaning? You must do it by selecting the meaning that you consider most valid. (The selection is usually done by the director, but the problem is the same.) You must establish the meaning that you will follow before you can present the play intelligibly on the stage, so do it before you begin to memorize your part.

We *can* learn meaningless sounds, of course, and when we were very young and had not built up a network of information in our memory storage, that was the only way we could learn. It was not as efficient as learning through meaning, but it worked. Our teachers taught us to sing "My Country 'Tis of Thee" by rote, mostly from the sounds. The tune and the rhythm helped. But many of us did not understand the word "tisothee," and I can still remember being puzzled by the word "country." My grandfather had a farm in the country, and that was the only usage of the word I knew. Were we singing something incomprehensible about Grandpa's farm? The pledge of allegiance was another mass of senseless sounds. Is "pledgeallegiance" one word or two or three? Is there something called a "legiance" that we were pledging?

At our age we have built up enough knowledge (and that means memories) to be able to understand all kinds of complicated ideas. We should take advantage of that when we face the task of memorizing a part for a play or a poem.

Verbatim learning

After you understand the play and your part in it, you must settle down to the tough job of memorizing the part verbatim. You have grasped the structure, now you must fill in the details.

Break the part into digestible units. These units — actors often call them "beats" — will usually be shorter than scenes. Each beat is a section that appears to you to be unified in some way; it appears to have an aim or an objective. In Act I, Scene 3 of *Hamlet*, Ophelia first talks with her brother, her aim being to bid him farewell. He leaves, and her father questions her about Hamlet. Now her aim is to satisfy her father by answering his questions. These could be considered two beats, each to be memorized separately; then, after each beat has been mastered, they can be put together into one whole.

Breaking a part into beats is an individual matter. You must decide how much you can handle at one time, and you must make divisions you consider logical.

Poetry can be memorized the same way. First be sure you understand the poem; then master the wording. Some people advise working on the entire poem as one unit because you will want to recite it as one unit. I am inclined to break the poem into beats as with a play. If the poet divided it into stanzas, I would use the stanzas as units to memorize. You can learn what strategy works best for you by trying various approaches.

A mechanical trick that you probably discovered as a child is to cover the poem you are working on and recite it a line at a time, uncovering the line after you have said it to be sure you got it right.

Multi-modal learning

Verbatim memorization calls for a lot of repetition: going over the words again and again. That is maintenance rehearsal. But you can also use elaborative rehearsal. Think about what you are repeating. Repeat it in different ways. Reading it and thinking about it is one way — or "mode."

Another mode consists of writing the words. Write out the poem. Write out your part of the play. That will focus your attention. In addition, you will not only think about the words, but you will see them.

Still another mode consists of speaking the lines aloud. When one of the leading actresses at the Stratford, Ontario, Festival was asked how she memorized her lines, she said that, in addition to what I have already mentioned, she spoke her lines aloud over and over, instead of simply repeating them mentally. In that way, she used her vocal chords and the muscles of her throat and mouth. Her input included not only the senses of sight and hearing, but of feeling as well. And speaking the lines gave her an additional boost: She would have to speak them on the stage, so practicing aloud came as close as possible to duplicating the actual performance.

Use imagery just as much as you possibly can. If you are learning a part for a play, "see" the characters you are speaking with. "See" the set. "See" everything you expect to see on the stage as you expect to see it — that is, from your own personal point of view. If you are memorizing a poem, "see" the setting and the action

— to the extent that the poem contains setting and action.

Listening to a recording of the poem or play offers another mode of learning. If you cannot find it on a record or tape, make a tape recording of yourself reciting it. If you have a tape player in your car, that is a wonderful place to work on it, and it gives you extra practice time that you would not have otherwise.

Obviously, we can combine all of these methods, and when we do, we strengthen the memory even more. When I listen to a recording of Maurice Evans reciting Hamlet's "How all occasions do inform against me, and spur my dull revenge!" I not only listen, which gives me aural input, but I read along with the record, which gives me visual input as well. The sound creates an aural image; when I recite the lines, I hear myself as Maurice Evans — even though I know, in my saner moments, that he sounds far better than I. Reading the lines rarely leaves me with a visual image of the printed page, as a photographic memory would, but, far better, I imagine the scene — as you should when reading an imaginative work — and I can visualize that when I recite. I see myself standing on a barren plain in Denmark, watching the Norwegian army march by.

Combine as many modes — meaning, visual, auditory, imagery — as you can. They reinforce one another.

Overlearning

When you have mastered the part for the play, don't stop working on it. Overlearn it.

If you get to the point where you can recite it perfectly, you know that the next day you will not be able to remember every word. You must fix it in your mind more firmly than that. Continue to practice just as you did before, until you have it so well in mind that there is no way you can forget it. That is what we mean by overlearning.

We discussed automatic processing in Chapters 4 and 6. The star tennis player practices the forehand drive until it becomes second nature — automatic. The pianist practices scales until they become second nature — automatic. The tennis player and the musician have overlearned their skills.

The skilled tennis player is free to concentrate on the tennis ball's angle of approach, the position of the opponent, the desired placement of the return, and many other things, where the novice must concentrate simply on hitting the ball. That is because the skilled player has overlearned the requirements for hitting the ball.

Overlearning a poem or a part for a play is similar. In this case, the structure and meaning of the poem or play act as cues, and, in addition, each word acts as a cue for the word that follows. (There are other cues, too, particularly in the case of a play, where such things as gestures, intonations, setting, and the actions of other actors act as cues.)

In Chapter 6, in the discussion of organization, we looked at these two strings of letters:

A I O Z T N G R N A O I

O R G A N I Z A T I O N

One reason the second string is easier to remember is that it is a word, and we have overlearned most of the words in our vocabulary. We have certainly over-learned "organization." The chances are that you cannot remember when you first learned it, but every time you have used it, you have reinforced your knowledge of it. It has finally become so thoroughly overlearned that it comes to mind instantly when you want to use it.

Language is perhaps the best example of overlearn-ing. We are not born knowing a language; we must learn language from those around us. But we over-learn it to the extent that words come automatically when we want them. On the few occasions that we cannot think of the word we want, we are perplexed. Not being able to think of the word is such an glaring exception that it puzzles us, when we *should* be puzzled by the amazing speed with which most words do come to mind when we need them.

Actors must overlearn their parts. All of the strategies should be used over and over till the actor can step onto the stage and (like the tennis player) concentrate on the important aspects of acting — creating the part in a way that convinces the audience

— instead of thinking about the strings of words that make up the part.

Jokes

One of the results of the questionnaire I discussed in Chapter 3 that surprised me is that the item selected as seventh most important (out of 30) by people over 60 is remembering jokes. I suppose I should not have been surprised that jokes ranked so high because I like to tell jokes myself, which means, of course, that I must remember them myself.

Remembering jokes is like remembering a poem or a part for a play, but it is easier. To begin with, be sure that you catch on to the joke. You can not expect to be funny unless you get the point of the joke yourself.

Example:

> The city council of a British provincial town was about to vote for the building of a public urinal. Only one alderman held out against it, and he could not be persuaded to change his mind till the man sitting next to him suddenly realized what the obstacle was. Leaning over and putting his mouth close to the hold-out's ear, he explained what the word "urinal" means.
>
> The hold-out changed his vote at once. "I'm in favor of the urinal," he said, "and I think we should build and arsenal as well."

To catch on to the joke, you must know what the words "urinal" and "arsenal" mean. And you must understand what the hold-out mistakenly thought "arsenal" means. And you must know enough about human nature to know that people often oppose things simply because they do not understand them.

A joke has two parts: the story and the punch line. The story need *not* be learned verbatim. The punch line must be.

The joke is seldom spoiled by changing wording of the story. You need only be sure that you get all of the essential information into it. But change the punch line and you will have no joke at all.

That is not strictly true, but it is a good operating rule. In my joke, the story must include the word "urinal," although I believe every other word could be changed as long as the resulting story contains the same information. The punch line could be altered a little without damaging the joke, but the words "urinal" and "arsenal" must be included.

Memorizing the punch line verbatim may not be absolutely essential, but if you do memorize it, you will avoid the embarrassment of telling the story up to that point, then messing up the punch line by forgetting one of the key words, or forgetting their relationship — which is what makes the joke.

So the recommended way to handle a joke is to understand it so that you can tell the story, and to memorize the punch line verbatim so that the joke goes off smoothly.

Jokes usually do not require a lot of rehearsal, although, if you think you are going to have trouble remembering your joke, rehearse it. Use all the devices I mentioned with regard to poems and plays. But remember: you do *not* have to remember the story verbatim, just the punch line.

A minister in one of my memory classes said that before he uses a joke in a sermon, he tries it out on some friends. That gives him practice and feedback. What I do is simply consider each telling a practice run. Maybe the reason I tell the same jokes so many times is that they get funnier each time because I improve my technique based on feedback.

At least *I* think they get funnier — and I hope my friends agree.

Memorizing music

Memorizing music is analogous to memorizing poetry. First you must understand the music, then you must work on the details, fitting each note into the structure you have learned.

Trained musicians can understand a piece of music from the sheet music, whereas most of us have to play it through or hear it played through. Listening to a record will give you an overall understanding of the music even if you disagree with the interpretation of the recording artist.

We can use three memory systems with music. One is aural — we "hear" the music in our mind.

I think of the second memory system as intellectual: our knowledge of the music in terms of the structure, melody, key, harmony, time signature, etc.

As with all memory tasks, mere repetition is less effective than thoughtful repetition. Think about the piece as you play it. Remember that if you want to memorize it, you must overlearn it.

Playing a piece of music requires the use of muscles, and the muscles seem to have a memory of their own. This is the third memory system. You develop it automatically as you practice, just as you do when you practice golf or tennis or any other sport. Although muscle memory (the technical term is "haptic memory") works well, depending on it alone is chancy. If the muscles forget, you will probably have to start over at the beginning.

For more detailed advice on memorizing music, see the reference for this page or see your music teacher or a friendly librarian.

Vocabulary

Increasing our vocabulary was high on the list of both young and old people who responded to my memory questionnaire. That's good. Words are important. We express most of our thoughts and many of our feelings in words. I have said many times that our minds are built to handle meanings. We usually handle meanings with words. Words express concepts. So if we want to understand what we hear and read, we must know words. We must have a strong vocabulary.

Furthermore, most of our remembering is in words. We also remember sights and sounds and smells, and haptic memory keeps us able to walk, run, and play tennis, but when we think about what we remember, we express most of our memories in words, even to ourselves.

Improving your vocabulary requires that you do two things: First, you must find new words to add, and second, you must memorize them. The second step can be broken down to understanding the meaning of the word and then overlearning it. You must *over* learn if you want to have the word on hand to use it when you want it.

Finding new words is not much of a problem. At our age, we have vast vocabularies, but we still run across new words in reading, conversing, listening to lectures, doing crossword puzzles, etc. Most of us do not want to learn every new word we run across. We want to learn the words that we find more than once or words that strike us as important — usually from the context in which we find them.

We can usually understand the meaning of a word fairly well from the context — the sentence in which we find it. But of course the best way to discover the meaning is by looking in the dictionary. The dictionary gives precise definitions, so that we learn what the word "really" means — that is, how the word is usually used.

Two problems: If we hear a word at a lecture, we do not have a dictionary handy to look it up, and second, if we are reading, we seldom want to interrupt our reading to look the word up. If we are reading a textbook or any other book that we take very seriously, we might have to stop to look up every word we do not know, but generally it is better to keep on reading.

You may be able to remember the new words you heard at a lecture, but you will do better if you can write them down. If possible, write the sentence in which the word occurred. Then follow the same procedure you would follow if you found the word when reading.

The procedure for learning words you find in your reading begins when you acquire a supply of 3" by 5" cards. You can buy them in a drugstore or stationery store. Mark them like this:

```
WORD
(broken into syllables)_____Plural_____
Pronunciation_____Part of speech_____
Sentence in which
word was found_____

_____

Definition_____

_____

_____

Derivation_____
```

Keep one or two cards in the book that you are reading. You can use them for bookmarks. When you find a new word that you want to know, write the entire sentence (not just the word) on the line that says: "Sentence in which word was found." Then return to your reading. Forget the word for the time being.

When you put the book down, go to the dictionary and look up the words in the sentences you have written on the cards. Fill in the card, with the word on the first line. Break it into syllables. Write down the plural if it is a noun. Write down the pronunciation and part of speech. Then fill in the definition. Finally, write in the derivation. Dictionaries often show the word in an illustrative sentence. Copy any such sentences on the back of the card. Also use the back for additional information such as related words, synonyms, antonyms, and to continue the original sentence and the definition if they are too long to fit on the front.

Why do you want all this information about the word? Elaborative rehearsal. You will use the card to review the word from time to time. The more you know about the word, the more you have to think about, and the more you can think about the word, the better it will stay in your memory. You will be able to associate it with several things, such as the derivation.

Derivations often help us associate groups of words. For example, "missile," "mission," and "missive" all come from the Latin *mittere*, which means "to send." That is not an important piece of information, but if you review the definition of all of the words in the group, knowing that they are related through the Latin "mittere" will give you a better understanding of all of them.

Because many English words come from Greek or Latin words, learning some of the more common Greek and Latin words makes it easy to build one's vocabulary. If we know that the Latin word "centum" means "hundred," it will be easy to remember the meanings of "century," "centennial," "centigrade," "centipede," and "centurion." This helps even though knowing the meaning of "centum" does not tell us what the other words mean unless we know what the other segments of the words mean.

Similarly, knowing the meanings of prefixes and suffixes helps us remember words. "Bi" means "two," so we can figure out that "bicentennial" has something to do with two hundred. "Re" means "again," and "memor" means "mindful." Put them together and we get "remember" — getting something into the mind again that was there before.

You will find prefixes and suffixes listed in the dictionary along with their definitions. They are organized in alphabetical order just as though each was a word. Suffixes are listed the same way. For example, my dictionary lists "-er" as though it were a complete word.

Latin and Greek roots — the basic part of the word — are not listed except in the derivation part of a definition, but they are usually given there along with an English equivalent.

Once you get accustomed to looking up derivations, you will find that your vocabulary will grow faster, and you will have more fun learning words in this way because it adds a new dimension of meaning.

Derivations in themselves can be dangerous, though. You can never assume that the derivation of a word gives you its present meaning. In fact, it may have nothing to do with the present meaning. For example, the word "nice" comes from the Latin "nescius" which means "ignorant." Nevertheless, the derivation gives you information about the word, and the more you know about anything, the better it will stay in your memory.

Remember the word "mnemonics" from the last chapter? Its derivation only vaguely suggests its meaning. It comes from the Greek word "mnemonikos" which means "relating to memory." In Greek mythology, Mnemosyne was the goddess of memory. It was the ancient Greeks who invented strategies for aiding our memories, and they called them by the Greek equivalent of our word "mnemonics," which explains the unusual spelling of the word.

None of this information about "mnemonics" explains its present-day meaning exactly, but all of it helps fix the word and its meaning in our minds.

A brief but important digression

One of the main reasons that I have not hesitated to use technical words about memory in this book is that I want you to learn them. I want you to learn new words in any subject that interests you, and I assume that memory interests you or you would not be reading this book. If you go on and read more books or articles about memory, you will run into those words, so you are better off learning them now.

Work on your vocabulary. The more words you know, the easier your reading and the clearer your thinking. Easy reading and clear thinking are good for your memory.

Back to the cards

Keep the vocabulary cards in alphabetical order and review them from time to time. You may want to keep them in two or more sets, putting the most recent words in one set, words you have worked on for some time in another. Or you may want to have sets for different kinds of words. If you are interested in knowing more about memory, you might keep all the new words pertaining to memory in one set. If you want to know more about architecture, keep all of the words pertaining to architecture in one set.

Carry some of the cards with you so that you can review them at odd moments. This provides the kind of distributed practice we discussed in Chapter 9. That is better than sitting down and going through the pack all at one time — and you are more likely to do it

The most important thing you can do to fix the word in your memory is to use it. Using the word makes it part of you. The greater your personal involvement with any word or any idea, the better you will remember it.

We all have a passive and an active vocabulary. The passive vocabulary consists of words that we can recognize and understand, but which we do not know well enough to use. The active vocabulary consists of the words that we actually use. Use your newly acquired words as often as you can until you are sure that they are part of your active vocabulary. That way, they will be available when you need them.

Foreign languages

Many older people travel more than they did when they were young. Many want to learn the language of the country they plan to visit. There was a time when people generally believed that you and I are too old to learn a new language, but that belief is a thing of the past. Older people are learning new languages every day.

Learning vocabulary is only a part of learning a foreign language, but it is an important part. The words must be put together in sentences, which means that you must learn grammar, too.

The native Spaniard does not have to learn Spanish grammar in order to speak any more than we had to learn English grammar before we could speak English. Why, then, must the student of Spanish learn Spanish grammar? If we immerse ourselves in Spanish and hear no other language, we will learn the language without learning the grammar. Otherwise, the rules of grammar are shortcuts to usage. We must master them either by living with the language for years or by studying them directly as taught in school — which may seem harder but is usually easier and quicker.

Understand the grammar. When the teacher talks about the dative case, be sure you know what the word "dative" means. It is in the dictionary, just like any other word. Use the rules for understanding that we discussed in Chapter 9. For instance: Think of examples of English datives.

You will have to memorize the rules of grammar, and, worse than that, you will have to memorize the exceptions to the rules. Rules are extracted from usage, and since native speakers often do not know the rules, they break them so often that there are many exceptions.

Foreign vocabulary

There are a few tricks you can use to memorize a foreign vocabulary. One is to break words into elements and look for connections between them and also between elements in the foreign words and English words.

Use English words as cues or reminders of the foreign words. Here are examples that you can use for Spanish and Latin, and that you can imitate for other languages. You will notice that the "Reminder" is an intermediate step between English and the foreign language. Many memory strategies use intermediate steps of this sort. The intermediate step resembles both the English and the foreign word in some way, either meaning, sound, appearance, or something else. You will strengthen your memory even more if you can create an image that combines the English and Spanish word.

English	Reminder	Spanish
alone	solitude	solo
ancient	antique	antiguo
cold	frigid	frio
dark	obscure	oscuro
door	portal	puerto
drink	imbibe	beber
follow	sequence	seguir
glad	content	contento
high	altitude	alto
sell	vend	vender
sleep	dormant	dormir
wash	lavatory	lavar

Try making images for these words. See yourself playing a solo piano piece with no one near — in solitude — alone. See an ancient fort — an antique fort. I would see it on the island of Antigua in the West Indies, which would add another intermediate step — from Antigua to antiguo.

Here are some examples from Latin:

English	Reminder	Latin
crown	coronation	corona
dog	canine	canis
father	paternal	pater
field	acre	ager
free	liberate	liber
head	cap	caput
horse	equine	equus
house	domicile	domus
land	territory	terra
man	human	homo
sour	acid	acer
think	cogitate	cogito

war	belligerent	bellum
water	aquatic	aqua
writer	scribe	scriba

Memorizing vocabulary requires review. Use 3 by 5 cards and write the word on one side with the English translation on the other side. You can buy cards like this, but you will do better to make your own. Writing them out yourself is another case of multi-modal rehearsing. Also make a note of the image you create for the reminder word.

Review the cards until you have overlearned the words. Carry them with you to review whenever you have a free moment. That will distribute the learning process over time, which is the best way to learn.

Bon voyage!

Chapter 11

Some Memory Tricks

Several years ago I attended a six-day seminar in Stratford, Ontario. I had been there in previous years for seminars, so that I had several friends among the hundred or so people in the group. But that year there was one man whom I had never met before, but who somehow seemed to pop up everywhere I went. He was always smiling, and he always had something irrelevant to say. I tried to avoid him, but found that impossible.

A few days into the seminar, I had occasion to introduce him to someone I knew. I was embarrassed. After all, I did not want to be rude to the man.

"I'm terribly sorry," I said, "but I seem to have forgotten your name."

"Dren," he said. And then he spelled it: "D-r-e- n."

It was an odd name. I had never heard it before this specimen introduced himself to me on the first day of the seminar, and I have never run into anyone since with that name. But of course that was not the real problem. I found him an annoying person, and I did not particularly want to know him or his name. I suppose that my unconscious blocked the name out of my memory.

Then he came out with a mnemonic that has enshrined his name in my memory forever. He smiled his vacuous smile and said, "Oh, it's an easy name to remember. All you have to do is think of 'nerd' spelled backwards."

I would like very much to forget Mr. Dren, but I'm afraid I never will.

Sometimes the long way around is the shortest

Mr. Dren's trick is a mnemonic strategy, and it illustrates the essential features of mnemonics. Instead of remembering the name directly when you see Mr. Dren, you take an intermediate step; you think of "nerd" and then spell it backwards. In other words, instead of the sight or sound of Mr. Dren acting as a cue to his name, the sight or sound acts as a cue to "nerd," and "nerd" acts as the cue to "Dren." I don't know if Mr. Dren understood how well his mnemonic worked; did he realize that the word "nerd" flashed through everyone's mind the moment they saw him? The perfect cue.

This is a paradox: Two things are easier to remember than one. How can putting extra information into memory make the memory work better? Why doesn't the extra information add a burden that slows memory down? The answer seems to be that when we have only poor cues to the information we want to know, the extra information — the intermediate step — gives us a better cue. Seeing Mr. Dren was not a good enough cue to bring his name to mind, but the sight of him immediately made me think of "nerd." "Nerd" instantly reminds me of the name "Dren."

Mnemonics are used with information that does not make much sense. The name "Dren" has no meaning except in relation to the man himself. Most names have no meaning in themselves — or they suggest the wrong meaning. I know a Mr. Short, but he is not short. Ms. Brown need not be brown, Mrs. Goodfriend may be someone you barely know, and Mr. Jolly may be a sourpuss. As a consequence, we usually need mnemonic strategies to help us remember names. We will look into names more deeply in Chapter 13; first we must learn more about mnemonics.

People sometimes object that mnemonics are artificial and that they can mislead us into remembering the wrong things. That is largely a matter of practice: the more we practice the mnemonic, the more effective it will be. It will never be perfect, but you will notice that the memory experts on TV rarely make mistakes.

Then there are people who think there is something morally wrong with mnemonics: if you must learn the names of the twelve cranial nerves, you should learn *them* and not some silly jingle that brings them to mind. True, your goal is to learn the names, but why not use every means you have? Anything that will help you realize your goal should be used, and mnemonic tricks can be a big help.

Limitations of mnemonics

Mnemonics have limitations, though. Writing a note can often be easier and more effective than applying a mnemonic. On the other hand, notes can be lost and overlooked, and we may not have the note with us when we need it.

Another problem is that we have to balance the extra effort of learning the mnemonic against the importance of remembering the information. The mnemonic must be cost effective, if we think of "cost" as the time and effort needed to learn the mnemonic.

Finally, as I mentioned before, if the information we want to remember is meaningful, we will remember it best by understanding it and studying it in the way that was explained in Chapter 9. Mnemonics are used primarily with information that does not make much sense, and you will see what kinds of things those are as you read through this chapter and the next. Even so, mnemonics are often helpful in reinforcing our memory for meaningful information.

But will you use them?

In a recent study, psychologists L. E. Woods and J. D. Pratt tested several subjects including a group aged 60 to 90 years old. They gave them memory tests, then had them use the pegword mnemonic that we will learn very shortly and tested them again. The test scores were much better when the subjects used the pegword mnemonic. But then they interviewed the subjects four months later and found that no one — but *no one* — was using the pegword system to improve their memory!

I hope you will do better than that.

Some simple mnemonics

Let's begin with some mnemonics that are so simple that the cost of learning them is low. "Thirty days hath September, April, June, and November. All the rest have thirty-one except February, which has twenty-eight, or, on leap-year, twenty-nine." We all know that jingle, and it seems simple enough to be worth knowing. But it was not easy to learn. It took me a long time, but that was so long ago that I can hardly remember the learning process. And I did not learn it as well as I might have. I know that the ending is correct in terms of the days in the month, but I think I have the wording wrong. However, it is close enough, and it serves my purpose.

You don't need two ways of remembering how many days there are in each month, but there is another simple way. Make your left hand into a fist. Then, with a finger from your right hand, touch the knuckle of your left index finger. That is January, a knuckle month. Touch the valley between the knuckle of your index finger and the knuckle of your big finger. That is February, which is *not* a knuckle month. Go on, touching knuckles and valleys in turn and naming the months as you go. You will find that the knuckle of your little finger is July.

Now start back, but start by touching the knuckle of the little finger again. Now that you are starting back, that knuckle is August. Continue through December, which is a knuckle month. All the knuckle months have thirty-one days, and the others have thirty — except February. But we all know about February.

This silly little device illustrates some important points. To begin, it ties a motor act (an act that involves moving something — in this case your hand) to a thought process. Whenever you can combine two modes, in this case speaking and acting, you strengthen the memory involved.

Secondly, it shows that the numbering is orderly. On the whole, each thirty-one day month is followed by a thirty day month. Only two exceptions: February and August. If you know only the "Thirty days hath..." method, this regularity may escape your notice.

Third, the association between knuckles and months is bizarre; it is an association we would not normally make. Bizarre associations are very effective as memory aids. In this case a third factor will probably do more than anything else to fix the technique in your memory: it is a funny procedure. I use it only as a kind of joke when I am talking with someone and the question of the number of days in a month comes up. If I am merely thinking to myself, I usually go through the jingle, "Thirty days hath September," simply because I learned that when I was young and have used it so many hundreds of times that it comes naturally to mind — I have overlearned it. But practice the knuckle month method, and the next time the question comes up when you are with a friend, demonstrate it. You'll enjoy it.

Rhyme and rhythm

Rhymes are often used for mnemonics, and the "Thirty days" jingle illustrates this. Rhythm also helps memory, and the "Thirty days" jingle has rhythm, too. Poetry is easier to remember verbatim than prose. Some scholars believe that poetry was used in the days before writing was invented so that people could remember things better. The story of Troy was composed in poetry, supposedly for this purpose, and the *Iliad* and the *Odyssey* were recited from memory long before they were written down.

We should notice that jingles and poems are intended to be remembered verbatim. The general idea that some months have thirty days and others have thirty-one is not enough; we want to know exactly which months have thirty and which have thirty-one. It is often verbatim information like this that requires mnemonics. Mnemonics are used primarily for meaningless information, but they are always helpful when we must memorize anything verbatim, even when the information is organized and meaningful.

So use mnemonics whenever you can. When trying to remember meaningful information, use meaning as the primary aid to memory, but if you can add a mnemonic, you will strengthen the memory.

How many wives did King Henry VIII have, and what was the fate of each?

> Divorced, beheaded, died;
> Divorced, beheaded, survived.

That is easy to remember, and it packs in quite a bit of information. It is not hard to add the names, although they do not fall into place quite so readily as the fates of the six women. (And you can see the mnemonics are great for remembering trivia.)

Songs offer another mnemonic technique for remembering verbatim. The tune acts as a cue for the words, and this adds to the cue provided by the previous words. So we have two different kinds of cues in songs, each reinforcing the other.

First letter mnemonics

Can you name the colors in the rainbow? You know them all by name. The trick is to select those that appear in the rainbow and to name them in order. Some genius invented the name Roy G. Biv to assist in this task. Read down the first letters of the list to find Roy's name:

> Red
> orange
> yellow
>
> Green
>
> Blue
> indigo
> violet

Using the word "homes" to recall the names of the Great Lakes in another example of first letter mnemonics. "Homes" has nothing to do with the Great Lakes, but you will remember it simply because it is one of those crazy things you can't forget.

Do-it-yourself mnemonics

The simple mnemonics I have discussed so far are meant less as tools to be used than as examples to guide you in devising tricks of your own. When you want to remember information that has virtually no meaning, work out a mnemonic of your own. Relate it to a jingle or a song. Devise a word or sentence from the first letters of the words. Your jingle may not be as clever as "Thirty days . . ." but you will remember it because you invested something of yourself in it, and that always makes things easier to remember.

The very next time you want to memorize one or a group of facts, devise a mnemonic strategy. You must practice if you want to benefit from your knowledge of mnemonics. Knowing about them is not enough. Invent some of your own. Use them. They will strengthen your memory.

How mnemonics work

Now that we have increased our understanding of mnemonics by going through some examples, we can understand better how they work.

1. Mnemonics make us think about the information that we want to remember. They force us into performing an elaborative rehearsal. At the same time,

they give us a way to organize the information we want to memorize. This strengthens the input process.

2. The intermediate step — jingle, song, first-letter trick, or other associations — will stick more firmly in memory than the new information we want to remember. This strengthens the storage process.

3. The intermediate step gives us cues that make recall easier. This strengthens the retrieval process.

So we can see that mnemonics works by strengthening the three memory processes that we always use.

Pegwords

The pegword strategy introduces two additional features that are widely used in mnemonics: a pre-learned mental structure into which new information is fitted, and the use of imagery in the intermediate step, where imagery might be all of the intermediate step or just a part of it. Both of these features are usually found in elaborate mnemonic techniques.

The pegword strategy has been around for a long time. It was described in the seventeenth century and probably goes back centuries before that.

The pegword strategy is easy to learn, easy to remember, and easy to use. And it has many uses, although the first example may make it look more like a game than a useful tool. I will mention some of its uses as I go along.

Pegwords requires that you learn ten words — and overlearn them so that they come to mind automatically. This is the "pre-learned mental structure" that

I mentioned above. The words are easy to learn because each one rhymes with its number. Here they are:

One is a bun
Two is a shoe
Three is a tree
Four is a door
Five is a hive
Six is sticks
Seven is heaven
Eight is a gate
Nine is a line
Ten is a hen

You can use the pegwords to memorize a list of items that have little or no relation to each other. The following list illustrates how pegwords work. It is probably not the kind of list that you would want to learn except to practice or to show off. It is easy because every item is a well known, concrete object. After you understand how to handle this list, I will explain how you can use pegwords to remember abstract words and names.

1. piano
2. dachshund
3. post card
4. milk shake
5. shirt
6. tent
7. basketball
8. wheel
9. rifle
10. soup

How do we encode the first word? We must create a mental image that includes our pegword, bun, and the target word, piano, interacting in some way. The interaction need not be logical, and, in fact, if it is logical, it might not be as easy to retrieve as an illogical, or at least a startling image. In any case, the image must be **VIVID**.

One logical image would consists of a grand piano with a hamburger bun lying on it. The trouble is that we can hardly see the bun for the piano. So why not make the bun as big as the piano. Bizarre — obviously impossible — but memorable. I prefer to image a huge hamburger bun with the piano in place of the hamburger. That's even more bizarre, but even more memorable.

The second word is dachshund, and our pegword is shoe. Since they have similar shapes, we could imagine a dachshund with its body being a shoe — a big shoe with four feet, a tail, and a head sticking out.

The third word is post card, and our pegword is tree. Close your eyes and see a huge post card the size of an outdoor road sign nailed to a tall tree. The stamp, the address, and a message must appear on the post card if we are not to confuse it with a sign such as a no trespassing sign.

How can we combine a milk shake and a door? Picture your own back door after your teen-age son came home carrying a milk shake which he spilt when trying to open the door with one hand and hold the shake with the other. Your nice clean door has gooey chocolate milkshake splattered all over it.

Which is better: a beehive hidden by a huge shirt, or a huge shirt with a beehive sticking out of the pocket?

Tent is easy. We use sticks driven into the ground as stakes to hold the ropes. We can go farther and visualize a big stick as the tent pole itself. Use a lot of sticks to hold your tent up and you will remember the target word, tent, more readily.

Basketball and heaven. What do they have in common? Well, it's heavenly to sink a shot, but that is not an image. Watching the ball go up into the basket will give you an image of the ball against the sky — assuming that the basket is outside. There you have heaven and a basketball in the same picture.

Have you ever seen a large wagon wheel used as a gate? Whether you have or not, you can see it in your mind's eye. I always picture a white picket fence with a gate. In this case, I see the wagon wheel hinged to a white gate post.

Rifle is easy because we can see a straight line running right through the barrel. The lines we use for images need not be straight. It depends on the word we are trying to remember. A spiral staircase might utilize a spiral line, and a penny might utilize a circular line. In this case, however, a straight line is perfect.

Finally, we must relate a hen to soup. I will leave that one to you, even at the risk of your coming up with "chicken" instead of "hen" when you test yourself.

Now test yourself. If you have not memorized the pegwords, use the list written out above as cues. Cover up the list of target words, and read down the list of pegwords. Does bun bring the first word to mind? Does shoe remind you of the second word. Go through the list and see if you don't remember more of the ten words than you would have with your un-aided memory.

Let's try again

All of the words on both the pegword list and the target list represented concrete objects. Concrete objects are easiest to remember, and they are best to practice with. But the pegword strategy can help us remember abstract words, too. For practice, here's another list that combines several kinds of words:

1. baseball
2. banana
3. smoking
4. liberty
5. runner
6. democracy
7. literacy
8. victory
9. communism
10. boxing

The first word, baseball, leaves us where we were — with a concrete object. You should be able to handle this and the second word without my help, but smoking is a new kind of word — a verbal noun. It refers to an activity, not an object. I once saw a forest fire, with the trees burning brightly and dense smoke rising from them. I was in an airplane near Anchorage,

Alaska. You only need to see a forest fire once to remember it all your life. I have no trouble creating an image that includes both trees and smoke — the trees are *smoking*.

Liberty is as abstract a noun as you'll ever run into. How can we combine "liberty" and "door" in one image? Easy. Let the Liberty Bell stand for "liberty," and put it smack in the middle of your dining room door so that no one can get around it. We simply found a concrete symbol for the abstract idea.

The fifth word, "runner" is concrete, but there is something odd about it. A man or woman is not enough; that man or woman must be *running*. How about a picture of a man running away from a swarm of bees. That will work best if we remember to have the beehive prominently in the picture. The bees are pouring out of the hive and swarming around the runner.

Democracy and sticks. They don't have much in common. Or do they? Remember Teddy Roosevelt, who warned our grandfathers to walk softly but carry a big stick? He was a Republican who staunchly defended democracy. We might remember a cartoon of Teddy striding across a map of the world carrying a big stick. Or we might imagine voting with sticks: a big stick for our candidate and a small stick for our opponent.

Literacy is a tough one. The cartoons often show St. Peter at the Pearly Gates studying a book to see if the newcomer is to be allowed in. Obviously he is literate; therefore literacy must be heavenly. Your image should emphasize the book with St. Peter *reading* it — with plenty of clouds in the background.

Victory and a gate. Can't you see Johnny come marching home, the happy, returning veterans in their blue or gray uniforms marching past the white picket gate, Johnny, arrived at last, rushing through the gate victorious?

Communism is easy because Communists follow the party line. (Or at least they did before *glasnost*.) But notice that this is not an image but a verbal association. However, it is so familiar to many of us that it will serve as well as an image. As usual, I am not as interested in sticking to the rules as in getting results.

Boxing is another verbal noun. It has no relation to hens. But we all know about cock fighting, and it isn't too far an imaginative journey from a fighting cock to a hen. We might even visualize a barnyard cockfight where the hen, standing in the background, is the prize. I don't know if it really works that way in the life of the barnyard, but it works that way in my imagination.

Using pegwords

Now that we've mastered the pegword strategy (maybe not at first reading, but it doesn't take long), what are we going to do with it? Answer: Lots of things.

I use it for taking tests in college courses — or any other kind of test. A history test may ask you to list six causes of the American Revolution. In studying for the test, you associate the causes with the pegwords.

Then you need only go down the list of pegwords to retrieve the six causes.

A test in philosophy may ask you to explain the philosophical arguments for the existence of God. In studying, you associate the name of each argument with the pegwords. In the test, the pegwords will enable you to retrieve the names. If you have understood the arguments, the names will be enough to permit you to retrieve them. (Notice that we have combined pegwords — to recall the list — with understanding — the technique discussed in Chapter 9.)

I have often had meetings with people in which I wanted to bring up several points. I could list the points on a piece of paper, but sometimes that is clumsy and disruptive to the flow of discussion. I use pegwords to remind myself of the points. In addition to enabling me to recall the points, the pegwords make it easy to remember which points have not yet been covered, even though they may have come up in an order different from my original pegword order.

If you give a speech, you should use notes to remind yourself of the points you want to cover. But if there is an occasion when you must give a speech and for some reason the use of notes is not appropriate, use pegwords to remind yourself of your points.

People often ask me how they can remember what they've read in a book or a magazine article. A simple way is to break the book or article into its important points, then use pegwords to remember them. If you can remember the points, and if you were interested in what you read, your mind will fill in much of the detail. If you want this information in your permanent memory store, be sure to review it occasionally.

This applies to such things as cultural and historical facts. If you want to remember recent movements in art, write them down in list form and link them to pegwords.

Believe it or not, you can hold many such lists in your mind without one blotting out the others. If you make two lists of artists, they may interfere with each other, but a list of artists and a list of the ideas that you found interesting in Lewis Thomas's *The Lives of a Cell* will not.

It takes practice for this technique or any other technique to run smoothly, but you will find the result worth the effort.

Sometimes when I am driving, a brilliant thought — sometimes more than one brilliant thought — may come into my mind. How can I remember it? Pegwords are the answer. Even with only one thought, I can use the pegword system. This also applies to thoughts that come while I am in the shower or anyplace else where I cannot write the thought down immediately.

More pegword practice

Pegwords are just complicated enough to require more practice. If you have had enough for the time being, skip to the section headed "The method of loci" and come back to this section later, when you decide that the time has come to master pegwords.

Current events: How do we remember the names of the Supreme Court Justices? With pegwords. Since I don't know what the judges look like, I have used their names to make associations with the pegwords. (My list is dated, but it will serve as an example.)

1.	William H. Rehnquist	Wren pecking a twisted bun
2.	Harry A. Blackmun	A bootblack shining shoes is a man
3.	Sandra Day O'Connor	Conifer — pine tree
4.	John Paul Stevens	Stevedore stoking furnace — fiery door
5.	Antonin Scalia	Hive covered with scales — hard flat plates, as on a fish
6.	Thurgood Marshall	A marshal's baton is a stick
7.	Anthony M. Kennedy	John Kennedy is in heaven
8.	Byron R. White, Jr.	White picket gate
9.	William J. Brennan, Jr.	Line formerly meant flax (compare with a fishing line) Linen comes from flax, and almost rhymes with Brennan

As I have used them here, the pegwords associate only with the last names except in the case of Justice Stevens. In his case, I image the stevedore to be on a ship, and ships remind me of John Paul Jones, our first great admiral. I find, though, that knowing the last name makes remembering the first name easier, so that I can usually go through the list and recall both.

You can also use pegwords to impress your daughter when she comes to visit. Ask her the names of the Supreme Court Justices, and when she runs out of steam after three names, you go down the list and remember them all. Who has the better memory then!

Or ask her to name the provinces of Canada, our giant neighbor to the north. She probably won't even be able to tell you how many there are. I approach them through the pegwords going from west to east — on a map that means reading from left to right, just as we read anything else.

1. British Columbia. B as in bun. This is the only province that begins with B. Vancouver is the best known city in BC, and I've been there, so it's easy for me to begin with British Columbia.

2. Alberta. I visualize a pair of hiking shoes climbing a rocky mountain — on the feet of a girl. (It helps to know that the Rocky Mountains are in Alberta and that this is the only province with a girl's name.)

3. Saskatchewan. I see one of those big vertical signs — the kind that make you twist your head ninety degrees to read them — on a tall tree. Saskatchewan has the longest name of all the provinces, so it takes a big tree to hold the sign.

4. Manitoba. Door — with a huge man standing in it, dominating the scene.

5. Ontario. Toronto is the busiest city I know — a beehive of activity. And of course Toronto is in Ontario.

6. Quebec. From the news we get, it seems as though the French in Quebec are always fighting their non-French fellow citizens. So why not imagine them fighting with sticks?

7. Newfoundland. What could be more heavenly than an unspoiled new-found land?

8. New Brunswick. New Brunswick is on the Bay of Fundy, which has tremendous tides. At high tide the salt water backs up into the rivers and streams, and the salt ruins the land for agriculture. To prevent this, the natives have built dams. But the dams must have valves — or gates — that permit the fresh water to flow out at low tide, yet prevent the salt water from backing up at high tide. These valves — which I think of as gates for the purpose of the pegword strategy — call New Brunswick to mind.

9. Nova Scotia. I visualize a line drawn across the map of the North Atlantic Ocean from Old Scotland to New Scotland — or, as the Canadians call it, Nova Scotia.

10. Prince Edward Island. There is a kind of hen called a Rhode Island Red. The word "island"

works well enough to bring the province name to my mind. Prince Edward Island is the only island province.

The more you know about any subject, the easier it is to remember new information about it. My knowledge of New Brunswick exemplifies this. If I had not known about the unusual dams there, I would have had a harder time finding a word to mediate between the pegword and the province name.

A short-cut

There is no real short-cut for pegwords, but sometimes I find that there are several things I know well enough, but I am afraid of missing one of them. For example, this morning I plan to go to the grocery store, the drug store, and the gas station for a fill-up. I make this same trip so often that I will have no problem remembering what to do as long as I remember that there I must do *three* things, not just one or two. On a simple task of this sort, I just have to remember the number 3: I have *three* things to do. This works well enough for me to give me the cue I need, relieving me of the job of going through a more elaborate mnemonic.

This short-cut works only because all three tasks are familiar, and I have done them together many times. If the number were 4 instead of 3, it would mean that I must stop at the hardware store, which is on the way home from the gas station.

The method of loci

If people did not love to use obscure words instead of simple words that mean the same thing, this would be called "the method of places." "Locus" (pronounced "low'- kus) means "place" in Latin, and "loci" (pronounced "low'-sigh") is the plural of "locus."

The method of loci is the oldest mnemonic known. It goes back about 2,500 years. It was first described by the Roman orator, Cicero, but it was almost 500 years old in his day.

Cicero used the method of loci to memorize the points in his speeches. In his day it was not unusual for an orator to make a speech that lasted for hours. Cicero could do that and remember every point in the correct order. Here is how he did it.

First he wrote out every point that he wanted to remember, and he listed them in the order in which he wanted to use them in his speech. Then he used a device that is similar to pegwords, but instead of words, he associated each point with a place in his house. After all, he could remember what his own house looked like as easily as one can remember the peg-words.

Cicero imagined himself coming home and walking through his house. As he "saw" (in his mind's eye — his image) each object that he encountered in his imaginary walk, he associated it with a point in his speech. Then, when he gave his speech, he simply re-imagined the walk through the house. As he "saw" each object in the house, the corresponding point of his speech came into his consciousness.

As you can see, the method of loci is similar to pegwords. Instead of memorizing a list of words for the pre-learned structure, we use something like our house, the details of which we know thoroughly. As with pegwords, we must create an image (or some other association, like a verbal association) that combines the thing we want to remember with the prelearned detail of the house.

Suppose you were asked to tell what this book is about. You would list the important points, then associate them with what you would see as you come home and walk through your house. In the example, I have used the chapter headings of the book for the major points to be remembered:

Locus	Chapter Title	Image
Driveway	Find Those Glasses	"See" yourself searching for your glasses along the driveway as you approach your garage
Garage door	Some Facts of (Older) Life	Since we think of the facts of life as relating to sex, imagine a dirty word scrawled on the garage door
Front door	What Do You Want to Remember?	Perhaps the window in the front door has the shape of a question mark
Coat closet	Dredging Things Out of Memory	Dredging things out of the closet (See yourself doing it!)

Locus	Chapter Title	Image
Fireplace	Two Magic Words and the Secret of Success	A smoky, spooky fireplace, where the smoke conceals magic and secrets
Easy chair	Strategies — The Tricks of The Trade	See yourself smoking your pipe (even though you don't smoke) and dreaming up strategies
TV	How to Find Things (Encoding)	TV encodes pictures as electric impulses. Or "see" a spy show with someone breaking the code
Book Case	Good Intentions	Visualize all the books that explain how to carry out our good intentions
Dining room	Information That Makes Sense	As you see yourself eating, see yourself explaining to someone that eating makes sense
Dining room	Word Perfect Memory	The sideboard is *perfectly* beautiful, and in *perfect* condition
Kitchen sink	Some Memory Tricks	Magician doing disappearing tricks — disappearing down the drain
Kitchen knife rack	More Memory Tricks	More tricks — this time with knives
Kitchen stove	Names	"See" the name of the stove in huge letters
First floor lavatory	Memory and Motivation	This is where you are motivated to go and reminisce in peace and quiet

As usual, the associations are not logical, but fanciful. You might prefer different images, and if you can make images of your own, they will work better for you than the ones I have suggested.

You may prefer the method of loci to pegwords. It has some advantages and some disadvantages. You do not have to memorize a list of pegwords because you already know what your house looks like, but you will have to decide exactly what objects you will use and in what order.

You might want to use an alternative approach: Instead of walking though the house, some memory experts use the parts of their body, beginning with hair, then forehead, eyebrows, eyes, ears, nose, mouth, and so on down to feet. The list can go on to as many items as you are ever likely to want. But once again, think about it and decide exactly what body parts you will use.

The method of loci can be expanded to include any number of items you want. Pegwords can be expanded, too, but not quite so easily. You can imagine two buns for eleven, a bun and a shoe for twelve, and so forth. Or you can add new words of your own: a ladder for eleven. The sides of a ladder look something like the number 11, but "ladder" does not rhyme with "eleven." It is easier to think of other associations than rhymes. For example, you can use eggs for 12 because we usually buy eggs by the dozen.

One advantage of pegwords over the method of loci is that it is easy to pick out any item from the list, say number seven. If you want the seventh item using the method of loci, you must begin with item 1 and go through the list, counting as you go.

*

Why can't you remember those four news stories you wanted to discuss with your friend? Because you left remembering to chance. You read the stories and wanted to remember them, but you assumed that they were so interesting you would never forget.

Lewis Carroll knew about your problem when he wrote *Through the Looking-Glass*:

"The horror of that moment," the King went on, "I shall never, *never*, forget!"

"You will, though," the Queen said, "if you don't make a memorandum of it."

If you do not write it down, use a mnemonic like pegwords to fix the news stories in your mind. Don't leave memory to chance. According to some psychologists, that is one of the most important reasons for older people having memory problems.

Chapter 12

More Memory Tricks

Many people think of mnemonics as tricks and question their value because they are nothing *but* tricks. However, if tricks help you remember something important, they have value for *you*. Use them when they can help you. Otherwise, ignore them. You will find some of the mnemonics in this chapter valuable, and you will find that some are not worth the effort to learn — for your purposes. Look them over and select those that will help you.

Linking strategies

Another method for remembering a series of items consists of linking them together with images. As an example, I will assume once again that you want to remember the contents of this book by being able to recall the chapter titles. If you find this method similar to the method of loci from the last chapter, you are right: all mnemonic strategies depend upon association, so there is a great deal of similarity between them. In every case, you should select the strategy that best suits your purpose and that you like the best.

Since you will catch on to this method quickly, I will go through only the first few chapters for illustration.

1. Imagine yourself searching for your glasses. That gives you the first cue to "Find Those Glasses." Be sure the image is vivid.

2. You must now link "Find Those Glasses" with "Some Facts of (Older) Life." If you imagined yourself searching along your driveway for your glasses, you can now imagine yourself coming across some dirty words scrawled on the pavement. This links the search for glasses with the facts of life.

3. Now link "Some Facts of (Older) Life" with "What Do You Want to Remember?" Perhaps you can see a big question mark drawn through the dirty words.

4. Next, you must link "What Do You Want to Remember?" with "Dredging Things Out of Memory." If my memory serves (as it sometimes does), dredges have booms that haul buckets of some sort up from the water they are dredging. I can see a dredge with a huge boom shaped like a question mark, which, of course, links the question with the dredge.

5. What do you think the dredge brought up? A mass of mud — magic mud — that conceals two magic words and a secret: the secret of success. (No better way to hide a secret than in a mass of mud.)

6. On the edge of the mud hole we see a man sitting in an armchair lost in thought — a strategist. Can't you

see the strategist working to break the code? Be sure your vision is vivid. Is the strategist a man or a woman? A good looking hero/heroine or a mean looking villain?

7. Let's identify the strategist. He or she is a person of good intentions — which links "Good Intentions." Most of us know people of such good intentions that we think of their goodness whenever we think of them. Use them for the strategist. If you have never met a person with good intentions (which I find hard to believe), you will have to imagine one. Imagine a caricature of a face that beams with good intentions.

I have gone far enough to give you the idea. Once again, if you can create your own images, you will remember the information better than if you use ready-made images. Don't labor over them. No one will know about them but you. If they are silly, so much the better. They usually stick better than sensible images.

One advantage to the linking mnemonic is that it can go on as long as your imagination holds up. It has the disadvantage that if you want to find the seventh item, you will have to begin at one and count through them to seven.

Stories

An easy way to create links is to tell a story. To remember the chapter titles of this book, make up a story about a woman who has lost her glasses. She searches around the driveway for them because she last remembers using them to read the mileage on her odometer just before she put the car in the garage. Searching around the driveway, she comes across some dirty words. Turning away in disgust, she wonders who could have done such an offensive thing as to scribble dirty words on her driveway. It occurs to her that she has lost her train of thought. What was it she was doing? What was she trying to remember?

Since she cannot remember, she goes into the house and into the basement, where she had left her laundry. She dredges it out of the tub where she had left it to soak.

That is enough story; I am sure you get the point. If you are good at dreaming up stories, this approach may appeal to you. Many people use it effectively.

Personally, I prefer the pegword mnemonic to the others. It gives me a ready-made structure on which to peg the new information I want to remember. That means that the images I make are suggested by the pegwords; I don't have to dream up images from scratch. In my own experience, I have found that I seldom need as many as ten pegs, and very, very rarely have I had to go above ten. Pegwords are my preference, but you may find that one of the other techniques works better for you. If so, that's the one for you to use.

In any case, you will find it useful to select one of these mnemonic strategies and learn to use it. When you have mastered it, you will find it very easy to use and very effective.

Spelling

English grew up by absorbing several European languages, and all of them have left their traces in the way we spell words. As one expert says, there are no reliable spelling rules, and those rules we have are plagued by exceptions.

The problem is that words are not spelled the way they sound. So if we spell by ear we will make many mistakes. We must spell by eye as well as by ear. The letters we have actually written must correspond to the letters shown in the dictionary for that word — or we have misspelled the word.

We have two ways to get around the problem. One is to reform English spelling so that the spelling corresponds exactly to the sound of the word, the other is to memorize the crazy spellings that exist. Back in April, 1957, *The Smithsonian Torch*, a slim house organ put out by the Smithsonian Institution for the museum set, wrote the article that should end all articles on simplified spelling. Remember, it was written in 1957.

> We are in complete accord with Bernard Shaw's campaign for a simplified alphabet. But instead of immediate drastic legislation, we advocate a modified plan.
>
> In 1957, for example, we would urge the substituting of 'S' for soft 'C'. Sertainly students in all sities of the land would be reseptive to this.
>
> In 1958, the hard 'C' would be replased by 'K' sinse both letters are pronounsed identikally. Not only

would this klarify the konfusion in the minds of spellers, but typewriters and linotypes kould all be built with one less letter and all the manpower and materials previously devoted to making the 'C's' kould be used to raise the national standard of living.

In the subsequent blaze of publisity it would be announsed that the troublesome 'PH' would henseforth be written 'F'. This would make words like 'fonograf' 20 persent shorter in print.

By 1959, publik interest in a fonetik alfabet kan be expekted to have reatshed a point where more radikal prosedures are indikated. We would urge at that time the elimination of all double leters whitsh have always ben a nuisanse and desided deterent to akurate speling.

We would al agre that the horible mes of silent 'E's' in our language is disgrasful. Therfor, in 1961, we kould drop thes and kontinu to read and writ merily along as though we wer in an atomik ag of edukation. Sins by this tim it would be four years sins anywun had used the leter 'C', we would sugest substituting 'C' for 'TH'.

Kontinuing cis proses year after year, we would eventuali hav a reali sensibl writen languag. By 1975, wi ventyur tu sa cer wud bi no mor uv ces teribli trublsum difikultis. Even Mr. Shaw, wi beliv, wud bi hapi in ce noleg cat his drims finali kam tru.

The other way

Of course, even if we wanted to reform English spelling, we could not do it as individuals. As individuals, we are doomed to the old fashioned spelling. (But at least we can read it.)

Although the rules of English spelling are not very helpful, they are sometimes better than nothing (and sometimes worse). The most well known is "*i* before *e* except after *c*, or when sounded as *a* as in *neighbor* or *weigh*." Notice that this rule obeys some of the mnemonic suggestions: it has both rhyme and rhythm. But then it falls apart because it has at least ten exceptions.

Since we have a mnemonic pattern in the rule, we should have a mnemonic device to help us remember the exceptions — if we think it important to remember them. Here is a suggestion. The boldface letters emphasize the part of the word that embodies the exception: "**Nei**ther **lei**sured for**ei**gn count**ei**feiter could s**ei**ze **ei**ther w**ei**rd h**ei**ght without forf**ei**ting prot**ei**n."

The mnemonic for the exceptions is tough to learn, but it is easier than no mnemonic at all. The fact is that if we want to be sure of the exceptions to the rule, we are faced with a tough assignment, and the mnemonic is the easiest way of handling it that I know.

Since most of us are willing to take our chances on misspelling a word now and then, I will not go on to give you the mnemonics for other spelling rules, but will refer you to the book in which I found them. If you really want to improve your spelling, you cannot do better than get a copy of *Demonic Mnemonics* by Murray Suid. (See Books for Further Reading in the back of this book.) Suid's book not only gives mnemonics for twelve spelling rules, but mnemonics for 800 individual words as well.

Even if we know all the rules, they are not enough. The final authority — rules or no rules — is the dictionary. If in doubt, look up the word in any dictionary. But if there are words that you write often but are not sure of, you will save yourself time and effort by learning to spell them correctly. That is where the mnemonics for 800 words in Suid's book will help. To give you an idea of what his mnemonics are like, I am listing a few that I find helpful for my own writing. I have added some comments of my own.

Some examples

The first example is the word "privilege." Suid presents it with a synonym in case you might confuse it with some other word that sounds or looks something like it. The synonym is not intended as a definition — use a dictionary if you need a definition. Here is how "privilege" is presented:

privilege: advantage

trouble spot: privi**le**ge

trick: It's **vile** that the rich have privi**le**ges

The "trouble spot" is the point where people are likely to misspell the word. In this case, many people tend to use an *e* where they should use an *i*.

The "trick" is the mnemonic that will help you remember the correct spelling.

Next, take the word "sincerely":

sincerely: honestly

    trouble spot: sincerely

    trick: **Since I rely** on you, **I sincerely** need you.

Here are several more examples:

judgment: decision

    trouble spot: jud**gm**ent (also *judgement*)

    trick: Use your own **judgment,** an **e** or not.

Note here that *judgment* can be spelled either of two ways: with an *e* after the *g* or without. In England it is usually spelled *judgement*, but in the United States, careful writers usually omit the *e*, although most dictionaries consider either spelling correct. Consequently, you can spell the word either way, although you will do better to omit the *e* if you are writing for an American audience.

chauffeur: driver of an automobile

    trouble spot: chau**ffeur**

    trick: Our chau**ffeur** hates the tra**ff**ic in
    Europe.

You may not use the word *chauffeur* very often, but this trick illustrates how mnemonics can help you remember a very unusual spelling.

sacrilegious: violating something sacred

    trouble spot: sacr**i**legious

trick: You **rile** me with your sac**ril**egious attitude.

The problem with *sacrilegious* is that we tend to think that it comes from the word *religious*, in which the two trouble vowels are reversed.

When do we write *principal*, and when do we write *principle*?

principal: head of a school

trouble spot: princi**pal**

trick: The school princi**pal** is your **pal**.

principle: rule

trouble spot: princi**ple**

trick: The princi**ple** that serves as a guideline is a **rule**.

These examples should be enough to illustrate how Mr. Suid's method works and how valuable it is to those of us who have spelling problems.

Home-made mnemonics

If you can make up your own mnemonic for spelling a word, you will have the advantage that always comes from figuring out something for yourself — you will remember it better. You may want to modify one of Mr. Suid's tricks, or you may make one up from scratch. You may have a problem word that he does not cover.

A problem that Suid does not take up is whether *all right* can be spelled *alright*. *Alright* is creeping into common usage, but discriminating writers still use *all right*. How to remember this?

Try: **All right** is spelled like **all wrong**.

I find the spelling of the two words, *compliment* and *complement* confusing, so I worked out my own mnemonic based on the fact that *compliment* is associated with the word *polite* (both with the letter *i*), and *complement* is associated with the word *complete* (both with the letter *e*).

If I go by sound, I am not sure whether the second vowel in *repetition* is an *e* or an *i*. But when I remember that it comes from the word *repeat*, it is clearly an *e*.

When do we write *stationary* (standing still — not moving), and when do we write *stationery* (writing paper)? Just remember that we buy stationery from a stationer. I cannot imagine writing *stationar*, so the mnemonic works — at least for me.

These examples are meant as nothing more than samples of what you can learn from Suid's book or what you can make up yourself. We each have our own trouble words, and those are the words we should work on.

Numbers

Not very many people indicated in their questionnaires that they wanted to be able to remember numbers better, so I will not devote a lot of time to them. I will give you some fairly easy tips; I will sketch out a complicated mnemonic that will enable anyone to become a memory whiz (if they spend countless hours mastering it); and if you need more help than I offer you here, I refer you to the Books for Further Reading. Numbers are hard to remember because they are abstract. We cannot visualize them the way we can visualize a bun or a shoe or a tree. So we use mnemonics to make them concrete or to associate them with something we already know.

Memory experts who can remember a twenty-digit number at a glance use various tricks of association. They break the number into chunks. Then they make associations — the same trick we have been using right along. Some simple examples may help you work out mnemonic tricks for the numbers you find important enough to remember.

Take the number 2176. Break it into two chunks: 21 and 76. Look for associations. Twenty-one is the age at which the individual becomes independent. Seventy-six (1776) is the year in which the United States became independent. If that number is important to you (if it is your bank PIN — personal identification number), that will give you a handle on it.

We all know the year that Columbus discovered America, so if you owe someone $14.92, you should be able to remember it. Or if your PIN is 1492, you should remember it.

How can you remember that Mount Fujiyama in Japan is 12,395 feet high? I have a unique method. It starts with a mistake. Somewhere (I forget where) I read that the height is 12, 365 (30 feet short), so that you could think of 12 as the number of months in the year and 365 as the number of days. Those associations, although not really relevant, readily bring 12,365 to mind. But of course that's the wrong number. The thing that tickles me about this is that I find that I can use that mnemonic trick, and I always remember the correction: I remember 12,365, then remember that the 6 must be changed to 9.

If 57 occurs alone or in combination, think of Heinz foods.

The telephone company chunks numbers for us: 991-0306 (my old telephone number) consists of a chunk of three digits and a chunk of four. In addition, the chunk of four can be broken down into 03 and 06. Both begin with 0, and 6 is twice 3. The 991 is not so easy to manipulate, but since it is the exchange for my area, many of the numbers I frequently call begin with it, so I am familiar with it.

The more you already know, the more you can learn — you've heard that before. My son pointed out that the second chunk of his telephone number is 1485, the year that Henry Tudor defeated Richard III at Bosworth Field. That may not mean much to you, but I am both a Shakespeare buff and an English history buff, so it means a lot to me. You probably have different interests from mine, but whatever they are, they probably involve numbers. Use mnemonics to remember them, and use them to build mnemonics to help you with new numbers.

If you like to play around with arithmetic, you can sometimes find simple operations that fix a number in your mind. For example, the number 3256 breaks into 32 (8 x 4) and 56 (8 x 7). The number 2496 breaks into 24 (12 x 2) and 96 (12 x 8).

In all of these tricks, we are playing around with the numbers. To put it in more technical language, we are employing elaborative rehearsal, and that is the most efficient way to encode information we want to remember.

Social security

Very few people seem to have trouble remembering their address, telephone number, or social security number, but for the sake of completeness: if you do, use the methods just suggested for remembering them. Your social security number and telephone number are already chunked for you, and address numbers are usually only four or five digits. A piece of cake.

A more thorough mnemonic for numbers

A system for memorizing numbers was first devised by Winckelman in 1648, using letters to represent numbers. The system was refined by Gregor von Feinaigle in 1813, using consonants that were similar in some way to the digits they represented. The system shown below was devised by Loisette in 1896.

In this system, you must first memorize the consonants that stand for each digit. It will help if you notice that both t and d have one downstroke, n has 2 downstrokes, and m has 3 downstrokes. The "r" sound dominates the word "four." The Roman numeral L equals 50 — so l is used for 5. The sounds for j, sh, and ch are somewhat suggestive of the sound of 6. K and g for 7 and f and v for 8 seem more arbitrary, but the appearance of b and p resembles in a fanciful way the appearance of 9. The s and z for 0 come from the word "zero." Here is a summary table of the translations:

```
1 2 3 4 5 6  7 8 9 0
t n m r l sh g f b s
d            j k v p c
             ch c    z
             g qu
```

The system works by using the letters in the order of the digit in the number you want to remember. Then fill in vowels to make words. The words have more meaning than the digits, so they are easier to remember. As with all mnemonics, the words need not make sense, and bizarre combinations will work well, so you need not be inhibited in making them up.

The way to begin learning this system is to take a number that is very important to you, translate it into a word, and use it. For example: Suppose the personal identification number that gives you access to the automatic teller machine at your bank is 5678. This translates to the letters: "l," "j (or sh or ch)," "k (or g)," "f (or v)". The trick is to dream up a word or words using those consonants in that order, which means filling in the spaces below with vowels and selecting appropriate consonants:

$$
\begin{array}{c}
j \\
l - sh - k - f \\
ch - g - v
\end{array}
$$

By juggling vowels with various consonant combinations, I came up with the words "logic off." Senseless, perhaps, but that is not the point. If your number is 5678 and you think up these words, they will come to you when you face the automatic teller machine, and you can then translate them back to your number.

Incidentally, you will note that double "f" is the same as a single "f," because the system uses sounds, not actual letters. In a word like "succeed," the two "c's" count as two sounds because they are different. They would stand for 7 and 0.

(In reality, if I had number 5678, I would use the fact that the four digits are in sequence. But this is just an example.)

Using the system requires that you master the translations to the point where you can translate very quickly from numbers to words and then back to numbers. That takes a great deal of study and practice. If remembering numbers is important to you, then the system is worth the time and trouble it takes to learn, because it very definitely will work. However, only you can decide whether remembering numbers is important enough to invest the effort it takes to master the system.

I do not use this system. At present, there are no numbers important enough to me to justify the time and effort it would take to master it. But the system works, and it is valuable to people who find it necessary to remember numbers.

What I do about numbers
When I was in business, I could remember prices of my products quite well. One reason was that I figured out the prices myself, and that helped fix them in my

mind. Secondly, I used them often in letters and in written quotations. Finally, if I had any doubt at all, I checked the price against a printed price sheet.

I make no attempt to remember telephone numbers. I keep a telephone index on my desk where I can refer to it so easily that it makes the slightest effort toward memorization ridiculous. If I have to make a telephone call when I am away from home, I find the telephone book a handy reference.

Similarly, I do not try to remember street addresses. Once I have visited a house, I can usually find it by landmarks, which seem to stick in my mind without effort. When I address a letter, I refer to the address book on my desk, which is bound to be more accurate than my memory.

All this is not to say that there are no circumstances when it is desirable to remember numbers. The personal identification number required to use an automatic bank teller is a case in point. Gasoline station attendants ask for our auto license plate number, and it is convenient to be able to remember it. When I mentioned that to a friend one time, he shrugged it off. "I just make up a number," he said. But I take life more seriously than that.

My present license plate number is almost impossible to remember. It is 614-GTQ. I've never figured out a mnemonic for that one, but I have had it long enough that I now remember it. When I first had it, I wrote out the number on a slip of paper and scotch taped the paper to my dashboard. This turned out to have a bonus benefit I had not anticipated.

I belong to a dinner club that has valet parking. The attendants park the car according to the license plate number, so when I leave the club, I give the number to the attendant, who then brings the car around.

One of the attendants at my club approached me with a very puzzled expression when I first had the number on my dashboard, and asked why I had stuck it there. When I told him, he burst out laughing. The upshot was that he remembered which car was mine from that time on. On stormy nights, when there is a crowd waiting for their cars, all pushing to be first, my attendant friend brings my car around at once, as soon as he sees me, without my even asking for it.

Transcribing numbers: A short-term memory problem

A friend of mine tells me she has a problem remembering numbers she is transcribing from her checkbook stubs to the book she uses to keep track of her expenses. This is different from the problem of memorizing numbers; she does not want to memorize the number, she just wants to remember it long enough to write it down. Then she wants to forget it so she can go on to the next number.

In other words, this is a short-term memory problem. You want the number to stay in your short-term memory, where you can hold it for just a few seconds. You do not want it in long- term memory, where you would be able to recall it some time in the future.

Conquering this problem involves attention and maintenance rehearsal.

To begin with, you must "get" the number — grasp it, apprehend it. That means paying attention to it. But it means more than simply paying attention.

Numbers are harder to read than words. We are so used to glancing at a word and grasping its meaning in an instant, that we tend to read numbers the same way. But not with the same results. When we see the word "number," we get its meaning without even thinking about it. Just to see it is to "get" it — to grasp it or apprehend it. But for most of us, getting a number takes thought. It takes effort. And it takes time.

The word "number" has seven letters in it, but we know what it is the moment we see it. The number 9326 has only four digits, but it seems longer and harder to grasp. In an important sense, it *is* longer. It takes four words to say it: "ninety-three twenty-six." Each digit is a separate word, and two of them are two-syllable words. A mathematician who is as familiar with numbers as most of us are with words can probably grasp the number 9326 as quickly as we can grasp the word "number," but most of us have to struggle through the four words that make up the number.

If we have trouble getting the number into short-term memory, it is probably because we automatically (without thinking) try to read it as one word — we try to take it in at a glance. But since it is actually four words, we don't really "get" it, so nothing goes into short-term memory. When we go to transcribe it, it isn't there. If the number is not solidly in short-term memory, we have nothing to hold there till we transcribe it.

The first step, then, is to pay attention to the number. Apprehend the number. "Get" it. That means slowing down. Speed is a deadly enemy of memory. Speed is a deadly enemy of accuracy. The draftsman in the company I worked for when I was young had a sign over his desk that read: "Do you want a quick answer, or do you want the right answer?"

So instead of "reading" the number like a word by just glancing at it, take enough time to see what the number is. Say it out loud: "Ninety-three twenty-six." You could say it silently, but it will work better if you say it out loud. It is too easy to cheat if you say it silently. You may slur over it. In addition, saying it out loud brings your vocal muscles into play, and brings your hearing into play. They will reinforce your memory of the number.

The second part of the problem is solved with maintenance rehearsal. Maintenance rehearsal means nothing more than saying the number over and over till you write it down. Just the way you do with a telephone number that you look up in the book. You say it over and over to yourself till you dial it. Do the same thing with any number you want to remember long enough to write down.

Historical dates

You can use the same mnemonic tricks for remembering dates as for remembering any other numbers, but I use a different approach. I begin with a few dates that I know well. I think of them as anchors. Then I fill in new dates that fall between the various anchors. Let me show you what I mean.

There are some historical dates that everyone knows. Our calendar begins with the year 1. All dates come before or after that — B.C. or A.D. If you are not a history student, you at least know 1492. And you should know 1776, the year we declared our independence from England. And you must know your birthday. Mine was 1917 — the year we entered World War I.

When was Lincoln elected president? It had to be after 1492, and I know it was before I was born. That's as much as the anchors tell me. When I look it up, I find that he was elected in 1860. That is a good date to add to my anchors because Lincoln was one of our most important presidents.

When did the Pilgrims land at Plymouth? After 1492 and before 1860. We have cut the span of time between our anchors.

And so we go on. Civil War buffs will use the dates of the war — 1861-1865 — and then learn the dates of every battle that took place within that time span, although they may not be able to date the reigns of the kings of England or the Caesars of Rome.

I have my own set of anchors that I know well enough to help me place historical events that interest me. I list it here as an example or what you might do if dates are important to you.

2940 B.C. Imhotep (architect) built the
oldest surviving pyramid

597 B.C. Nebuchadnezzar captured Jerusalem

399 B.C. Death of Socrates

44 B.C. Death of Julius Caesar

1 A.D. Birth of Jesus used for establishing our calendar

410 Sack of Rome by Alaric the Visigoth

479 Fall of the western Roman empire. A convenient date to mark the beginning of the Middle Ages, although the transitions into the Middle Ages and from the Middle Ages to the Renaissance are too vague to be pinned down to a specific date.

800 Coronation of Charlemagne

1066 William the Conqueror defeated Harold at the Battle of Hastings

1453 Fall of Constantinople to the Turks. A convenient date to mark the end of the Middle Ages — a span of about 1,000 years.

1492 Columbus discovered America

1620 Pilgrims land at Plymouth Rock

1776 Declaration of Independence

1860 Election of Abraham Lincoln

1914 Beginning of World War I

1917 My birthday

If you are interested in a particular period, pick dates from that period for your anchors and fill in the dates that are important to you.

Chapter 13

Names

I used to have trouble remembering names until I took that Sam Carnegie course.
　　　　　　—Jack C. Taylor

Most of us have trouble remembering names, and I am no exception. I have a terrible time with names. But I am not as bad as I used to be. There are many tricks that help. I have mastered some of them, and I am working on more.

External strategies, such as writing names down, do not help very much. When you run into people you know, you do not want to pull out a reference file to look up their names. So we must depend on internal strategies, and if there is any deterioration of memory with age, it affects the internal strategies. If there is no deterioration of memory, there is almost always a slowing down. It takes us longer to retrieve memories, and usually, when we need to remember a name, we need to remember it right now, not tomorrow or even an hour later, so slowing down is almost as bad as not remembering at all. A good part of my optimism about the memory of older people comes from the fact that we can use notes and files to compensate for many memory problems. But not for names.

We can begin to improve our memory for names by clarifying our goal: To retrieve the name when we see or think about the person.

Obviously, then, we must use something that we see or think about as a cue to bring back the name. And that points to our old friend *association*.

Why names are hard to remember

Using association sounds easy enough, but we all know that it is not that easy. It may help us get started if we consider why names are so hard to remember. I have discussed the difference between recognition and recall earlier in the book, and names offer us the best example of the difference. When we run into a neighbor at the supermarket, her face is right there in front of us. The only question is: do we recognize her or not? Yes or no. But where is her name? We can't see it, the way we can see her face. We have to recall her name from somewhere in that vast network of stored memories somewhere in our minds. How can we find it? What is associated with it that will act as a hook to fish it out? Obviously, the best time to work on the name is when we are learning it, not when we are suddenly confronted with the task of retrieving it.

What associations do we have to work with? Unfortunately, names are essentially meaningless. Very few short people are named "Short," and Mr. Clipperman is not likely to be a barber (although, believe it or not, I do patronize a barber by that name).

We usually have to learn some tricks to give meaning to names if we want to make strong associations.

Another reason it is hard to remember names comes out of the situation in which you meet someone. It takes less than a second to pronounce that person's name — you hear it for less than a second. But the person's face is there for the duration of the conversation. That gives you a good chance to become familiar with the face, but almost no chance at all to become familiar with the name.

And there is often some confusion when introductions are being made. Introductions often come in the middle of a conversation. Do you listen to the name or follow the conversation? Normally, the name has nothing to do with the conversation, so that you must shift mental gears to attend to it. There is not likely to be anything in the conversation that you can use to associate the new name with the new face.

Emotional problems, too

To make matters worse, our emotions often work against us when we are introduced to someone. Because we are afraid of muffing our part in the introduction, we sometimes concentrate on what we are supposed to be doing rather than concentrating on the new name. Egocentrism enters into this problem.

Egocentrism can range from simply trying not to behave foolishly to trying so hard to make a good impression that we have no mental capacity left to take in the other person's name.

Egocentrism harms memory in many situations. For practical purposes, we can attend to only one thing at a time. So if you are paying attention to yourself, and to the impression you are making, you will not be able to pay attention to names or to any other information that you would like to remember.

If getting your own name remembered is important to you, use some tricks that you work out in advance so that you do not have to think about them at the time introductions are made. One that struck me as effective was the person who said, "My name's Hank Nisbett, but you won't remember it." That acted as a challenge, and I *did* remember it.

Tell something about yourself. That is one reason people tell what they do for a living — what you do is a good part of what you are. "I'm Harrison Otway, president of the Eighty-third National Bank." Or, if you think your position not exalted enough: "I'm Joe Schultz. I'm a busboy a the Kneeaction Bar and Grill. I broke more dishes last week than anybody who's ever worked there."

We all have *something* that sets us apart.

Try a mnemonic. Remember my friend, Mr. Dren? What can you do with your name. I had another friend, a salesman whom I liked a great deal, whose name was Omar McDowell. Omar confided in me that he had hated his name when he was a child; he was always getting into fights about it. But when he grew up and became a salesman it was great. No customer ever forgot him.

Telling people something that helps them remember your name has a plus value: it may remind them of something about their own name that will help you remember it.

I sometimes find myself repeating my name. "Mendelson. You know: My Uncle Felix wrote the Spring Song."

"I'm Fred Clouse. My Uncle Sandy used to bring you presents at Christmas."

Motivation

Do you really care to remember the name of the person you just met? If the person means nothing to you, there is a good chance that you will forget the name.

You are at a huge reception. You know hardly anyone there. You are introduced to a dozen people or more. How many will you remember?

"Meet Katherine Ortega," someone says. You go through the motions. She is just one more name to forget.

But suppose it goes like this:

"Meet Katherine Ortega. She's the Treasurer of the United States."

You will remember that name. Why? Because Ms. Ortega now means something to you. You have met an important person, and you don't want to forget it. And you don't want your friends to forget it, either; you make sure you remember her name so you can brag about meeting her.

You were motivated to remember Ms. Ortega's name. But what about Ms. Kretschmer, the mousy lady in the appalling print dress? Can you motivate yourself to remember her name, too?

You can if you talk to her. Find out something about her. Does she work? You might know the company she works for. You might have friends there. Does she have a family? Perhaps her children know your children. It turns out that her chief interest in life is bowling, and you haven't bowled for fifty years. Well, find out what's new in bowling. You may be no better off for knowing it, but you certainly won't be worse off. Associate her name with her appearance and her love of bowling.

Dredging names up from memory storage

But you do not talk with her, and two months later you go to another huge reception, and there she is. You grasp for her name, but nothing comes up. Your mind is a blank. Now don't you wish you had followed my advice?

All you can do is fall back on the techniques we discussed before. Run through the alphabet. Do you find a letter than resonates?

You do have some cues right in front of you: her face and her general appearance. They are enough to tell you that you met her before, and they might clue you into her name. Study her appearance.

Try reconstruction. Where did you meet her before? When? Who introduced you?

Can you remember her occupation? Do you remember if she engages in any civic activities?

If all else fails, try this social strategy: Walk up to her, give her a big smile, extend your hand, and say, "Hi. I'm Jerry Warbeck," as though you assumed that she forgot your name.

The worst that can happen is that she will smile, shake your hand, and say, "Oh, yes. We met before." But there's a good chance that she'll say, "Oh, yes. I'm Gertie Kretschmer. We met last week."

If all else fails, ask for the name. That is usually embarrassing, but in the long run it is less embarrassing than not knowing the name. Besides, most of us would rather have you ask for our name than ignore it. Our names are important to us. We want people to know them. If you keep that in mind, asking someone to repeat their name will be easier.

You can also fall back on your age. I have objected to the notion that we lose our memories simply because we have grown old, but since that is a common belief, why not take advantage of it when it works in our favor? I think old folks like me should take advantage of every break that comes our way. I use my Golden Age card to get a discount on groceries by shopping at Dave's Supermarket on Wednesdays. I use my Senior Citizen Identification Card to ride public transportation at low fares. And when I find myself in the uncomfortable position of forgetting someone's name, I sometimes fall back on the excuse of old age to cover my embarrassment.

That is all the help I can offer you concerning retrieval of names. The best way to handle names, of course, is to encode them so that the person's face will act as a cue to bring the name to mind. That will be the burden of the rest of this chapter.

Two essentials of encoding names

The two essentials of encoding names are our old friends: the magic words and the secret of success. Pay attention and make associations.

If you do not hear the name to begin with, how can you possibly remember it afterwards? So when you are introduced to someone, listen carefully for the name. If you do not get it, ask the person to repeat it. Ask him/her to spell it. Repeat the name aloud, and repeat it to yourself. Just this one technique can increase your ability to remember names. Some experts estimate the improvement at well over fifty percent.

Use the name as often as you can. This may not seem to be part of "pay attention," but it is certainly part of the encoding process. Using the name helps fix it in your mind. It also makes certain that you heard the name correctly.

When you use the name, speak up. Don't mumble. If you speak up and get the name wrong, that is embarrassing, but at least it offers an opportunity for correction, and then you will have the name right. If you mumble and get the name wrong, you may have lost your chance for correction, and you may think you know the name when you really don't. Whenever you meet people, call them by name so that you reinforce it in your memory. Also use the occasion to learn more about them. That will reinforce the name, too.

The secret of success for remembering names

Make associations. The secret of success for remembering names or anything else lies in encoding the name with associations. The associations will act as cues to bring the name to mind when you want it.

Memory experts use a complicated technique involving visual imagery that I will explain in a moment, but first consider straightforward visual imagery. If you meet Mr. Short, and he is short, you can make a visual association of the name and the man's appearance. If you meet Mrs. Tomak, and she has a big stomach, use that for your association.

The Mrs. Tomak example gets us back into mnemonics, and I will make a short digression. People sometimes object to mnemonics because they might be misleading. When you see Mrs. Tomak, your mnemonic may mislead you into saying, "Good morning, Mrs. Kelly." (Belly — get it?) There is no doubt that can happen, but it does not happen very often. Usually the mnemonic brings you closer to the name than your unaided memory. And what if you do call her Kelly? Is that any worse than forgetting completely? I don't think so. The mnemonic will usually help, and even if it fails, you won't be any worse off that you would have been without it.

Practice mnemonics. As you develop your skill in using them, your chances of making mistakes will diminish greatly.

Another association comes from people's importance to you. Who are they, and what do they mean in your life? What is their occupation?

Where and when did you meet them? Tie the context into your association. This may be distracting if you meet them in a different context, but even then it will give you a cue, however faint it may become.

Do they have special accomplishments, like playing the piano, macraméing wall hangings, or throwing pottery? Are they involved in civic activities, politics? Who is their spouse? Family? Friends? What kind of reputation do they enjoy among your acquaintances?

These questions help two ways: They increase our motivation, as I mentioned before, and they increase the number of associations that tie the name to the person.

The four-step strategy

You want to use any association that promises to work for you. But what do you do with a name like Bernardinelli attached to a pleasant woman about whom you know nothing? Memory experts have worked out a four-step strategy that will help you remember any name. It is a tough mnemonic strategy to learn, and, frankly, I have not mastered it, but if remembering names is really important to you, it will be worth your while to learn it because it really works. It is the technique that the memory prodigies use.

Step 1.

Listen to the name and get it right.

I have already covered this step, but it is worth repeating some of the key points it includes. Pay attention to the name when you hear it. If you realize, a minute or two after the introduction, that you cannot repeat the name, say something like, "We were introduced so quickly that I really didn't have a chance to get your name."

Talk about the name if possible. It used to bother me that people I met would make remarks they thought were funny — and I thought were stupid — about the Spring Song. I realize now that they were simply looking for hooks onto which to hang my name to make it retrievable.

Use the name in the conversation as frequently as you can. Use it when speaking to other people in the group.

Think about the name. Is it unusual in some way? Funny? Is it a common name? Does the name fit the person? In what way?

If you have trouble getting the name right, ask the person to spell it for you, and repeat the spelling. This will insure your having it right, and it provides some elaborative rehearsal by adding to your store of information about the name.

We just met Ms. Bernardinelli — remember? I would consider that an unusual name but not a difficult one. It is long, but assuming that she accents the second and fourth syllables, it is rhythmical. I presume that it is an Italian name, but that does not necessarily mean that Ms. Bernardinelli is Italian. She might be a Scotch lady married to an Italian man. Maybe we can learn more about her.

Step 2.

Convert the name into some "imageable substitute." The chances are that you don't know what an "imageable substitute" is, but here I am asking you to convert the name into one.

We all know what a substitute is, so Step 2 evidently tells us to replace the name with something else. What kind of "something else"?

Something that we can make an image of. The image will be in our imagination. (Image — imagination. Right?)

This is a crucial step in our four-step strategy, so let's plunge into it. Can we make an image of "Bernardinelli"? No. So how about substituting "St. Bernard"? At this point we do not know what our image will be, but we know that we can make an image of a St. Bernard dog if we have to. We might even be able to make an image of the Saint himself.

Please note that the imageable substitute sounds a great deal like the name. That is important, because it must remind us of the name.

Imageable substitutes are likely to be ridiculous. In fact, I am often embarrassed when I give some examples, so, as I do with my classes, where I must look people in the eye when I give them examples, I will use examples that I found in other books. Please keep in mind that I am not responsible for them.

What do you do with a name like Patrick? Try "pat trick." Far fetched, perhaps, but you *can* make an image with it.

"Ryan" is more versatile. "Cryin'," "rind," and "Rhine" can be used.

"Calahan" is a tough one. My source suggests "call a hand." Can't you picture someone calling a hand at a poker game. Even if you've never played poker, you must have seen enough movies for a vivid picture to come into your mind.

"Simmons" introduces another kind of image. In addition to "simmers," we can use "mattress," because Simmons mattresses are so well known to most of us that we automatically think of them together.

"Alexander" is the most far fetched name on this list. Try "lick sander." Absurd. But imageable. And there is nothing wrong with absurdity in mnemonics. Many experts believe that the more absurd the image the more useful it is as a cue to bring back the memory you want.

Break "Perlmutter" into "pearl mutter." For "Rafferty" try "rap for tea."

If these sound too far fetched, dream up your own. You are always better off to create your own mnemonic; because you created it, you will remember it.

And practice. At first, it will take so much time and effort thinking up the imageable substitute that you will mess up the entire procedure, but with practice you can master it. And the experts practice it to the point where making the imageable substitute comes close to being automatic; they do it fast and with so little effort that they can follow whatever conversation is going on at the same time.

Step 3.

Note a prominent physical feature of the person

Actually, this should begin even before you are introduced to the person. You are standing in a theater lobby at intermission, talking to your friend. A man approaches with that expectant look that indicates that he knows your friend and expects to have a conversation. As he approaches, look at him. (Many people look away out of shyness or modesty or something — I don't know what.)

When you are introduced, look the new acquaintance right in the face. No matter how strong the impulse, do not look away. Examine the face. Drink it in.

What are you looking for? An individuating feature. Something about that person that sets him or her apart from others. You want to find the most prominent feature of face or body, a feature that you will recognize the next time you see the person. Look at the eyes, nose, mouth, hair, chin. Look at the shape of the head, shape of the neck and ears. Is the person unusually short or tall or fat or thin? Is there a birthmark in evidence? A deformation?

If you met Long John Silver, you would notice at once that he had only one leg. If you met Sherlock Holmes, you would probably be so taken by his deerstalker cap, his cloak, and his great curved meerschaum pipe that he would have no trouble deceiving you next time by wearing a disguise. So beware of using clothes or hair style for your distinguishing marks.

Clothes have very little value as distinguishing features, but they have some. We all have our own taste in clothes, so that one of our outfits usually resemble others that we select. Nevertheless, clothes change, so be careful using them for clues. Hair has somewhat more value as a distinguishing feature, although a woman may change her hair style, and a man may shave off his beard or mustache.

You are not through when you have selected an outstanding feature. Now you must exaggerate it in your imagination. You must become a political cartoonist who draws a caricature of President Bush which may look nothing like him when examined closely, but which you can recognize at once because of the way his features have been exaggerated. Look at caricatures in the newspaper to see how it is done; then do it yourself. You will not be as skillful as the professional caricaturist, but you can develop a good enough skill to help you remember names.

What will we do with Ms. Bernardinelli? It would be a lucky break if she wore a sad expression on her face, because we could exaggerate that to the point where it looks like the sad expression on the face of a St. Bernard dog. If she wears a perpetual smile, we might caricature the dog: a St. Bernard dog smiling from ear to ear.

Perhaps she has beautiful hair that is almost the tan color of the St. Bernard, or white hair the color of the white on the dog. If she is unusually big, we could "see" her towering over her St. Bernard lap dog.

But I am anticipating Step 4.

Step 4.

Make some association between the person's appearance and name so that the appearance acts as a cue to bring the name to mind.

In this step, we must form an image that links the cue — the individuating feature that we have exaggerated — with the name or the imageable substitute. I already did that with Ms. Bernardinelli. What about Long John Silver? Well, if we concentrated on his missing leg, we might have misled ourselves. He was a tall man — a "long" man — and "long" makes an easy association with his name.

Do you see the resemblance between this four-step procedure and pegwords? In pegwords, the pegword is an additional step that provides us with an image that, in turn, brings to mind the thing we want to remember. In our four-step procedure, the imageable substitute provides us with an image that brings to mind the name we want to remember.

Suppose the last name of that man you met at the theater is Cameron. He has piercing eyes. Look directly into them. See each one as the lens of a camera. Your image of the eyes as cameras creates the link between the appearance and the name. His appearance cues the image, and the image cues the name.

But what if the name is Popowski? Do his eyes pop? Probably not. Then can you imagine him as the fatherly type — Pop? Probably yes. Turn his nose into the big feature of your caricature — a ski slope — and "see" Pop skiing down it.

Three things to keep in mind: 1) Make the image vivid. Do you know what Mr. Popowski is wearing as he skis down his own nose? Well, figure it out and put it in the picture. 2) Absurd images are great. No one but you will ever know what they are, so you can make them silly, unflattering, anything you wish, as long as they are vivid. 3) Images you make up yourself will help you more than images you read in books like this. I consider the images I mention as models. You will find more images in other memory improvement books. I recommend that you read them, but again only as models, not as examples for you to use. Make up your own.

Sometimes you can make an image directly with the name. You will not need an imageable substitute for Mr. Biggs if he is big or for Mrs. Bright with the sparkly eyes. Or for Ms. Schwartz if she has a big head of shiny black hair. That brings up a warning: If you use the black hair for Ms. Schwartz, and then meet a Ms. Black, you should try for a different image. Otherwise you may confuse the two ladies.

If you want to remember the names of people you meet even when you meet several at a time, you must master the four-step procedure so thoroughly that you can go through all the steps in the short time between introductions. It can be done. It takes hard, thoughtful practice. You will have to start out slowly, keeping every step in mind, just as you did when you learned tennis or typewriting or playing the piano. Your goal is to make it an automatic process like the others.

First names

Most of us want to remember first names as well as last names. First names present something of a problem because there are so may duplicates. When I was young, most boys were either Bob, Bill, or Jack. Mary was a popular girl's name then and still is.

My first suggestion is that you take one thing at a time. While you are learning the technique, decide whether you will concentrate on first names or last names and let the other go till you have become somewhat adept at applying the four-step strategy.

When you think you can handle both, try to run the names together into one imageable substitute. Remember the imageable substitute for Jacob Cass? Some movie of my youth worked it into the story. For those of you who don't remember, it is "jackass." If you mean Jean Bluestein, you might make an image combining blue jeans with a beer stein — depending, of course, on what prominent feature of Jean's appearance you can tie in.

First names complicate the procedure, so the only thing we can do is break the procedure into two stages and master them one at a time.

Other associations

Although images usually prove the best means of linking a cue with a name, other associations are better under some special circumstances. If you meet a man named Mr. Reagan, and he is a dead ringer for our recent president, you need not work up an imageable substitute to bring his name to mind. The names of prominent people and even of friends can sometimes be used as the intermediate link between a person's appearance and name.

A mixture of names and characteristics can work. For an aggressive man named Kaiser, try the Kaiser who embroiled Europe in World War I; for a milquetoast — Neville Chamberlain and his umbrella.

People whose names are the same as the names of political or historical figures, movie stars, and athletes offer easy associations. Take advantage of them.

You can use fictitious characters, too. Eddie Silver can become Long John if you can find a resemblance. Jane is a hard name to remember simply because it is so common. If Jane Wolanski is a teacher, she can become Jane Eyre. That will not help with her last name, but it accomplishes half the job.

Wolanski sounds Polish to me, and that might be the lead to a cue for her last name. Many nations are caricatured in the newspapers, and we can use them as guides. The English bulldog and the tall, bearded Uncle Sam come to mind. I would try to tie a Polish name into Solidarity or Lech Walesa. And there's nothing wrong with Frédéric Chopin or Ignace Jan Paderewski.

Names that also name occupations can be used for links. If Miss Miller is pasty-faced, it is because she has been busy milling flour. If Mr. Smith has bulging muscles, he is a blacksmith — and you can see the muscles bulge in your caricature even if the real Mr. Smith is puny.

Work out place associations with Ms. Paris, Mr. London, and Mrs. Patterson — New Jersey.

Finally, there are completely irrational associations. I have never read about them in any memory improvement book, and they would never have occurred to me had I not discussed my writing of this book with a Cleveland State University professor friend. He said that he can remember the names of every person in his classes after only one or two sessions. He uses the craziest system I've ever heard of.

"I make up associations," he told me.

"Like for instance?"

"Well, when I go through the attendance roll the first day, I take a good look at the student and make up an association. I look at a girl and say to myself that she likes Chinese food. I associate her with Chinese food. The next name is a young man. He drives a Mercedes."

"But how do you know she likes Chinese food or that he drives a Mercedes?"

"I don't. They probably don't. But that's the way I see them. She looks to me like someone who likes Chinese food, and he look like someone who drives a Mercedes. I just think of them that way. It always works."

Of stereotypes and such

Caricatures come close to stereotypes — the rigid forms that we try to fit people into. Stereotypes can be used successfully to make imageable substitutes. The stereotype of the Englishman that is caricatured by John Bull is of someone very stubborn. Use it if it helps you remember someone's name, but don't believe that it characterizes the person.

The trouble with stereotypes is, for example, that Englishmen are no more or less stubborn than anyone else. But knowing that, use the stereotype if it will help you remember Mr. Thatcher's name. Similarly, although America is the home of the brave and the free, not all Americans are brave, but if you can make that description fit Mr. Amerbach, take advantage of it.

Imagining someone as stupid is dangerous. Use it if it helps you remember the person's name, but be careful that it does not influence your judgment of the person. That can happen. No one but you will ever know your mnemonic for the person — but *you* will know, and *you* are the one who will be in danger of being misled.

Review

Review everything you want to remember, including names. On your way home from a party, discuss the people you met and use their names. When you come home from a meeting, tell your spouse whom you met. Use their names.

If you did not work up mnemonics for the names at the time you met the new people, do it when you get home or whenever you have a spare minute or two.

When you go to bed, think of the people you met and name them if you can. Review your mnemonics for their names. It often helps to do this even with people you know. People change over the years. Their appearance changes. A review will keep you up to date.

External aids have limited value with names because you cannot carry a card file with you and look up names when you meet people. But writing a name down gives it another reinforcement. Use a notebook or use 3 x 5 cards. In addition to giving you a permanent record, writing the name adds to your review, the act of writing gives the name motor reinforcement, and seeing it on paper gives it visual reinforcement. They all help.

Anticipate

Whenever you plan to meet a group of people, review their names in advance if you can. If you attend a business meeting or a club meeting, you will often have a list of the people who are likely to attend. Read over the list. Try to visualize the people named. Review your mnemonics for them.

Before you go to your school reunion, review your old year book.

Before you go to a family reunion — if it will be a big one — review the names, particularly of the children you do not know well.

Categories of names

You can chunk or categorize groups of names so that the category or any name in it will act to cue in the other names. Do that with families or members of a club or employees at a company.

My friend Connie has three sisters, Anne, Molly, and Phyllis. They use the word "CAMP," made from the first letters of their name, to remind people of their names and the order of their ages, Connie being the oldest and Phyllis the youngest.

A last word

How hard should you work at mastering the strategies I have discussed in this chapter? As hard as you think it worth the effort. If you want to master it, keep working till it becomes automatic. With enough practice, you will be able to go through the steps so fast that you will have one name properly stored before your host introduces you to the next person in the group. If names are really important to you, that should be your goal.

Chapter 14

Sherlock Holmes and the Art of Forgetting

Psychologists disagree on so many things that whenever you read a statement that begins, "Psychologists say . . . " it is a good idea to question it. There is one thing, however, that I believe all psychologists would agree on: Sherlock Holmes's theory of memory is hopelessly wrong.

"A Study in Scarlet" tells about the first meeting of Dr. Watson and Sherlock Holmes. Watson describes his new acquaintance and tries to figure out what kind of man Holmes is and what he does for a living. He is amazed at Holmes's vast knowledge, but — but I will let Watson explain:

> His [Holmes's] ignorance was as remarkable as his knowledge. Of contemporary literature, philosophy and

politics he appeared to know next to nothing. Upon my quoting Thomas Carlyle, he inquired in the naïvest way who he might be and what he had done. My surprise reached a climax, however, when I found incidentally that he was ignorant of the Copernican Theory and of the composition of the Solar System. That any civilized human being in this nineteenth century should not be aware that the earth traveled round the sun appeared to be to me such an extraordinary fact that I could hardly realize it.

"You appear to be astonished," he said, smiling at my expression of surprise. "Now that I do know it I shall do my best to forget it."

"To forget it!"

"You see," he explained, "I consider that a man's brain originally is like a little empty attic, and you have to stock it with such furniture as you choose. A fool takes in all the lumber of every sort that he comes across, so that the knowledge which might be useful to him gets crowded out, or at best is jumbled up with a lot of other things, so that he has a difficulty in laying his hands upon it. Now the skilled workman is very careful indeed as to what he takes into his brain-attic. He will have nothing but the tools which may help him in doing his work, but of these he has a large assortment, and all in the most perfect order. It is a mistake to think that that little room has elastic walls and can distend to any extent. Depend upon it there comes a time when for every addition of knowledge you forget something that you knew before. It is of the highest importance, therefore, not to have useless facts elbowing out the useful ones."

"But the Solar System!" I protested.

"What the deuce is it to me?" he interrupted impatiently: "you say that we go round the sun. If we went round the moon it would not make a pennyworth of difference to me or to my work."

The expanding room

If you want to think of memory as a room in which you store memories, you must think of it as a room that is constantly expanding. Holmes is utterly wrong: the walls *do* distend and will continue to distend as long as the mind is active and in working order. Psychologists have never found a person who has reached the limits of his or her memory storage. Because of this, they often speak of memory storage as infinite.

I have said before, and I will repeat again, that the more information we have in our storage network, the more additional things we will be able to remember, because it is easier to make associations between old knowledge and new.

Holmes does raise a fascinating question, though, when he says: "Now that I do know it I shall do my best to forget it." How does one go about forgetting something? If I want to forget something, how can I do it? You are reading this book because you believe that you forget a lot of things unintentionally. But Holmes seems to suggest that we can easily forget things on purpose. Can we?

The essayist, Montaigne, said, "Nothing so deeply imprints anything in our memory as the desire to forget it." Maybe forgetting is not so easy after all.

First let's look at how we forget things involuntarily. That should help us figure out how to forget voluntarily. And it may help us learn to remember better, too.

Are there things we want to forget?

First we should be sure that there are things we want to forget. The fact is, there are many such things, whether we are aware of them or not. William James explained this a hundred years ago. I quoted part of his comment in Chapter 3, but it is so appropriate that it is worth repeating:

> In the practical use of our intellect, forgetting is as important a function as remembering. . . . If we remembered everything, we should on most occasions be as ill off as if we remembered nothing. It would take as long for us to recall a space of time as it took the original time to elapse, and we should never get ahead with our thinking. [James then goes on to quote a M. Ribot.] "We thus reach the paradoxical result that one condition of remembering is that we should forget."

It is worth taking special notice of that profound remark: *One condition of remembering is that we should forget.*

It is not hard to see what James and Ribot are talking about. When I park at the supermarket, I want to remember where I left my car. But I do not want to remember where I parked it the last time I was there — or the time before that, or the time before that. If I go there twice a week, do I want to remember all 104 locations where I parked over the past year? If I do, I will have to sort out all those memories when I go to get the car this time. Life is a lot simpler if I just forget all the other places.

If I labored this point any more, I would risk boring you into forgetting what I was saying, but I must point out a paradox that is more complicated that Ribot's because, unless I do, you may think that I have goofed.

Ribot said that we must forget if we want to remember. This seems to contradict the maxim I keep repeating: *The more we remember, the easier it is to remember new material.* The two statements seem contradictory because they are both condensed. Expanding them will clear up the seeming contradiction.

Ribot's maxim expands to: We must forget trivial information that has little importance to us if we want to remember matters that are important; remembering everything wastes time and energy and may lead to trivial memories interfering with important memories. My statement expands to: The more pathways we make in our network of memory, and the stronger those pathways become, the easier it will be to retrieve information that we have stored in the network. The trivial, irrelevant information Ribot refers to will create pathways that lead to dead ends (and to interference, which I will explain in a moment); significant information creates pathways that lead us to significant information we want to remember.

Some explanations of forgetting

Psychologists have offered several different explanations of forgetting. No one of the explanations seems to be complete, but each adds something to our understanding of forgetting.

Women and elephants — and men

Dorothy Parker maintained that women and elephants never forget. Quite a few psychologists agree with that, and they would add that men never forget either. The idea is simply that one never forgets anything — a notion I have a hard time agreeing with.

Sherlock Holmes believed that we forget because the room gets so stuffed with memories that we finally get to the place where every memory that goes in pushes another memory out. The psychologists I am now talking about believe exactly the opposite; they believe that no matter how many memories we stuff into the room, every single memory stays right there forever.

There seems to be a germ of truth in that. Every once in a while, we remember something that we were sure we had forgotten forever. This fact leads some psychologists to conclude that we remember everything even though we cannot retrieve it all.

Then what does it mean to say that I forget an appointment? I remembered it the next day. Too late to be of help, but it shows that the knowledge that I had the appointment was in my memory. That kind of forgetting seems to be more a matter of timing than of actually forgetting. The information was in my memory storage, but I failed to retrieve it at the right time. I did retrieve it — but too late.

The trouble with the theory that we never forget anything is that there is no way of proving whether it is true or false. I have argued with some people who believe it, and when I say, "There are things that I simply can't remember," they reply, "You can't retrieve them at the moment, but they're there whether you can retrieve them or not." That gets us no place.

My reason for rejecting the idea starts from my understanding of evolution. Evolution preserves traits that help us survive and prosper in the world; it weeds out traits that work against survival. It seems to me that remembering everything, no matter how trivial, would work to our disadvantage. Irrelevant memories — where I parked at 2:24 on August 7, 1968, and similar mental trash — outnumber important memories many, many times and would create a tangle of interference. (Don't give up; I'm coming to interference very soon.)

Instead of arguing the matter — since no argument can be conclusive — I believe we should simply rule any piece of information that we cannot retrieve as forgotten. Maybe it will come back to us some day, and maybe it won't. But if we can't dredge it out of memory no matter how hard we try and no matter how long we wait, let's consider it forgotten.

So the question remains: How do we forget?

Decay

The oldest and most persistent explanation is that memories simply decay. Every day the memory gets a little weaker until finally it is gone. A hundred years ago, a psychologist named Hermann Ebbinghaus worked out "curves of forgetting" that tell us that if we learn something today, we will forget much of it by tomorrow. The next day we will forget more, but not as much as we forgot the first day. Every day thereafter we forget some more, but each day we forget less than we did the day before.

Ebbinghaus's conclusions are valuable because he also pointed out that if we review the information, our memory will bounce back to where it was the first day. We will forget it again, but the second time we will forget more slowly than the first time. The information will stick in our memory better after we have reviewed it.

Ebbinghaus's conclusions fit in with the idea of memory decay, but this explanation has fallen out of favor with psychologists. Still, I think it has merit. If we think of memory as a network of connections that get stronger with use, it seems reasonable that they would get weaker with disuse. I believe, though, that decay is simply one factor that enters into forgetting, and that there are other factors.

A problem with the decay explanation

There is a serious problem with the notion of decay. If decay were the only cause of forgetting, then we would expect our oldest memories to fade before recent memories, but we know that does not always happen. In addition, a simple memory experiment indicates that time is not the only factor in forgetting. The psychologist has two groups of people memorize a list of words. One group goes about its regular business for two hours and is then tested to see how much they remember. The second group goes to sleep for two hours and then gets the same test to see how much they remember. The second group will remember more words (on the average) than the first group, even though the decay time was the same for both. Why? Interference.

Interference

Today the most popular explanation of forgetting among research psychologists is interference. A large number of well designed experiments have shown that interference has a strong influence on memory.

The idea of interference is quite simple: one memory interferes with another. If you are introduced to one person, you can probably remember the name, at least for a little while. But if you are introduced to twenty people, the first name you hear will interfere with the second and so on, and you often end up being unable to remember any of them.

You have learned to speak Spanish well enough to get around in Mexico with no difficulty. You decide to visit Italy, so you study Italian. Sometimes when you try to think of an Italian word, the corresponding Spanish word pops into your mind. The Spanish word interferes with the Italian word.

Every once in a while, someone designs a typewriter keyboard that is much more efficient than the conventional keyboard. You have been typing competently for forty years. You try the new keyboard, and you can hardly type at all. More efficient? No way! The promoter of the new keyboard will explain that you must first unlearn your present method of typing; then you can learn the new keyboard. "Unlearning" simply means eliminating the interference of the old with the new method.

At this point I must amend something I said before. Sherlock Holmes was not completely wrong. He did point out that when a man puts new information into a crowded memory "room," each new memory gets "jumbled up with a lot of other things, so that he has a difficulty in laying his hands upon it." The old memories interfere with the new one. If Holmes had presented his theory of interference without the idea of an overstocked attic room with rigid walls, he would have had a sound theory of forgetting.

Interference and age

Interference slows us old folks down when we try to remember something. A young friend in his twenties told me that he found a history lesson interesting in which he learned about the 1948 election in which Truman upset Dewey. He remembers that fact. I remember it, too, but I remember many other "facts" about the election. I remember standing on Superior Avenue in front of the Cleveland Public Library watching Dewey parade through the city and wondering why there were so few people out to see him. I remember the arguments I had with my parents and with friends about the relative merits of the candidates.

My young friend may remember from his history lesson that our Air Force began airlifting supplies into West Berlin that year. But he does not remember that General Tunner commanded the operation with stunning success, and he does not remember that General Tunner commanded the Air Transport Command when I was assigned to it during World War II. But I remember these things and many, many more.

Where my young friend remembers two or three facts about 1948, my memory is crowded with facts and impressions. My older son was born that year. (My young friend had not yet been born.) My wife was active in the League of Women Voters. I remember our house and our yard and our neighbors. All of this vast body of memories has the potential to interfere with other memories, so that I sometimes act like a doddering old idiot whose mind has slipped as I search through that mass of memories for the one I want at that moment. My young friend pops out with his one fact quickly because he has nothing else in his memory to interfere with it. Whose memory is better?

Some things that affect interference

There are two factors that tend to make the effects of interference greater or less. One is the intensity of thinking that occupies the mind between the time of learning information and the time of trying to remember it. I mentioned above that psychologists find that people remember better after two hours of sleep than after two hours of activity. Activity involves the mind; what we see and hear and learn interferes with the earlier memories.

The other factor is similarity. When you were introduced to those twenty people mentioned above, the fact that they were all people, all with the kinds of names people have, made the names difficult to remember. If, in the middle of the introductions, someone led an elephant into the room and told his name was Apyornis, you would remember his name even though it was a kind of name you had never heard before.

One reason I discourage people from memorizing shopping lists instead of writing them down is that one list is similar to another. Was the broccoli on today's list or last week's list? Similarity can be confusing.

To help us remember

We can use interference theory to help us remember. Sherlock Holmes made an important point about jumble and disorder. When you want to remember a piece of information, think about the information till it is clear in your mind and distinct from other information, especially similar information. Jumble and disorder increase interference. Good memory takes clear and orderly thinking.

To help us forget

The opposite kind of behavior will help us forget. Occupy the mind with other things; they will interfere with the memory. We all know how the rejected lover travels to Paris or explores the source of the Amazon to forget his (or her) sorrows. Some people — not the ones you read about in romances — dig into their work. By filling their mind with their work they forget their troubles.

Obviously the methods we learned from the ideas of decay and interference can work together. In fact, they work best when they are used together. How can you avoid reviewing a memory you want to forget? If you find yourself thinking about it, busy your mind with something else.

A common method of creating interference — or at least it is often talked about — is drowning one's sorrow in booze. That is definitely not recommended — which is the burden of the next section.

Brain damage

Brain damage can cause forgetting, and it can cause anything from slight forgetting to almost complete obliteration of everything we know. How much help can we get from knowing that? Not much if the brain damage results from an automobile accident — except to warn us to drive more carefully. But brain damage also results from alcohol, and we *can* do something about that. There is a condition called "Korsakoff's syndrome," that comes from too much booze and too little vitamin B_1. The victim loses most of his memories and cannot form new ones. He/she also has trouble seeing and hearing, becomes lethargic, and talks a great deal without making any sense. You can avoid that one if you are smart enough to see it coming and do something about it like joining AA.

If you are on illegal drugs such as cocaine or heroin or even marijuana — forget it. You are only kidding yourself into thinking you want to improve your memory. You can do nothing to improve your memory unless and until you kick the habit. There is nothing more to be said on the subject.

Unfortunately, age can also cause brain damage. Between five and ten percent of the elderly develop enough brain deterioration to affect memory. People who have brain damage must be treated medically. They can often be helped, if not cured, by the kind of memory aids and mnemonics that we learned from earlier chapters of this book, but the person suffering from that kind of problem cannot make it through self help from a book. He or she must be helped by a professional therapist.

Sigmund Freud

Freud was one of the most important psychologists in history, and his ideas about forgetting are among his most important ideas. Freud believed that many things (but not everything) remain in memory even though we think we have forgotten them and cannot retrieve them. The things that interested him most are those that are so important to us, and so threatening to us, that we repress them without even knowing that we repress them. We repress them unconsciously. It is essential to the understanding of Freud that we fully appreciate the fact that we have no control over the process of repression. We are not even aware that it happens. It is completely and utterly involuntary.

Freud's theory is too complex to go into here, and it won't do us any good anyway. Our goal is to find a way to forget things voluntarily, that is, when we *want* to forget them. Repression will not let us do that. It will not serve our purpose. It is vain to *try* to repress a memory. Repeating the quotation from Montaigne, because it is important in this context: "Nothing so deeply imprints anything in our memory as the desire to forget it."

Following Freud's ideas, we know that emotions affect memory. We not only repress unpleasant things unconsciously, but we twist — or reconstruct — what we do remember. Take the man who has been in an automobile accident: He tells us that it was "the other guy's" fault. And what was "the other guy" telling his friends? You know as well as I. Similarly, when we watch a football game, whose team plays dirty? Ours or theirs?

Do we remember better when we are emotionally aroused or when we are calm and collected? Unfortunately, the relationship between arousal and memory is so complex that there is no one answer. It depends on the specifics of your emotional state both at the time you learn — or see — or hear — something and the time you try to remember it. Some things are remembered better, some worse; and when strong emotions are involved, things often get twisted in your memory. Freud discusses many of the effects of emotions on memory in the second lecture of his book, *A General Introduction to Psychoanalysis*.

It does seem, though, that we remember pleasant things better than unpleasant. When I think back, for example, on my army days, I know that I had some very unpleasant times (although I was never in combat), but I remember the pleasant times, the funny incidents, and the good friends that I made.

The fact that we remember pleasant things better than unpleasant things suggests a warning. I have noticed that I (and others I know well enough to have this kind of information about them) am more likely to forget a dentist appointment than to forget to go to a symphony concert. I have learned to take extra precautions to remember the dentist appointment. I not only write it in my calendar, but I write myself other reminders that I stick on the wall above my desk and put on the dresser where I keep my wallet at night.

The Zeigarnik effect

With a name like Zeigarnik, it's got to be good. And it is. The best introduction to this intriguing concept is through a delightful anecdote about Kurt Lewin, who was one of the outstanding psychologists of this century.

> Lewin and his friends were in a restaurant in Berlin, in the sort of prolonged conversation which always surrounded Lewin. It was a long time since they had ordered and the waiter hovered in the distance. Lewin called him over, asked what he owed, was told instantly and paid, but the conversation went on. Presently Lewin had an insight. He called the waiter back and asked him how much he had been paid. The waiter no longer knew.

The question is, of course, why the waiter could remember when he was asked originally, but could not remember later. And the answer is that once he had completed his task, he lost the memory of it.

Bluma Zeigarnik was a student of Lewin. She took on the job of studying memory for completed tasks and uncompleted tasks. She found that memory for uncompleted tasks is far better than for completed tasks. That seems reasonable enough when you think about it. The information has no value once the task is completed. What good would it do the waiter to remember the cost of each meal once the meals have been paid for? That information would only interfere with his memories for the cost of other meals that he would serve

The importance of value

The Zeigarnik effect is an important cause of forgetting. We can expand the notion to cover more than completed tasks. It occurs whenever an item of information has lost its value, interest, importance, or utility to us. Information about the uncompleted task has utility to us because we need it to complete the task. It has value because we need it. But it loses its value and its utility as soon as the task is completed, so we forget it — assuming it has no value for other tasks.

I remember that when I was a young man, I heard an elderly man complain that he was having trouble with his memory. When he drove to work, he would be appalled, upon his arrival, to realize that he had completely forgotten the drive; he could remember nothing about the sights and sounds of the road; he could not recall seeing the other cars on the road. It frightened him for two reasons: he was afraid that he was losing his memory, and he was afraid that he was not driving carefully, since he could not remember anything he had done during the drive. Actually, this was a perfect example of Zeigarnik forgetting. He had completed the task, and so the memory of it vanished. Of what value would be the memories of the other cars on the road, or the scenery, or the details of his own driving, once he had completed the trip?

After I have taken my car out of the parking lot, that task is complete, and the memory of the parking place does not stay very long in my memory. The memory has absolutely no value to me. Keeping it in memory will only build up interference that may make it difficult for me to find my car the next time I park somewhere.

Did Queen Elizabeth really forget?

Isn't it interesting that all of us are concerned about remembering things, and psychologists have worked out all sorts of devices to help us remember, but it is almost impossible to forget things at will, and there is almost no help for it?

About all we can do to forget the terrible faux pas we made at our mother-in-law's formal dinner twenty years ago is to occupy our minds with something else whenever the memory pops up, and to hope that another twenty years will bury our embarrassment. Do nothing to reinforce the memory, and concentrate on other things that will interfere with it.

The story about Queen Elizabeth I is too good to pass up, even though it includes vulgar language. Did she really forget, or was she only being polite? I repeat the story exactly as it was written by the seventeenth century biographer, John Aubrey — the language (and the spelling) is his, not mine:

> This Earle of Oxford, making of his low obeissance to Queen Elizabeth, happened to let a Fart, at which he was so abashed and ashamed that he went to Travell, 7 yeares. On his return the

Queen welcomed him home, and sayd,
My Lord, I had forgott the Fart.

Excruciatingly correct behavior

Since the conduct of a monarch establishes the etiquette of her (or his) time, we cannot fault the Queen, however much her remark may amuse us. In our own time and country, we must consult books of etiquette for current practices. There are many good books. *Miss Manners' Guide to Excruciatingly Correct Behavior* (by Judith Martin) makes good sense, and her delightful humor makes it enjoyable reading. If questions of conduct concern you, select a book of etiquette and follow the reading suggestions on pages 201-208, studying to whatever degree of intensity you think appropriate.

Chapter 15

Memory and Motivation

"Nobuddy ever fergits where he buried a hatchet."

We encountered that saying back in Chapter 5. It's a catchy saying, but is it true? Well, there's enough truth in the statement for us to recognize it and smile inwardly at our foibles.

To the extent that it is true, what is it that makes memories of past quarrels so persistent? Can we use it to make our memories for other things equally persistent?

The something that makes those memories persistent is motivation. We are motivated by our feelings of anger or resentment to hold the memory of the quarrel in our minds.

So why not use that something — motivation — to make our memories for other things equally persistent?

Motivation

Motivation is what makes you do something. It determines the amount of effort and energy you put into a task. You will remember things better if you are motivated to remember them. In fact, you will work harder to remember them the more highly motivated you are.

Motivation refers to rewards for doing good work, and it also refers to inner urges or desires that move you to do something. Rewards can be money — like salary, or like the dollar we offer our child for a good grade in school — or rewards can be fame and adulation. Inner urges are such things as drives to gain satisfaction from a job well done or drives to improve our performance in such things as memory. In the case of memory improvement, since no one is likely to offer us rewards, we must rely on internal motivation.

I believe that one reason older people have memory problems is that they lack the motivation to apply themselves to improving their memories. Many of us seem to believe that we have paid our dues; now that we have reached the golden age, we can rest on our laurels. I suggest that you think about your own motivation. Do you *really* want to improve your memory? You can. But only if you really want to.

How motivation works

Motivation focuses attention on the task we want to do. Because I am engaged in writing a book on memory improvement, I am motivated to learn everything I can on the subject. When I read the newspaper, if there is a mention of memory, it jumps out at me. I find information about memory in all kinds of magazines and books, although before I began to study memory, I never noticed that anyone mentioned it.

Motivation enhances concentration. I can read about memory for hours, whereas I quickly get tired of reading almost anything else, particularly at the present time, when my interest is focused on memory.

Interest

Interest is closely related to motivation. When we are interested in a subject, we are motivated to learn more about it. We are (or, if retired, we were) interested in our jobs. This gives us the motivation to learn everything we can about them. You must know many people — I certainly do — who can talk intelligently about their jobs at great length, but if you get them on an unrelated subject they sound like morons. That is because they have been motivated for years to learn about their jobs. For most of us, our job is our life as well as our livelihood. It establishes who we are in the world. The problem with our moron friends (who are not really morons by any means) is that they lack motivation to learn about music or politics or whatever. Because of their interest and attention over a long period of years, they have built up a vast network of information about their jobs in their memory storage, but they have very little information in that network about other things.

Another way of saying this is that some subjects seem important to us, and we find it easy to work on them, whereas other subjects are not important. I believe that one big reason that older people do not look as good on memory tests as young people is that the tests are not important to older people, whereas young people as so accustomed to being tested that they take the tests in stride. In addition, the young people often find the tests novel and consequently interesting, whereas the older people find them trivial and annoying.

Understanding your motivation can help your memory. Suppose you decide to memorize the pegwords. Ask yourself why you want to remember them. If it is just for a memory exercise, it will not be worth the trouble. But if you have uses for them, reviewing the uses can be helpful. You may be called upon to give a speech, and for some good reason you do not want to use notes. If you memorize the pegwords thoroughly, you can use them to memorize the points of the speech.

Now that you have a clear understanding of the reason for memorizing the pegwords, you will find them easier to remember. You will go at the work with more energy.

Different people, different interests

We all know that different people have different interests. That is why the businessman often knows little about art and why the artist is often a poor businessman. Your interests are different from mine. Keep that in mind in using this book. I have included a lot of information that may not be of interest to you.

Don't waste your time working on the strategies that you never expect to use. If you believe that the method of loci will do more for you than pegwords, forget pegwords and work on the method of loci.

The general principles that I have discussed throughout the book apply to all memory improvement, but the specific strategies do not. Select those of interest, work on them, master them. Forget the others.

Interest is as close as we come to a magic method of memory improvement. Take advantage of it.

Improving motivation

Since motivation is what moves you to remember, improving motivation will improve memory. The best place to begin improving your motivation is with clarifying your goal. If, in the case we just looked at, you decide that you might as well use notes for your speech, then there is no point — at least no immediate point — in learning the pegwords. So work on something else. But if you decide that it will be better to use pegwords, then you have boosted your motivation for learning them.

Set yourself tasks that you will be able to perform. Do not try to remember everything, because it cannot be done. Tackle one strategy at a time. Select the one of greatest interest to you and work on it.

Set yourself tasks that you *want* to perform. Work on things that are important and useful to you. Usefulness is a strong motivator.

Why do some kinds of information interest you? Usually because they are useful to you in one way or another. So if you have to learn some information that bores you, consider whether the information will prove to be useful. What will you do with it? If you can find genuine utility in it, that utility will stimulate interest, which will stimulate memory.

If you have nothing else to associate with a piece of information, you might ponder the reason you want to remember it. Tie that reason to the information itself, and that may be the association that will call it back to mind when you need it.

Motivated study

If you decide to follow a line of study — say memory — plan your approach. If you take a college course, the professor will do the planning for you, but if you attempt a subject on your own, you must do the planning. Set goals and deadlines, just as your professor would do. If you are reading a book, set time limits for reading each chapter. Schedule your work. Do not be too rigid, but keep to your schedule as well as you reasonably can.

Measure your progress. One advantage to a college course is that the periodic tests measure the progress you have made and tell you whether you are catching on or not.

Any subject that you study, be it contract bridge, calculus, or art history, requires thinking. Memory and thinking are interwoven; you can't have one without the other. You can memorize information by rote practice, but it is not efficient. Rote practice involves some thinking, but very little. Whenever you can, apply one of the strategies you have read about in this book.

Ordinarily, you will study a subject of interest to you, and I encourage that. I do not believe in studying subjects that are not of interest on some vague theory of mental discipline. Learning should be enjoyable — certainly when you are our age you should be beyond having to study things that are distasteful to you. You will get all the discipline you need from something of interest. I assume that if you have read this far, memory must be a subject of interest to you, so I will use it to illustrate some of the things you should do to master a subject.

Begin with work that is easy enough that you will not be discouraged. One of the best books on memory is the Ashcraft book which I have listed in "Books for Further Reading" at the end of this book. But it is not for beginners. A good place to begin the study of any subject is in an encyclopedia like *The World Book*. It was written for children, so the style is simple and clear, but the content is accurate. The two pages on memory will give you a straightforward overview of the subject.

Then progress to more difficult reading. Two other books in the "Books for Further Reading" are good: Loftus and Baddeley. After reading one of them, you will be ready for Ashcraft, if you want to go on.

This procedure has two advantages: It lets you advance by easily comprehensible stages, and it gives you different approaches to the subject, different points of view that will broaden your own point of view and your own understanding.

College courses

Many states permit older persons to audit college courses in state universities without charge. "Audit" simply means that you can take the course, but you will not get college credit for it or receive a grade. Most programs of this sort allow you to take examinations and turn in papers if you wish — but they are not required.

College courses are the most efficient way for most of us to learn. They set the schedules for us, both the deadlines that force us to move along and the examinations that measure our progress. I highly recommend them — if you can find some on subjects of interest to you.

Motivation for boring subjects

Sometimes we have to study subjects about which we could not care less. That can happen on the job or if we are pursuing a degree at a university, and I suppose there are other occasions, too. Can anything be done to motivate us to learn subjects that we find dull and boring? I believe there is.

First, we can remind ourselves of our purpose. If that purpose is important to us, it will motivate us. If it is not important, we should consider changing our plans. Why invest time and effort in work of no importance?

Secondly, our interest in a subject grows as we learn more about it. So if we can begin to learn something about a subject, we usually become interested in it.

That is not likely to be your problem with the study of memory, although, after you have finished this book, you may feel that you have had enough. But let's assume that you have some pressing reason to study something that you have no interest in. How should you begin?

Try to find some aspect of the subject that is of interest. If you have to take a course in finance and you hate the subject, look for an article or book about big financiers and the dirty tricks they used to push their way in the world. If you have to take a course in biology and you cannot stand the subject, perhaps an article or a chapter on sexual selection will get you into it. With regard to the study of memory, if you have no burning interest in it, but think you should learn more about it, try the book by Loftus listed in "Books for Further Reading." Dr. Loftus is one of the leading authorities on memory, and she writes in a style that is easy to understand and pleasant to read. She draws on her courtroom experience, where she has served as an expert witness, to assess the value of eye-witness testimony, which gives the book an extra fillip that makes it more attractive to the general reader.

To make sure of keeping up your interest, you might want to set up a system of rewards, just in case interest flags. Set up sub-goals, such as grades on examinations (for a college course) or completing a chapter (if you are reading a book). Reward yourself each time you achieve a sub-goal by indulging some whim: a hot fudge sundae or a new hat.

Egocentrism again

If you take a course in college (or in a high-school or library program for adults) keep in mind that you are there to learn, not to teach. You and I know a great deal from the experiences of a lifetime, and we often feel the urge to pass our knowledge and wisdom on to the younger generation. The trick is to find the right audience, and a school classroom is not it.

Your teacher may well turn out to be younger than your children. My advisor in graduate school is, and I know more about many things than he does. But he knows a lot more about psychology than I do, and that's what counts in our relationship.

Unless you put aside your vanity and respect the teacher's knowledge in your field of study, you are not likely to learn much. And you will not endear yourself to your fellow students with stories that drift off the subject. This caveat applies to any new group you get into, whether it be college, the Red Cross, the Urban League, or any other that you plan to work with. Sometimes your stories will be appropriate, and you should tell them. Often they will not be, and you should save them for a more suitable occasions.

The good old days

A harmless form of egocentrism is reminiscing about the good old days. At least, it's harmless if we don't take it too seriously. As the years go by, we tend to forget the unpleasant and remember the pleasant, so that reminiscing can be one of the pleasures of our older years. When we think back to those good old days, and see that mess the world is in today, we can warn our grandchildren that the world is going to hell in a handbasket without doing much harm, because in their innocence they don't believe us anyway.

Not many people responding to my questionnaire (in Chapter 3) indicated that they wanted to be able to reminisce better, but a word or two may be in order. In my own experience it works best either when I am with old friends, or when I am alone without anything serious on my mind. Reminiscing with an old high school sweetheart is fun because you can say things now that you never could have mentioned fifty years ago. I have had my eyes opened many times through this process.

In my sister's later years, when she had been widowed, we spent many hours reminiscing about our childhood and our family. That may have been what impressed me so about the subjective nature of memory: we would talk about the same incident, but have two contradictory sets of facts about it. We never got our conflicting memories straightened out, but we had many a pleasant evening.

To remember the past, make yourself comfortable, turn down the lights, and relax. Forget about the worries of the day, and let the memories flow.

Mood and memory

Mood seems to be related to motivation, although the relationship is far from clear. A headline in the November, 1987, American Psychological Association *Monitor* read: "Mood's role in memory still puzzling." A couple of things do seem clear, however.

Moods that distract our attention obviously have a bad effect on memory, as we noted in Chapter 5. If we feel depressed, we are likely to be thinking about our woes and not about the information we want to remember. If we are in the mood to study we will remember more than when we are in the mood to play golf or loaf.

Can you change your mood to make yourself more productive? To some extent. Robust health is likely to put you in a good mood. Even doing some physical exercise can change your mood from glum to sunny. If you have mood problems, go swimming, jogging, or golfing. Ride your bicycle. Or just take a good, long walk.

Nervousness

People usually get nervous when faced with giving a speech or acting in a play or taking an examination. Up to a point, that is good. The nervousness keys you up, so that you are likely to perform better. If you are completely relaxed, you may be too lethargic to do your best. And if you are too nervous, you may forget information you would otherwise remember with no trouble at all. But how can you reach the middle ground, the proper amount of nervousness? If lethargy is your problem, remind yourself of the importance of the task you are about to perform. If nervousness seems to be the problem, remind yourself that nervousness — in moderation — will help you do a better job. That will often bring the level of nervousness down to a level at which it is helpful.

A related mood problem can arise when you visit your doctor. You have several questions to ask, but when you are face to face, your nervousness blocks some of them out of your mind. At one time I tried using pegwords to be sure that I asked all the questions that had bothered me, but I soon realized that it is far easier to write a list of questions. The doctor may have thought I was getting forgetful because I needed a written list, but the fact is that I was getting smart.

You CAN improve your memory

Try harder. If you put more effort into improving your memory, you will improve it. You have mental skills; make the most of them. Use the ideas in this book as a guide so you don't waste your effort — and work on them. They will work if you work to make them work.

Keep active mentally and physically. Giving up is the surest way to go into a decline. Unused machinery gets rusty till it freezes tight and can't be used. I had a friend who did nothing but sit in front of his television set after he retired. He sat there, doing nothing active, for several years. The last I heard of him, they had taken him to the hospital for physical rehabilitation because his muscles had atrophied to the point where he could hardly walk. He had not been ill, he had just been inactive.

The same thing applies to mind: don't use it and soon you won't be able to use it. Read the newspapers to keep up with what's going on. TV news is all right, but it is too passive to help your mind. The TV newscasters spoonfeed us. Spoonfeeding is all right for infants, but if you live on spoonfed information, you must expect your mind to slip back towards infancy. Read the news articles that interest you. Read the details and evaluate them: Do they support the conclusions you drew when you first heard the news item?

Read magazine articles and books about the subjects that interest you. If you don't, you will soon lose interest and become a couch potato vegging out in front of the idiot box.

Work at improving your mind and that part of your mind we call memory. Use external aids whenever you can. They will not let your mind grow rusty. Far from it. External aids assist the memory. Use your mind to think up new, ingenious memory aids. It is fun; it keeps your brain in shape; and it helps you remember important things.

Live an organized life. Use your ingenuity to improve the way you have organized you life. Organization frees you from the boring details of living and gives you time to enjoy the things you like. Take advantage of that.

Summary and review

I have no intention of summarizing or reviewing the book for you. You have the book in your hand; the best way to master the parts of it that are of value to you is for *you* to review them and practice them till you learn them.

But I am not quite through. I want to urge you to use the book as a guide to the development of good memory habits. The strategies I have explained will be of no use unless you practice them till they become automatic. It will not help a bit to know that you should put your car keys on the stove every time you come into the house unless you make a habit of it.

Remember my distinction between biological and functional memory? Your biological memory may deteriorate, but you can compensate by developing your functional memory.

Remember this: Habits are an essential part of the kind of orderly life that older people must develop to compensate for any loss of biological memory.

Three parting words

1. A cautionary tale: A man went to New York on business. While there, he discovered that there was to be a concert at Carnegie Hall that sounded worthwhile. He telephoned and was able to get a ticket. The bell captain told him that Carnegie Hall was easy walking distance from the hotel, and he told the man how to get there.

But the man got lost. With time running out, he stopped a stranger to ask the way. (Although the man loved music, in his distress, he did not recognize the stranger as Jascha Heifetz.)

"How do you get to Carnegie Hall?" he asked the stranger.

"Practice," the great violinist replied.

If you want to improve your memory, you must practice; if you do not practice, you will see very little improvement if any. That is not a new idea: way back in 1562, a man named Guglielmo Gratiorolo wrote a book called, *The Castel of Memorie* in which he said:

> An often callinge to mynde of things seene or hard, both strengthe and confirme the Memorie: for there is nothing that is so soone increased by diligence or diminshed by negligance, as Memorie it selfe is: because except it be thoroughlye [strengthened] with a continual meditation, it is soone corrupted by sluggishenes.

For best results, space your practice sessions. Two spaced study periods are about twice as effective as the same amount of study time spent continuously.

2. Take it easy: Take your time. Rushing means forgetting. Don't get flustered. When you forget something, shrug it off. Everybody forgets.

Shrug it off the way one of the characters in Alan Ayckbourn's farce *Taking Steps* does. At one point, he says: "Ah, well. It's a great life if you don't slacken. Weaken. Some people say weaken, I say slacken."

At another point, he says: (taking a long drink) "Ah, that's better. This is the real McKay. McCoy. Some people say McCoy. I say McKay."

Those remarks get a good laugh on the stage, but the spirit behind them is worth emulating. Weaken — slacken, McKay — McCoy; will the world come to an end if you get them mixed up? Enjoy the humor of the goof, even if it means laughing at yourself. What's wrong with that?

3. Think of your successes: Think of all the things you *do* remember. You can't think of a word, or, like Roland, you get the word mixed up? You have about fifty thousand words in your memory. If you forget one, what's the big deal? You have or had a job for many years. Think of all the things you remembered as a part of that job, many of which you still remember.

Practice so you can do your best. But don't get upset when something slips your mind.

A long but important digression: Enjoying old age

We need three basic things to make old age enjoyable: health, wealth, and a social support system. They are all essential underpinnings to our wellbeing. Our general wellbeing affects memory, so health, wealth, and the social support system underpin memory as well.

A recent nation-wide survey taken by the Los Angeles Times showed that a larger proportion of older people are happy — or at least contented — than younger people. They are said to be freer from worry and nowhere near as fearful as they are usually portrayed. I have some doubts about the survey, but I am sure that old age *can* be a time of contentment if we go about it right.

We all know that the average life expectancy is much higher than it has ever been in the history of the world. The *maximum* life expectancy age has not gone up, but more of us will get close to that maximum age. Scientists now know that old age does not automatically bring with it a decline of body function efficiency. Since most of us can expect to live a long, long time, we should plan for a better quality of life in our later years.

George Burns said that if he had known that he was going to live so long, he would have taken better care of himself. He was talking about his health, but his observation applies to wealth and the social support system, too.

The three requisites are not entirely under our control, but to the extent that we can control them, it is worth the effort. (Young people should read this book because the best time to begin to improve your health, build up your wealth, and acquire a social support system is when you are young.)

Health

Food: We know what to do, but do we do it? Eat a balanced diet: no fast foods, no junk foods. You need proteins (fish and chicken are high in protein, low in cholesterol), and you need a variety of vegetables and fruits. Avoid animal fats, including whole milk and cheese. Don't like skim milk? You'll learn to like it. It cuts down the calories, too.

Keep you bowels open. Drink beaucoup water. Eat roughage: less white bread, more whole wheat and rye.

You don't need alcohol. You don't need tobacco. You can — and should — get by with little sugar and salt.

Your body was built to be used; you need exercise to keep it in good working order. Exercise at least twenty minutes at a stretch, three times a week. (More is better.) If you can't do anything else, walk. Walk as briskly as you can. Of course, if you like tennis or golf or any other sport, that is the way to go.

We can control our mental health to a large extent. One of the foundation stones of mental health is the enjoyment of life. Of course, if you have poor mental health, telling you to enjoy life will not accomplish much, but if you can get yourself to stand back (from yourself) and see the amusing things in your life, you might be able to break away from the worries, anxieties, and all those other bad things that are getting you down.

Laughter and leisure are two important aspects of life; don't miss them. Take time off to see funny movies and read funny books. Relax when you are delayed at a traffic light. Think of it as leisure time, a time when you are free to look around at things you've always seen but never noticed. The other cars. The intense, overstrained people in them. The ugly buildings along the road — and the beautiful buildings along the road.

"Boredom," wrote Bertrand Russell "as a factor in human behavior has received, in my opinion, far less attention than it deserves. It has been, I believe, one of the great motive powers throughout the historical epoch, and is so at the present day more than ever." Russell is the only writer I have come across who acknowledges that the need for excitement is very deep-seated in human beings. We need excitement; we need adventure. But how can we get them?

Most of us get our adventure vicariously through movies, spectator sports, and books. Nothing wrong with that; we should do more of it. When I discussed food a moment ago, I recommended cutting out a lot of things that we all enjoy. We can't cut them out without substituting something else for them. Substitute adventure. Instead of overeating, read a good book, go to the movies, watch a football game, or jog around the block.

Many people travel for adventure. Games and gambling, if they don't get out of control, are great adventures. Social activities at senior citizens centers, at your private club, or anywhere else will bring new friends, too, and each new friend is an adventure. We need adventure in whatever form is possible and practical.

Participation in civic activities provides an outlet for our energies and for the wisdom we have acquired over a lifetime, and it throws us into contact with new people and new situations. It gives us a sense of accomplishment and the feeling of being part of the community. It is important work, and there is nothing like doing important work to make one feel good.

Wealth

Wealth is the second of the three requisites for a comfortable old age. Not great wealth, but enough to let us live comfortably. Unfortunately, by the time we reach old age and retire, there is not much we can do about this important factor other than to husband carefully whatever resources we have. Don't gamble on the horses or on speculative stocks in the hopes of making it big. Don't fall for the many phony business schemes you'll find in the classified ads. Hold on to what you have.

We tend to equate wealth with the number of dollars in the bank, but there are other, completely different ways of thinking about wealth. I enjoy reading Shakespeare and Tolstoy and Mark Twain. No one in the world, no matter how much money he has, can read better literature than I can: I can get all the books I want free at the library. Do you enjoy music? The cost of a radio is within reach of almost everyone. Do you enjoy sports? A television set costs a little more, but not that much.

I do not mean that books and television can take the place of cold cash. The best things in life may be free, but we need the lesser things, too, and they cost money. Social Security is one of the most important things in the life of an older person. My own life would be tightly restricted without it. My chances of seeing

Shakespeare on the stage would be fewer and farther between. And many people depend on Social Security entirely. That is why the threats against it must be fought and fought hard. An important institution in the lives of older citizens is the American Association of Retired Persons (better known as AARP), 1909 "K" Street, N.W., Washington, D. C. 20049. It gives us older folks a strong voice in Washington, fighting for the preservation of Social Security and for other rights and benefits. I urge you to join it. It is not expensive, and it helps us all by speaking up for us where we cannot be heard as individuals.

A social support system

The third requisite for a comfortable old age, a social support system, includes friends, relatives, and community institutions to which we can turn in time of need. The need may be anything from companionship to brain surgery.

The first line of support comes from our relatives and friends. It saddens me whenever I see relatives or friends fall out. This is a prime mistake that should be remedied at all cost. Each friend that we have is irreplaceable and should be treasured. These are the people who will give us the warmest help in time of need.

I mentioned the American Association of Retired Persons (AARP) earlier. It is one of the most powerful support institutions we have. You will find many other, smaller, support organizations in your community. You may have a problem finding the one that can help you in time of need, but between asking friends and telephoning whatever institution you think can help, you will eventually get to the right place.

Many people move to a warmer climate — to Florida or California — when they retire. Before you decide to make that move, consider how many friends and relatives you will leave behind. Friends are more important than climate. The sun can warm your epidermis, but only friends can warm your heart.

Before you make that move, consider how familiar you are with your home town resources, and how familiar they are with you. The move may be a good thing, but it is not always a good thing for everyone. The trick is to be sure your needs will be met, whether you move or stay at home.

Whether you stay home or move, you need a social support system. Take a look at what you have — in addition to relatives and friends, your doctor, your hospital, your clubs, your bank, the baseball team, library, recreation center, local TV shows and personalities, newspaper. If you stay home, learn more about your area, what it has to offer in the way of entertainment for the good days and help for the not-so-good days. If you move, see what's available in your new locality — before you make the move. It will make all the difference in the world in the comfort and security in which you live.

*

One more thing that helps make age pleasant is memory — memory for past events that we enjoyed

and can now look back on with pleasure, and memory
in the sense of our ability to function well in the world.

*

And so, farewell. . . and pleasant memories . . .

Books for Further Reading

The books are listed in alphabetical order by author. I urge you to read at least one or two of them to supplement what you have learned in my book.

Ashcraft, Mark H. (1989). *Human Memory and Cognition*. Glenview, Illinois: Scott, Foresman and Company.

This is the most scholarly book on the list. It was written as a textbook for students of cognitive psychology, so it covers far more than memory. It is easier to understand and more enjoyable to read than any other textbook I know of. If you want to go beyond memory and learn what cognitive psychology is all about, this is your best bet.

Baddeley, Alan (1982). *Your Memory: A User's Guide*. New York: Macmillan Publishing Co., Inc. (A large paperback)

Baddeley, one of the big names in memory psychology, presents virtually all the knowledge that we have about memory. Written in a popular style, with many relevant color photographs, it includes a great deal of detail and theory. Consequently, it is valuable only when you have reached the point where you want to know more about memory than Cermak, Loftus, or Lorayne can give you.

Cermak, Laird S. (1976) *Improving Your Memory.* New York: McGraw-Hill Book Company. (Paperback)

If you read only one additional book on memory improvement, read this one. Cermak has organized his book in an unusual— and unusually helpful—way. If you want to know more about memorizing numbers, this book will help. It is short and very, very good.

Loftus, Elizabeth (1980). *Memory.* Reading, Massachu setts: Addison-Wesley Publishing Company. (Paperback)

Loftus manages to tell a great deal about the psychology of memory in relatively few pages and in an easy style. She is particularly good on the fallibility of memory—her specialty. Her chapter on "Memory in Older People" is not quite up to date, but it is good, and the book makes interesting reading

Lorayne, Harry, and Lucas, Jerry (1974). *The Memory Book.* New York: Ballantine Books #32510. (Paperback)

This is a practical book with almost no theory. The authors present a system that works—if *you* work at mastering it. If you are particularly interested in remembering names, try this book. It is also good on remembering numbers.

Suid, Murray (1981). *Demonic Mnemonics.* Belmont, California: Fearon Teacher Aids, a division of David S. Lake Publishers. (Paperback)

If you are seriously interested in improving your spelling (as we all should be), you will find this book invaluable. In addition, it will give you some good ideas for inventing your own mnemonics for other things. The street address for Fearon Teacher Aids is 1850 Ralston Avenue, and the zip code is 94002.

References

Because this is not a work of scholarship, I have avoided footnotes. I have added this section for those who wish to check the many quotations, etc. found in the text.

page 10 The recent findings about brains and aging were reported by Susan Chollar in *Psychology Today*, December, 1988, p. 22.

page 11 Dr. Samuel Johnson, quoted in W. H. Auden and Louis Kronenberger: *The Viking Book of Aphorisms*. Dorset Press, p. 391.

page 12 Hulicka, I. M. (1982). Memory functioning in late adulthood. In F. I. M. Craik & S. Trehub (Eds.), *Aging and cognitive processes*. New York: Plenum

page 13 *The Cleveland Plain Dealer* for July 16, 1989, carried the story about Vice President Quayle.

page 14 Less than 6% of people over 65 have Alzheimer's or anything that serious. B. F. Skinner and M. E. Vaughan (1983). *Enjoy old age*. New York: W. W. Norton & Company, p. 123. See also Zarit, Stephen H. (1980). *Aging and mental disorders*. New York: The Free Press, p. 32.

page 15 Alan Baddeley (1982). *Your memory: a user's guide*. New York: Macmillan Publishing Co., Inc., pp. 141-44.

page 15 "The best opinion . . . " See: Labouvie-Veif, G. (1985). Intelligence and Cognition. In Birren, J. E., & Schaie, K. W. (Eds.). (1985). *Handbook of the psychology of aging* (2nd ed.). New York: Van Nostrand Reinhold Company. Also see: Meer, J. (1986). The reason of age. *Psychology Today*, June, 1986, 60-64.

page 15 In Zarit (see ref. for pg. 14), pp. 42 and 140.

page 16   Regarding slowing down, see Salthouse, T. A. (1985). Speed of behavior and its implications for cognition. In Birren & Schaie (see ref. for pg. 15)

page 17   Depression is ". . . the single most common mental complaint of the elderly . . . " Skinner and Vaughn (see ref. for pg. 14).

page 17   DeAngelis, T., (1990). Study on aging paints rosy picture. *APA Monitor*, August, 1990, p. 11.

page 19   Evans, B. (1978). *Dictionary of quotations*. New York: Avenel Books. P. 442.

page 19   The "recent study" was: Cavanaugh, J. C., Grady, J. G., & Perlmutter, M. (1983). Forgetting and use of memory aids in 20 to 70 year olds everyday life. *International Journal of Aging and Human Development, 17*, 113-22.

page 20   "The average adult is said to have a use-and-recog nition vocabulary of 30,000 to 60,000 words, and a highly literate adult is not likely to go much beyond 100,000." Krech, D., Crutchfield, R. S., & Livson, N. (1974). *Elements of psychology*. New York: Alfred A. Knopf. P. 108. I have used a very rough "average" of a very rough estimate.

page 20   Perlmutter, M. (1978). What is memory aging the aging of? *Developmental Psychology, 14*, 330-345.

page 23   Elbert Hubbard. I learned this story from my father, who attributed it to Elbert Hubbard, a writer who was popular when my father was young. I have no idea where to find it in Hubbard's work, and I'll be dinged if I'm going to read all that stuff just to find a reference.

page 27   "I Remember It Well" is from *Gigi*. Lyrics by Alan Jay Lerner; music by Frederick Loewe. Publisher: Chappell & Co., Inc. Reprinted here by kind permission of the publisher.

page 34   Skinner and Vaughn (see ref. for pg. 14).

page 34   Thomas Hardy. Weber, J. C. (1963). *Hardy's love poems*. London: Macmillan & Co Ltd.

page 36   Hulicka: see ref for pg. 14.   Also, with regard to confidence, see Meer (ref. for pg. 15). The paper by Burke, Worthley, & Martin, discussed on page 43 is also relevant.

page 38   H. J. Eysenck (1965). *Fact and fiction in psy chology*. Baltimore: Penguin Books Ltd., 232-33.

page 41 Burke, D. M., Worthley, J. & Martin, J. (1988). Never forget what's-her-name: Adult's tip-of-tongue experiences in everyday life. In M. M. Gruneberg, P. E. Morris & J. N. Sykes, (Eds.), *Practical aspects of memory: Current research and issues:* Vol 2: *Clinical and educational implications.* Pp. 113-118. Chichester: John Wiley & Sons.

page 43 Perlmutter (see ref. for pg. 20).

page 45 The two psychologists are Wilkinds, A. J., and Badde ley, A. D. (1979). Remembering to recall in everyday life: an approach to absent-mindedness. In Gruneberg, Morris & Sykes (see ref. for pg. 41).

page 45 Baddeley, A. See reference for page 15.

page 45 Meer, J., (1986). *Psychology Today,* Pp. 60-64.

page 46 Although most psychologists seem to agree that older persons become less efficient as problem solvers, see Reese, H. W. and Rodeheaver, D. (1985), Problem solving and complex decision making, in Birren & Schaie (see ref. for pg. 15), for many serious questions about the validity of the evi dence on which this agreement is based. For problem finding, see Rybash, J. M., Hoyer, W. J., & Roodin, P. A. (1986). *Adult cognition and aging.* New York: Perga mon Press.

page 49 The information about semantic, implicit, and episodic memory was found in an article in the *Richmond Times-Dispatch* of Sunday, April 1, 1990 from the *New York Times Service,* written by Daniel Goleman, and based on an article by Peter Graf in the *Psychonomic Society Bulletin* (not yet published at the time of writing).

page 53 Ring Lardner (1929). *Round up; The stories of Ring W. Lardner.* New York: The Literary Guild. ("The Golden Honeymoon" can also be found in many short story anthologies.)

page 54 James, W. (1892) *Psychology: Briefer Course.* New York: Henry Holt and Company.

page 54 Laurence Sterne (1935). *The Life & Opinions of Tristram Shandy, Gentleman.* Many editions of this famous work are available.

page 56 Pi. *The Cleveland Plain Dealer* for August 27, 1989, carried an Associated Press article by Nancy Shulins about Rajan Srinivasen Mahadevan and his unusual memory.

page 57 Photographic memory: 7% of school children. Baddeley, A. (1976). *The psychology of memory*. New York: Basic Books, Inc., Publishers. Pg. 220.

page 57 Stratton, G. The mnemonic feat of the "Shass Pollak." In Neisser, U. (Ed.) (1982) *Memory observed*. San Francisco: W. H. Freeman and Company. pp. 311ff.

page 58 Baddeley. (See ref. for pg. 15)

page 58 R. L. Kahn. Kahn, et. al. p. 42 in Zarit (see ref. for pg. 14), page 59 Three kinds of things: This approach to memory was adapted from Morris, P. E. (1979). Strategies for learning and recall. In Gruneberg, Morris & Sykes (see ref. for pg. 41).

page 68 In James (see ref. for pg. 54), p. 297.

page 71 Recent work on the physiology of the brain was reported by Kent, D. (1991). How does learning make physical changes in the brain. APS Observer, 4(5), 8-9.

page 72 Freud, S. The notions of the unconscious and repressed memories pervade Freud's works. See *New introductory lectures on psychoanalysis*. (1965). (J. Strachey, Trans.). New York: W. W. Norton & Company. (Original work published 1933)

page 76   For the failure of older people to use strategies, see Hasher, L., & Zacks, R. T. (1979). Automatic and effortful processes in memory. *Journal of Experimental Psychology: General, 108,* 356-388. Also see Smith, A. D. Age differences in encoding, storage, and retrieval. For criti cism of this view, see Salthouse, T. A. Age and memory: strategies for localizing the loss. And for comments on both, see Arenberg, D. Comments on the processes that account for memory declines with age. These papers can be found in L. W. Poon, J. L. Fozard, L. S. Cermak, D. Aren berg, and L. W. Thompson (Eds.) *New directions in memory and aging*, Hillsdale, New Jersey: Lawrence Erlbaum Associates, Publishers.

page 87   Absent mindedness and education: see Wilkinds and Baddeley, (see ref. for pg. 45).

page 93 . . . the harder you work . . . Those who fear that this general rule might not apply to memory can consult Tyler, S. W., Hertal, P. T., McCallum, M. C., & Ellis, H. C. (1979). Cognitive effort and memory. *Journal of Experimental Psychology, 5,* 607-617.

page 95 Freud (see ref. for pg. 72).

page 95 "Nobuddy ever forgets . . ." Hawes, D. S. (Ed.). (1984). *The best of Kin Hubbard*. Bloomington: Indiana University Press. p. 28.

page 96 Depression Ellis, H. C. & Hunt, R. R., (1972). *Fundamentals of human memory and cognition*. Dubuque, Iowa: Wm. C. Brown Company Publishers. p. 127. This reference covers both the comment that depression make people complain about memory loss and the quotation about mood state.

page 98 Quotations and comments about hypnosis and truth serums from Loftus, E. (1980). *Memory; surprising new insights into how we remember and why we forget*. Reading, MA: Addison-Wesley Publishing Company. pp. 54-62.

page 104 Network theory is explained in all recent texts on cognitive psychology, e.g. Ashcraft, M. H. (1989). *Human memory and cognition*. Glenview, Illinois: Scott, Foresman and Company.

page 108 James (see ref. for pg. 54), p. 294.

page 109 James Mill, quoted in James, pp. 289-90.

page 114 The definition of "strategy" is adapted from Perlmutter (scc rcf. for pg. 20).

page 118 Stern, L. (1985). *The structures and strategies of human memory*. Homewood, Illinois: The Dorsey Press. P. 175.

page 121 The ancient rules of association come from Aristotle, *On the associative nature of memory*. The modern rules come from Brown, T. (1820). *Lectures on the philosophy of the human mind*. Both can be found in R. J. Herrnstein and E. G. Boring (Eds.) *A source book in the history of psychology*. Cambridge, Massachusetts: Harvard University Press.

page 127 "divide and conquer" Bower (1970). Quoted in Gregg, V. H. (1986). *Introduction to human memory*. London: Routledge & Kegan Paul, p. 134.

page 128 Miller, G. A. (1956). The magical number seven, plus or minus two: Some limits on our capacity for processing information. *Psychological review*, 63, 81-97. page 130 The quotation is from West, R. (1985) *Memory Fitness Over 40*. Gainesville, Florida: Triad Publishing Company. p. 151-52. This is a good book and worth reading.

page 155 The friend is Bea Lawyer (Mrs. Herbert) of Chagrin Falls, Ohio. The telephone index was an original idea on her part, and, in my opinion, a very good one.

page 167 The Chinese proverb is in Stevenson, B. (1948). *The home book of proverbs, maxims and familiar phrases*. New York: The Macmillan Company. P. 1561. I have changed the wording slightly.

page 187   Harris, J. E. (1978).   External memory aids.   In Gruneberg, Morris & Sykes (see ref. for pg. 41).

page 190 Spinoza: *Tractatus de Intellectus Emendatione*, quoted in Bartlett, J. (1955). *Familiar Quotations*, Thirteenth Edition. p. 283.

page 190 The psychologist is P. E. Morris (1979). Strategies for learning and recall. In Gruneberg, Morris & Sykes (see ref. for pg. 41).

page 191 The 7 criteria for understanding come from Holt, J. (1964). *How children fail*. New York: Pitman Publishing Corporation. p. 104.

page 192 The definition of "mnemonics" is from Ashcraft (see ref. for pg. 104), page 177. For the ability of older people to comprehend reading, see Meer (see ref. for pg. 15).

page 203 Distributed learning is discussed with additional references in Dempster, F. N. (1988). The spacing effect. *American Psychologist*. August, 1988, p. 627.

page 205 Thurlow Weed. The quotation is from James, W. (1890). *The principles of psychology*. New York: Henry Holt and Company. Vol. 1, p. 665.

page 211 James (see ref. for pg. 54). p. 297.

page 219   I found this delightful story years ago in Reginald Reynolds (1946). *Cleanliness and Godliness*. Garden City, NY: Doubleday and Company, Inc. If you can find a copy, it makes good reading, and Reynold's argument for sanitation and the recycling of waste is as pertinent today as it was in 1946.

page 221 I based some of the discussion on memorizing music on conversations with musicians, and some on Cooke, C. (1941). *Playing the piano for pleasure*. New York: Simon and Schuster.

page 234 Information about the mechanism and the value of mnemonics is based largely on Ashcraft (see ref. for pg. 104), pp. 192-197.

page 236 Wood, L. E. & Pratt, J. D. (1987). Pegword mnemonic as an aid to memory in the elderly: a comparison of four age groups. *Educational Gerontology, 13:325-000*, 325-339.

page 264 The "expert" is Vallins, G. H. revised by Scragg, D. G. (1965), *Spelling*. London: Andre Deutsch Limited. P. 15.

page 264 *The Smithsonian Torch*, April, 1957. Washington, D. C.: Smithsonian Institution. Quoted with permission.

page 267 Suid, Murray (1981), *Demonic mnemonics*. Belmont, California: Fearon Teacher Aids a division of David S. Lake Publishers. Quoted with permission.

page 269 Information about *judgment* and *alright* is from *Webster's Dictionary of English usage*. Spring field, Massachusetts: Merriam-Webster Inc., Publishers. (1989).

page 273 Winckelman, von Feinaigle, and much of the other information in this section is based on Morris, P. E. (1979). Strategies for learning and recall. In M. M. Gruneberg & P. E. Morris (Eds.), *Applied problems in memory*. Lon don: Academic Press.

For Loisette's exposition of this technique, see Loisette, A. (1969). Another method for remembering dates and figures. In D. A. Norman (Ed.), *Memory and Attention*, (pp. 143-147). New York: John Wiley & Sons, Inc.,

page 274 The table of translations is from James (see ref. for pg. 54), p. 299.

page 282 I do not know who Jack C. Taylor is, and I do not remember where I found the quotation, but I like it.

page 289 I do not have a reference for the "experts" who estimate that memory for names will increase 50% with improved attention. I have read it in more than one memory book, but I did not bother to document it because I am sure these were guesses, although I would expect the percentage would be higher than 50% if a test could be made.

page 293 The "other books" from which I took the examples are listed in "Books for Further Reading."

page 305 Doyle, A. C. "A Study in Scarlet." This famous story is available in many editions. The story was originally published in 1890.

page 308 James (see ref. for pg. 54), pg. 300.

page 310 Although Dorothy Parker proclaimed that women and elephants never forget, the idea is ancient. The Greeks referred to a camel. In modern times the elephant was substituted, and before long women were added. See Stevenson, B. (1948). *The home book of proverbs maxims and familiar phrases*. New York: The Macmillan Company. Page 675, No. 8.

page 312 Ebbinghaus, H. (1964). *Memory: A contribution to experimental psychology*. New York: Dover Publications, Inc. Originally published 1885.

page 318 Korsakoff's syndrome is described in most abnormal psychology text such as Sarason, I. G. & Sarason, B. R. (1984). *Abnormal psychology*, Englewood Cliffs, New Jersey: Prentice-Hall, Inc.

page 320 Freud, S. (1938). *A general introduction to psychoanalysis*. (J. Riviere, Trans.) Garden City, New York: Garden City Publishing Company, Inc. (Original work published 1920).

page 321 The story about Kurt Lewin is told in Boring, E. G. (1957). A history of experimental psychology. New York: Appleton-Century-Crofts, Inc. Page 734.

page 323 Dick, O. L. (Ed.). (1957). *Aubrey's Brief Lives*. Ann Arbor: The University of Michigan Press, pg. 305.

page 333 Loftus (see ref. for pg. 98), pg. 106.

page 340 Guglielmo Gratorolo: The Castel of Memorie (1562), quoted in Schacter, D. L. (1982). *Stranger Behind the Engram*. Hillsdale, NJ: Lawrence Erlbaum Associates, Publishers.

page 340 Ayckbourn, A. (1981). *Taking steps; a farce*. London: Samuel French.

page 341 The nation-wide survey was reported in the *Cleveland Plain Dealer* for May 5, 1989.

page 342 Life expectancy information is widely known. I took my information from a lecture by Richard Adelman, Director of the Institute of Gerontology at the University of Michigan, reported in the *Cauldron*, a student publication of Cleveland State University for November 13, 1986.

page 344 Russell, B. (1930). *The Conquest of Happiness*. New York: The Book League of America. P. 56.

Index of Questionnaire Items

Items have been rearranged into alphebetical order. (Only the more important page references are listed.)

General Index

This index has been designed to help the reader improve his or her memory. Entries that might appear in a more scholarly work have been omitted to make the index easier to use. Where many page references appear along with one reference of greater impor tance, the more important reference has been boldfaced.

A specialized index listing only the questionnaire items appears immediately preceding this general index.

H

Habit(s), 4, 8, **101-104**, 115, 141-142, 145, 151-152, 165, 170, 185, 186 (habitual), 187, 339

Haptic memory, 222, 223

Harris, J. E., 187

Harvard Magazine 34

Haste as the enemy of memory, 41-43, 141-142, 145, 279

Health, 16-17, 97-98, 336, 341, 342-345

Historical information, (dates and facts), 69, 79, 250, 279-281

Holmes's, Sherlock, 295, 305-308, 310, 314, 316

Hubbard, Elbert, 23

Hubbard, Kin, 95

Hulicka, Irene, 12, 36-37

Humorist, (Kin Hubbard), 95

Hypnosis, 98-99

I

Imageable substitute, 293-295, 297-300, 302

Imagery (images), **131-136** 142, 143, 181, 183, 184, 215-216, 230- 232, 242, 244-245, 247-248, 251, 255-256, 258, 260-263, 290, 293-295, 297-299

Implicit memory, 49

Income tax, 159, 171, 172

Independence, Declaration of, 281

Information for job, school, etc., 188-208, 233-236

Initial-letter strategy, 82-83, 240-242, 287, 304

Input, **70-76**, 86, 93-95, 215-216, 242

Intentions (one of three kinds of things to remember), **66-67, 69,** 163-187

Interest and motivation, 44-45, 99-100, 111, **325-334,**